BESIDE YOU IN TIME

BESIDE YOU
in TIME

SENSE METHODS
& Queer Sociabilities

IN THE AMERICAN

19TH CENTURY

ELIZABETH FREEMAN

DUKE UNIVERSITY PRESS
Durham and London
2019

© 2019 Duke University Press
All rights reserved
Printed in the United States of America on acid-free paper ∞
Text design by Amy Ruth Buchanan. Cover design by
Amy Ruth Buchanan and Courtney Baker.
Typeset in Garamond Premier Pro and Din Std by
Westchester Publishing Services

Library of Congress Cataloging-in-Publication Data
Names: Freeman, Elizabeth, [date] author.
Title: Beside you in time : sense methods and queer sociabilities
in the American nineteenth century / Elizabeth Freeman.
Description: Durham : Duke University Press, 2019. |
Includes bibliographical references and index.
Identifiers: LCCN 2018061092 (print) | LCCN 2019013604
(ebook)
ISBN 9781478006350 (ebook)
ISBN 9781478005049 (hardcover : alk. paper)
ISBN 9781478005674 (paperback : alk. paper)
Subjects: LCSH: Time—Social aspects—United States—
History—19th century. | Homosexuality—Social aspects—
United States—History—19th century. | Time perception in
literature. | Human body in literature. | American literature—
African American authors—19th century—History and
criticism. | Literature and society—United States—History—
19th century. | Queer theory.
Classification: LCC HM656 (ebook) | LCC HM656 .F73 2019
(print) | DDC 306.7601—dc23
LC Record available at https://lccn.loc.gov/2018061092

Cover art: Susan Grabel, *Confluence*, 2006. Collagraph
monoprint, 23 ½ × 21 inches. Courtesy of the artist.

CONTENTS

ACKNOWLEDGMENTS

The writing of this book was supported most generously by a grant from the American Council of Learned Societies in fall quarter 2015 and winter quarter 2016. I also thank the Davis Humanities Institute for a Faculty Fellowship course release in spring 2015, and the University of California, Davis, for several Small Grants in Aid of Research. My department, the Department of English, is as intellectually rigorous, convivial, and supportive a place as I could hope to work, and I am grateful to my colleagues and students there; I only refrain from singling out individuals because I would not want to accidentally slight any member of a department that I am so proud to be a part of. Outside of my department but still at UC Davis, Liz Constable, Sarah Giordano, Ari Kelman, and Rana Jaleel have all been ballasts.

I've felt great intellectual sustenance from C19, the Society of Nineteenth-Century Americanists, whose members have revitalized the field in ways that make it feel newly capacious and habitable for me. Hester Blum deserves special mention here; I have been grateful for her friendship and for her work at C19, of which I feel myself to be a direct beneficiary. In nineteenth-century American literary/cultural studies, sometimes intersecting with queer and feminist theory, I have also felt especially indebted to and inspired by Lara Cohen, Peter Coviello, Brigitte Fielder, Stephanie Foote, Naomi Greyser, Nat Hurley, Jeffrey Insko, Dana Luciano, Molly McGarry, Justine Murison, Eden Osucha, Lloyd Pratt,

Mark Rifkin, Britt Rusert, Bethany Schneider, Martha Schoolman, Kyla Schuller, Dana Seitler, Gus Stadler, Jordan Stein, Pam Thurschwell, Kyla Wazana Tompkins, and Ivy Wilson, all pre-1900 Americanists whose friendship, interlocution, and work have been vital to my life in the academy, and whom I feel lucky to know. The recent renewal of my friendship and collegial life with Dana Seitler has been an especial joy. Nancy Bentley and Cindy Weinstein continue to be guiding stars; I could not ask for more generous and thoughtful mentors and friends. Molly Ball, Michael Borgstrom, Daniel Grace, John Mac Kilgore, Samaine Lockwood, Jodi Schorb, Melissa Strong, and Julie Wilhelm, former students and now impressive pre-1900 Americanist colleagues, continue to enliven and inspire my thinking. Kara Thompson may have wandered off to the twentieth/twenty-first century, but I count her as well among my cherished former student interlocutors in the field. Krystyna Michael is a new nineteenth-century Americanist colleague whose work on rhythm has pushed my thinking, as has the work of James Salazar. Brigitte Fielder and Jonathan Senchyne have provided me with food, wine, and intellectual life in Wisconsin. I also owe a great deal to some very fine scholars who are editors in the field: Cindy Weinstein edited a version of chapter 1 for her collection *A Question of Time;* Dana Luciano and Ivy Wilson edited a portion of chapter 3 for their collection *Unsettled States;* Peter Coviello and Jared Hickman edited a version of chapter 5 for their special issue of *American Literature.* In other fields: I could not have thought about Protestantism and the sacramental without early modernists Colby Gordon, Margie Ferguson, and Ari Friedlander; Rebecca Schneider has been both kind to me personally and vital to my thinking about historiographic performance; Joel Burges and Amy Elias have helped me think about time; Sianne Ngai just makes everyone she meets a little bit smarter; and a portion of chapter 4 was edited by Autumn Fiester and Lance Wahlert for a special issue of the *Journal of Homosexuality*, "Mapping Queer Bioethics."

....

The writing of this book has overlapped almost exactly with my work coediting GLQ: *A Journal of Lesbian and Gay Studies* from 2011 to 2017. I am grateful to Ann Cvetkovich and Annamarie Jagose for showing me how to continue to produce scholarship while maintaining high editorial standards, to Nayan Shah and Marcia Ochoa for being spectacular coeditors, to the subeditors of the journal—Kadji Amin, Noreen Giffney, Alexandra Juhasz, Benjamin Kahan, Kara Keeling, Dana Luciano, Eithne Luibhéid, Ming-Yuen S. Ma, and Martin Manalansan—for work that made my job easier, and to all the special issue editors, authors, and managing editors who bore with me. In the field of queer studies, I feel especially indebted to the brilliance and collegiality (much of it mediated by Facebook) of Kadji Amin, Iben Englehardt Andersen, Anjali Arondekar, Anne Gladys Balay, Toby Beauchamp, Lauren Berlant, Robin Bernstein, Roland Betancourt, Michael Bibler, Abigail Boggs, Tyler Bradway, Joshua Branciforte, S. Pearl Brilmeyer, Marissa Brostoff, Steven Bruhm, Julia Bryan-Wilson, Jill Casid, Christopher Castiglia, Zahid R. Chaudhary, Mel Chen, Michael Cobb, Gino Conti, Alex Corey, Alicia Cox, Ashon Crawley, Mathias Danbolt, Ben Davies, Carolyn Dinshaw, Lisa Duggan, Jennifer Doyle, Ramzi Fawaz, Carla Freccero, Brennan Gerard, Bishnupriya Ghosh, Noreen Giffney, Gayatri Gopinath, Joshua Javier Guzmán, Jack Halberstam, Gillian Harkins, Brian Herrera, Scott Herring, Lucas Hilderbrand, Gil Hochberg, Sharon Holland, Janet Jakobsen, Miranda Joseph, Eileen and Aranye Fradenburg Joy, Benjamin Kahan, Kara Keeling, Ryan Kelly, Katie Kent, Tirza Latimer, Eng-Beng Lim, Christopher Looby, Heather Love, M. Shadee Malaklou, Joseph A. Marchal, Jeffrey Masten, Robert McRuer, Victor Roman Mendoza, Julie Avril Minich, Liz Montegary, Amber Musser, Christopher Nealon, Nguyen Tan Hoang, Tavia Nyong'o, Michael O'Rourke, Geeta Patel, Ann Pellegrini, Christopher Peterson, Shane Phelan, Jasbir Puar, Iván Ramos, Chandan Reddy, Vanita Reddy, Takeo Rivera, Juana María Rodríguez, Gabriel Rosenberg, Jordy Rosenberg, Gayle Salamon, Shanté Smalls, Michael Snediker, C. Riley Snorton, Sandy Soto, Eric Stanley, Tina Takemoto, Karen Tongson, Zeb Tortorici, Fillippo Trentin, Mikko Tuhkanen, Jeanne Vaccaro, Deb Vargas, Christine Varnado, Patricia White, Hentyle Yapp, Damon Young, Mary Zaborskis, and Xiang Zairong. I miss the late and cherished José Esteban Muñoz, who, the last time I saw him, stood with me holding hands and giggling about being queer teen grandparents. Sarah Blackwood and Sarah Mesle have been kind editors of other work of mine, and inspire me to write as beautifully as I can. Amy Ruth Buchanan has designed every one of my book covers, and I am so glad we are friends now, too.

I'm indebted to the research assistance, without which I could not have done this work, of Lindsay Baltus, Michael Clearwater, Matt Franks, Katje Jylkka, Jessica Krzeminski, Danielle McManus, Teresa Nelson, George Thomas, and Kaitlin Walker.

I have also been lucky to present in-progress versions of much of this work to colleagues, and I thank very helpful audiences at the American Studies Association; Brown University; Cornell University; the Drew University Theological Seminary; Duke University; Georgetown University; the Intercultural Institute Berlin; Indiana University; Occidental College; the The(e)ories: Critical Theory and Sexuality Studies Seminar at the University College of Dublin; the Center for Gender and Sexuality Studies at the University of California, Berkeley; the University of California, Merced's Interdisciplinary Humanities Program; the University of Illinois Chicago; the "Queer Bioethics" symposium of 2012 by the Bioethics, Sexuality, and Gender Studies Consortium at the University of Pennsylvania; Tulane University; the *Chewing the Scenery* exhibit at the 2011 Venice Bienniale; Washington University in St. Louis; and Yale University.

Jennifer DeVere Brody, Kyla Tompkins, and Peter Coviello, especially, got me through a year I did not think I would survive, when my spouse was catastrophically ill, my marriage was ending, my child was still young, and even my poodle was in and out of the hospital. They continue to make me possible, and I thank them for their friendship. Also crucial to that year and beyond, on Facebook and in the woods: Mandy Berry and Fiona Brideoake, Lisa Beskin and Robin Klein, Katherine Biers and Katherine Lieber, Hester Blum and Jonathan Eburne along with the great Adelaide, Stephanie Foote and Cris Mayo, Karo and Jeff Engstrom, Geoff Gilbert, Susan Gregson and Frank Ridgway, Michael and Britt Metivier, Pam Thurschwell, Sarah Leamon Turula, and Joan Stroer White, all of whom know that it's okay to pee outside. On Facebook also, a group of phenomenal parent-colleague-friends too numerous to name buoyed me up and continue to do so: ANAs, you know who you are. Far away, but crucial to my sanity then and beyond, are H. N. Lukes and Molly McGarry, Sarah Miller, Deb Schwartz, Alison Shonkwiler, and A. K. Summers. In the Bay Area, Suzuki Cady, Birgitte Gilliland, Heather Hadlock, Jing Jacobs, Claire Jarvis, Daphne Magnawa, Pennington Ahlstrand Neuhaus, Tramy Nguyen and Sebastian Diessel, Shannon Steen, Nikki Stoddart, Mie and

Dav Yaginuma, and Kay Young made that year bearable, and continue to make parenting while working a more convivial project. Jan Adams and Rebecca Gordon have also provided San Francisco sustenance, politics, intellectual life, and laughter. Most recently, Nat Hurley has taught me more than she knows, and I thank her for her infinite clarity. Patti Forster, Lori Lamma, Rachel Roberson, and Allison Cain remain the godmamas who bring the light—and without my coparent, Jackie Cherry, there would be no book at all. The latter is not quite true of my daughter, Caroline "Firefly" Freeman-Cherry, but without her there would be no reason for a book, or for much of anything else.

I finished this book by keeping together in time with a very special group of friends I'll call the Pomeranians—you, too, know who you are. Several times a week, a group of us would gather virtually, via a group text, and time our writing sessions and breaks so that we were working and breaking in synch. It sounds like the worst kind of neoliberal productivity maximization, and perhaps it has been, but it has also mitigated the incredible loneliness and self-doubt that writing can produce, and I'm so grateful to the Poms for getting me through the last haul.

I'm indebted to Peter Coviello and Dana Luciano, each of whom read this manuscript through with generosity and rigor, Pam Thurschwell for comments on Chapter 1, Jennifer DeVere Brody for comments on a very early draft of Chapter 2, and Kyla Wazana Tompkins for comments on an early draft of Chapter 5. Finally, I'm very proud of my long association with Duke University Press, and with Ken Wissoker in particular. Ken has been a generous, scrupulous, thoughtful editor and colleague, always believing in my work even when I could not.

....

Chapter 1 is a revised version of an essay that appears in earlier and different form in Cindy Weinstein, ed., *A Question of Time* (Cambridge: Cambridge University Press, 2018).

A portion of chapter 3 appeared in earlier and different form as "Connecticut Yankings: Mark Twain and the Masturbating Dude," in Dana Luciano and Ivy G. Wilson, eds., *Unsettled States: Nineteenth-Century American Literary Studies* (New York: New York University Press, 2014), 275–97.

A portion of chapter 4 appeared in earlier and different form as "Hopeless Cases: Queer Chronicities and Gertrude Stein's 'Melanctha,'" in "Mapping Queer Bioethics," ed. Autumn Fiester and Lance Wahlberg, a special issue of the *Journal of Homosexuality* 63 (2016): 329–48.

Chapter 5 appeared in earlier and different form as "Sacra/mentality in Djuna Barnes's *Nightwood*," in "After the Post-Secular," ed. Peter Coviello and Jared Hickman, a special issue of *American Literature* 86 (December 2014): 737–65.

INTRODUCTION

In his study of the rise of the modern penal system, *Discipline and Punish* (1979, 6–7), Michel Foucault juxtaposes two modes of punishment: a spectacular and grisly execution from 1757, and a prison timetable from 1837. During this relatively short period, to rehearse his well-known argument, the predominating power modes of an emerging liberalism shifted away from public torture, with its focus on the visibly suffering body, and toward self-regulation. In the latter mode of power, subjects (of whom the prisoner was paradigmatic) were supposed to internalize a sense of constantly being supervised, such that they managed their own behavior. Their bodies took meaningful shape and intentionality in relation to, and ideally by incorporating as second nature, an externally imposed order of minute differentiations, emblematized by the timetable.

It is surprising in some ways that Foucault's figure for this external order is a timetable, because timetables greatly preceded the shift he describes, originating as they did in early monastic communities.[1] But as Foucault tells it, the period from the mid-1700s to the mid-1800s saw the rise of a technique of power—he calls it, famously, discipline—whose method and modality temporalized the human body more completely, more thoroughly, and more minutely than ever before.[2] His focus is thus less on the organization *of* time that the timetable seems to represent than on the regulation and instrumentalization of human capacity *through* time. That is, the aspects of the timetable that interest him are not units such as the day or the hour but the fact of collective human punctuality itself: specific actions, such as rising and dressing in silence, lining up to a sequence of drum rolls, and submitting to inspection, were to be performed by groups, within allotted and very specific times, in an unchanging sequence, at regular intervals. Indeed, Foucault speaks of the "three great methods" of control enabled by the timetable: more than simply demarcating the hours, the timetable was part of a project that intended to "establish rhythms, impose particular occupations, [and] regulate the cycles of repetition" of human activities (Foucault 1979, 149). Though all three of these aims take the body as their object, the first and last are matters of timing that body in relation to other bodies as well as to the clock, in a choreographed chronometrics. In short, the timetable is less another iteration of the calendar than it is the representation of a newly systematized body moving deliberately in concert with other bodies.

In Foucault's eye, what distinguished modern institutions of power from their medieval counterparts was that precision of time was met by precision of bodily movement, such that even gestures came under the control of "collective and obligatory rhythm[s]" (Foucault 1979, 152). Discipline's quintessential procedure was the exercise, in which the body itself was broken down into parts, each of whose forces was rearticulated in relation to other parts, objects, and bodies, thereby recomposing the body into, itself, a part-object in relation to a larger machine. This was accomplished in the military through the drill; in schools through increasingly organized physical activities culminating in gymnastics and eurythmics in the late nineteenth century (see, e.g., Budd 1997); and in workplaces through management techniques that peaked with Taylorism, also in the late nineteenth century (see, e.g., Seltzer 1992). These processes were matters, not exclusively but foremostly, of timing: of flesh coming into meaningful embodiment and connectivity through adjusting itself to particular rhythms, that is, particular muscle memories whose accomplishment and automation felt like a form of both selfhood and community (see McNeill 1997).

To sum up the temporal aspect of *Discipline and Punish:* Foucault argues that during the eighteenth century "[a] sort of anatomo-chronological schema of behavior is defined. . . . . Time penetrates the body and with it all the meticulous controls of power" (Foucault 1979, 152). Here, time is both the dominant instrument of control and a means by which other forms of control, such as occupational training, enter the body and come to feel organic, as body parts are coordinated and choreographed in their relation to other body parts, to the body as a whole, to other bodies, and to external stimuli. In fact, Foucault goes so far as to argue that this process formed a "new object" (155): a body that was felt and understood as natural, as agential and enduring, and as prior to any operations enacted upon it, even as these operations were also understood to bring out the body's true arrangement, capacities, and functions. The instrumentalization of time, coextensive with the temporalization of the body, (re)produced the "true" body. This newly naturalized body, Foucault writes, was "composed of solids and assigned movements"; that is, it was stable, measurable, and separate from other bodies. In other words, discipline's "docile body," as Foucault (135) calls it, was profoundly individualized, insofar as discipline isolated and specified not only singular human beings but also minute gestures. This is the Foucauldian body we know and have critiqued for decades in queer, feminist, and antihumanist theory: the singular body proper to the atomized subject of liberal rationality.[3]

But this newly timed body is also, Foucault goes on to say somewhat enigmatically, one of "speculative physics . . . imbued with animal spirits. . . . [a body] of rational mechanics" (Foucault 1979, 155).[4] His tilt toward speculation, the animal, and the mechanical thus also invokes a combinatorial ethics, hinting at the way that the disciplined body was newly imagined as, and trained to be, both porous to and associative with other bodies, objects, and machines. That is, the disciplinary techniques of the military, schools, factories, and so on worked to collate and to instrumentalize the time of individuals in order to amalgamate them into new kinds of massified *forces*: armies, student bodies, and workers whose

carefully arranged combinations of human energy maximized production and effect.[5] The temporalized body of *Discipline and Punish,* then,
was also collectivized in new ways prior to, and eventually alongside of, its
biopolitical management as population: population, we might say, was
the horizon of engroupment produced by the state, but it was made flesh
by, and also contested through, smaller forms of association. And as Kyla
Schuller (2017, 20) notes, in the nineteenth-century United States these
smaller forms of association—"private sector sites such as the plantation, slave ship, church, orphanage, domestic home, domestic novel, factory, women's auxiliary societies, reform movements, and extranational
settlements"—were just as vital to the operations of power as were explicitly state-run institutions such as schools, hospitals, prisons, and the
military. Local forms of sociability and agency shaped the capacities of
individual US American bodies into small-scale forces: constellations of
nonstate, collective actors.

What Foucault describes in *Discipline and Punish,* then, is something
like a Deleuzian assemblage, a collectivized body that represents a contingent gathering of connected forces whose component parts shift in
relation to one another and whose interior and exterior are not stable—
albeit one that discipline immediately reterritorializes for the state, the
market, and other entities of control (see Deleuze and Guattari 1988).
This early Foucault also has in common with Deleuze an understanding of
how bodies communicate with other bodies to form alliances and modes
of being together without passing through cognition or through the linguistic forms of identity—and thus intersects with some of the concepts
foundational to contemporary fields such as the new materialisms and affect studies, both of which turn away from the social constructionist position that language determines the field of action, being, and collective
possibility. The new materialisms are most concerned with the agential
properties of matter, the processes by which matter becomes meaningful,
and the interactions between the human and the inhuman world. Stacy
Alaimo's (2010, 2) new materialist concept of "trans-corporeality," for example, captures some of the porosity of human bodies that Foucauldian
discipline makes it possible to apprehend, though Alaimo is concerned
with the interface between bodies and environments. Affect studies,
too, focuses on the body as a "sensitive interface" (Gregg and Seigworth
2010, 12), exploring thresholds of sensation that may or may not be dis-

cursively codified as emotion, that blur subject-object and mind-body distinctions, and that constitute "asubjective forces" for sociopolitical action (Gibbs 2010, 187). Congruent with the aspect of discipline that I am describing here, and crucial to at least some versions of affect studies, is Marcel Mauss's "habitus," or the learned disposition of the body that allows culture to feel like nature and to be "passed on" from body to body (Mauss 1973; Bourdieu 1977).[6] Similarly, the temporal remaking of bodies into forces entails the idea that bodies communicate directly, in what affect theorist Davide Panagia calls "somacognition" (Panagia 2009). Finally, the scientific concept of "entrainment," or the tendency of rhythmic patterns to synchronize and, more broadly, of moving bodies to align with one another, has been fundamental to affect studies (see, e.g., Brennan 2004, 9–11, 68–73). None of these theories of materialism or of affect draws directly from *Discipline and Punish*, yet the process Foucault describes, of timing the body, seems vital to all of them.

To return, then, to Foucault, the invention of the subject, a modern body with an interior life understood as separate from that body, was, at the same time, the invention of the possibility of local assemblages, novel and contingent forms of belonging that neither required nor resulted in a subject. Yet the genealogy of queer theory that has taken up the porous, combinatorial body as a wedge against the liberal politics of identity has generally followed Deleuze and Guattari's interest in space, or "planar relations" (E. Sedgwick 2003, 8), and thus has not taken up the role of timing in making assemblages possible. Leo Bersani (in Dean, Foster, Silverman, and Bersani 1997, 14), for example, imagines engroupment formally, in terms of visual and tactile correspondences between bodies, as "a kind of solidarity not of identities but of positionings and configurations in space." Eve Sedgwick, in *Touching Feeling* (2003, 8), pivots from a hermeneutics of "beneath" to a politics of "beside," another spatial relation. In *Queer Phenomenology,* Sara Ahmed (2006) dissolves the boundary between bodies and objects through interrogating the normative spatial arrangements that naturalize and reproduce some bodies at the expense of others. Even Jasbir Puar (2007), in *Terrorist Assemblages,* is predominantly interested in the role of the assemblage in deconstructing linear-progressive time through its juxtapositional logic, as opposed to the role of timing in making assemblages possible in the first place.

In contrast, I maintain that the *temporalized* invention of the subject, which is simultaneously the dissolution of the subject, should be of interest to any scholar of sexuality. Indeed, it seems crucial that the body was understood as being fully penetrable by time before it was understood as being fully penetrable by desire: discipline's temporalization-subjectification precedes and then overlaps with the solidification of sexuality as such, or what Foucault elsewhere (1990a, 129) calls "the regime of sexuality"—by which I understand him to mean, briefly, the bundling of anatomy, object-choice, desire, fantasy, gender expression, and sex practice (among other things) into a specific kind of person, narrowing by the middle of the twentieth century into the heterosexual/homosexual binary. Foucault's account of the disciplined body as something whose potentialities were latent and brought out through applied techniques—penetrations of power—that retroactively confirmed the very innateness of those possibilities sounds very much like his account of how sex came to be installed as the true meaning of personhood, and indeed the two intersect and coarticulate.

But in his shift to the study of sexuality, Foucault himself also loses time. He describes the invention of sexuality as a series of predominantly spatial techniques: implantation, interiority, proliferation, distribution, annexation, peripheries, dissemination, penetration, saturation, areas, surfaces, networks, and spirals. Only in his suggestions about the *ars erotica*—in cultures he describes in his four-volume *History of Sexuality* as either non-Western or premodern, in which the practice of pleasure in the pursuit of truth includes attention to the frequency, pacing, rhythm, and duration of sensual activities—can we see the timing of erotic life as a central part of how subjectivity and personhood come into being.[7] In Foucault's ([1976] 1997, 240) work on modern Western biopolitics, on the other hand, the chronometrics of the body disappear into a large-scale "state control of the biological" focused on sequence and duration. In biopolitics, populations—masses of bodies—are created and managed through temporal techniques that change the arrival time, order, and length of life and life events. These include birth control or fertility enhancement, policies designed to promote or delay marriage, reduction of the morbidities associated with chronic illnesses, and so on (243). And, of course, as the work of Ann Laura Stoler (1995) has clarified, this is a partial treatment of the role of temporality in biopolitics in any case, for

Foucault does not account for the role of sequential or durational time in the eighteenth and nineteenth centuries' racialization of sexuality, which is equally the sexualization of race, in which colonized populations were cast as primitive and savage—as both developmentally behind and historically prior to their colonizers. But even in bringing out this history, Stoler follows Foucault in imagining the work of time on sex and sociability only on a very large scale and not in terms of rhythm, synchrony, timing, or metronomics.

To sum up, Foucault offers no description of the role of time between the two poles he describes for the organization of life: the individualizing work of anatomo(chrono)politics that depends on timing specific bodies, and the massifying work of biopolitics whose temporal aspects seem limited to rearranging life events or periodizing populations. There is no explicit account in Foucault of how social formations are temporally created and regulated by forces other than the state, as they so clearly were in the United States; as Dana Luciano (2007, 11–12) puts it in her call for an affective history of sexuality, "[a] different analysis [of power and 'sex'] might have been produced had Foucault incorporated other addresses to the body within this chronology [of the movement from anatomo-politics to biopolitics]." The temporalizing address to the body clarified in *Discipline and Punish,* then, clearly involves bio*power,* or the work of organizing the sensorium and the physical habits that give rise to it (see Lemke 2011, 36), but may not be apprehensible under the state-centered understandings of bio*politics* that have emerged after Foucault, such as those of Giorgio Agamben (1998) and Achille Mbembe (2003).[8] Nor does Foucault explore how the timing of bodies in local instances might disrupt the rhythms, durations, and sequences imposed by the state and other large-scale institutions. Only in Foucault's early descriptions of bodies as accumulating into forces do we see a glimpse of what we might call an *ars sociabilis,* or the attention to frequency, pacing, rhythm, and duration that tunes bodies to one another even in the absence of physical contact. We need a story of how discipline's temporalized body met other bodies in modern social formations reducible neither to institution nor population, neither to identities nor genital sex—but in ephemeral relationalities organizing and expressing themselves through time.

This book is that story. It identifies sites of temporal control, of the rupture of that control, and of the temporal rupture of other forms of control, which are bigger than the individual body and for the most part smaller than populations. It is most interested in small-scale techniques that might be conceptualized as coming between anatomopolitics and biopolitics; that may be aimed at subjectification but may produce a small-scale collective consciousness instead of an individual, interiorized subjectivity; that may be produced within, by, and even for a biopolitical project but that do not necessarily serve it at all times. Foucault's theory of discipline teaches us that the body may be a site of inscription, but also makes it possible to see the body as an instrument in and for acts that cannot be reduced to identities but are social nonetheless, in a process that I will eventually link to incipiently queer modes of belonging and becoming. Similarly, the proliferating inclinations between the bodies that discipline fosters do not necessarily solidify into a figure or a form of being but may stay entirely in the register of doing. Finally, we can see through *Discipline and Punish* that temporality is a nonreproductive, but nevertheless somatic and material, mode of sensory receptivity that collates bodies in relations of affinity across space and, I would add to Foucault's analysis, even across historical period.

Beside You in Time contends, then, that subjugated knowledge is often lodged in the flesh itself, and lives as timed bodiliness and as styles of temporally inflected sociability, predominant in the nineteenth century, that we have forgotten, or never learned, how to see.[9] Broadly, the sites of temporal control and response to that control that I discuss in this book are religious rituals (those of the Shakers in chapter 1, and Catholics in chapter 5), racialization (slavery in chapter 2, and racial uplift in chapter 4), historiography (chapter 3), health and conservation culture (chapter 4), and sexuality (chapter 5), all appearing or intensifying during a period that I call the very long nineteenth century, whose contours I will outline more carefully below. Within these sites, fictional characters and actual historical actors struggle both to inhabit the dominant temporalities that organize them, and to tap into other rhythms, other ways of feeling like they belong to a history, and/or other modes of arranging past, present, and future, that will foster new forms of being and belonging. In what follows, I call these temporal encounters *sense-methods*, foregrounding time itself as a visceral, haptic, proprioceptive mode of apprehension—a way of feeling and organizing the world through and with the individual body, often in concert with other bodies.

On Sentimentality and Sense-Methods

Any theory of the time-sense as a method for creating sociability in the nineteenth century must be squared with the extant work on sentimental culture, for as numerous critics have shown, the latter was the nineteenth-century United States' dominant machine of sociability and intimacy—its *scientia sociabilis,* to riff again on Foucault's (1990a) *History of Sexuality.* By "sentimental culture," I mean the wide variety of institutions and discourses that turned what were understood as raw physical sensations into meaningful emotional concord with others, with those meanings organized and recontained around, or reterritorialized in and as, race, buttressed by gender, class, nationality, religion, and sexuality (and of course this list could go on).[10] The promise of sentimental culture was, and remains, its capacity to extend face-to-face rituals and practices into forms of belonging that affiliated people beyond immediate community, to build cohorts of fellow feeling (Kete 2000; Coviello 2005). But its ideological currency was, and remains, a highly racialized language of emotion, whereby white people's, particularly white women's, fragility, interiority, receptivity, porosity, and expressivity are produced and maintained in relation to other subjects and populations cast as overly susceptible to their sensations or as impervious to feeling.[11]

This book's object of analysis, in contrast with sentimental studies, is neither raw sensation nor the nineteenth century's codified language of emotion and its attendant identities. *Beside You in Time* turns from the passions back to the body receiving sensations and puts the body at the center of analysis, but focuses on ways of using and tuning the body in relation to other bodies present, past, and future, in an extension of Foucauldian discipline toward ends that may not serve identity or dominant forms of the social. However, the best recent work on nineteenth-century American sentimentality has also illuminated something crucial for this project: how biopower takes shape through culture's management of the affects, particularly the sense of time, in processes that sometimes historically precede the state's relatively more brute interventions on the physical body and sometimes justify the latter. Dana Luciano's *Arranging Grief* (2007), for example, clarifies how non-state-centered rituals and symbols of mourning conscripted the body for a form of slow, nonlinear time that seemed to be a bulwark against both national-progressive and commodity-capitalist time, even as it clearly buttressed them. For Luciano, biopower, or what she calls "chronobiopolitics," involves the production of "life" in the coordinated temporal terms of linear reproduction, accumulation, and accomplishment on the one hand, and a replenishing cyclical and sacred domesticity on the other (10). Luciano's work on the "temporalities of social belonging" (17) demonstrates that time and its regulating functions take shape in and through collective bodily praxes that are not coterminous with the state's inventions of and interventions into populations—an insight key to this book.

In a related project, Kyla Schuller's *The Biopolitics of Feeling* (2017, 2) asserts that sentimentalism "operates as a fundamental mechanism of biopower." As with Luciano's work, Schuller argues that this affective form of biopower preceded state-centered biopolitics in the United States, and provided a means for the latter to operate: "the tasks of the biopolitical state," writes Schuller, "evolved out of the private institutions of sentiment" (21). These institutions, in Schuller's view, focused on the capacity of the body to receive and coordinate external stimuli. The scientific discourse of impressibility, or the capacity of the body to receive sensations and incorporate them into heritable qualities, Schuller argues, was used to differentiate "civilized" subjects, who could progress through time, from "savage" ones who were "suspended in the eternal state of flesh and linger[ed] on as unwanted remnants of prehistory" (8). Impressibility was understood as a literal binding mechanism, connecting bodies to their environment and to each other in ways that were eventually managed by the state as race, gender, and sexuality. Furthermore, impressibility organized linear-historical time through the rubric of heritability.

What brings these two projects together, and makes them so important to this one, is their understanding of the role of bodily sensation, prior to the regime of "sexuality" and expanding our understanding of biopower to include affect, in disposing subjects toward one another socially. As Schuller puts it, "Sex before sexuality manifested as a proliferating dynamic between bodies" (2017, 34). I've attempted to capture this dynamic with the term "sense-methods." Sense-methods consist of bodywork, of inarticulated or unspoken, carnal forms of knowledge, intervention, and affiliation inhabited and performed either in groups or on behalf of them. They are nonverbal, and often nonideational—not so much Foucault's ([1976] 1997, 7) "non-conceptual knowledges," which are unsystematic or seemingly unsophisticated ideas that merely rank below the knowledge systems of elites, but rather somatic manifestations that are not, however codified they might be on their own physical terms, typically understood as concepts or methods at all. Neither are sense-methods necessarily keyed to the traditional five senses of sight, sound, touch, smell, and taste. Instead, they might be synaesthetic, or entirely beyond those five senses, insofar as they often involve the visceral, the proprioceptive, or muscle memory—and in this book, I am particularly interested in a sixth sense, the sense of timing, or synchronization (temporal coincidence) and alternation (turn taking), which, though some scientists have described it as innate (Trevarthen 1999/2000, cited in Gibbs 2010, 198; see also Strogatz 2004), seems a site wherein the cultural and the biological meet one another.

Sense-methods do not necessarily operate from the top down, as Foucault would have it in *Discipline and Punish* and beyond. Curiously, *Discipline and Punish* has virtually no theory of resistance, and even in the first volume of *The History of Sexuality* (1990a), in which Foucault does theorize resistance, the idea of "reverse discourse" shears the term "discourse" of any but its linguistic aspects, insofar as it names the way that individuals could reappropriate a form of selfhood by claiming the terms and concepts produced by the institutions of law, medicine, and psychiatry, rather than by arrogating techniques of power that were applied directly to the body: there is, for example, no "reverse implantation" in Foucault. But amassed and recombined human energies—engrouped, disciplined bodies—can certainly turn together against the very institutions in which they were organized, as in the factory strike that turns the sociability of wage workers against the owners of production, or the urban flash mob that turns the anonymous consumer crowd into a juggernaut. Judith Butler (2015, 8) calls this "concerted bodily enactment, a plural form of performativity," focusing on "forms of coordinated action, whose condition and aim is the reconstitution of plural forms of agency and social practices of resistance" (9). Butler's horizon is the demonstration aimed at the official national-political sphere, where bodies gather and do things in concert in order to signify and to perform their persistence in the face of being relegated to the biopolitical status of disposability: notably, according to Butler, plural actions intervene in a specifically temporal way, showcasing the quality of endurance. Butler's heuristic is the performative, or the way that popular sovereignty can be enacted in advance of or as a relay to its achievement as policy. My horizons and heuristics are somewhat broader: in my view, coordinated, informal sense-methods can effect any number of social possibilities, and enactment of a national ideal is only one of them. They can also generate social forms that do not respond to or mimic an official, legible version. In other words, if Butler's performative theory of assembly focuses on the embodiment of "the people" through protests and occupations, my own theory of sense-methods focuses on the embodiment of a relationality that does not always refer to or result in a stable social form but instead *moves*, with and against, dominant timings and times.

On Queer Hypersociability and Method

"Sense-methods" comprise, above all, a queer theory of relationality and sociability. If engroupment is a sensory matter, one particularly inflected by the senses of time and timing, this is because the senses are necessarily more promiscuous than the discourses that reterritorialize sensations into identities and populations. In their treatise *The Undercommons,* Stefano Harney and Fred Moten (2013, 15) describe the social in some of the terms that I am after, gesturing toward "the re-routing encoded in the work of art: in the anachoreographic reset of a shoulder, in the quiet extremities that animate a range of social chromaticisms." In these brief, evocative phrases I can see several elements of what I mean by sense-methods: an emphasis on body parts (shoulders, extremities) as metaphors for and means of rearticulating the social; a compositional theory of the social itself (here, it is imagined through choreography, through the jazz technique of chromaticism, and through color theory, whereas my predominant rubrics are temporal); an unpredictable sense of direction (the prefix *ana-* meaning upward, backward, again, against). *Beside You in Time,* in keeping with these elements, tracks a series of social reroutings that take place through embodied temporal recalibrations. These reroutings are extensive, as centrifugal as they are centripetal: sense-methods, I contend, are key to imagining queerness as not antisocial or antirelational, as in recent work by Lee Edelman and others, but *hyper*social.

To briefly rehearse the antisocial thesis of queer theory: foundational to it is Lacan's (1999, 126) dictum that "there is no such thing as a sexual relation," meaning that desire is a series of self-projections onto the Other, in which the Other's subjectivity has no place or real impact. Early gay male theorists such as Guy Hocquenghem ([1972] 1993) and Harold Beaver (1981), who theorized the antirelational aspect of homosexuality in advance of its contemporary articulations, understood homosexuality as, precisely, a breaking of the social contract through which imaginary identities recognize and enter into exchange with one another. Extending the Lacanian formulation and borrowing from Laplanche ([1970] 1976) the idea of sexuality as "unbinding" the energy that the ego seeks to bind into coherence and functionality, Leo Bersani (1987) has famously posited the receptive sex act—the state of being penetrated sexually— as fundamentally anticommunitarian and antiidentitarian. Sex, in Bersani's view, is anti- or nonrelational not just because desire is a hall of mirrors but also because receptive sex shatters the contours of the bodily imago and of the ego, which is at first a bodily one and the grounds from which we enter into relations with others. Receptive sex, then, is a figure for the promisingly destructive potential of all sex, a theoretical insight that spans Bersani's work from at least *The Freudian Body* ([1986] 1990) through *Homos* (1995). For Lee Edelman (2004), this destructive potential, which Edelman links tightly to the figuration of queers as avatars of death and to the Freudian death drive, makes queerness into a wedge against a particularly US American form of futurity in which reproductive heterosexuality and the figure of the child are the horizon for politics, for life, for the politics of life.

For my part, and despite how compelling I find these formulations, I see queerness less in terms of the pulsations of the death drive that insistently undermine the coherence of ego, identity, and politics—or what Lynne Huffer (2009, xvii) calls the "ironic" mode—and more in terms of a drive toward connectivity, conjugation, and coalescence that produces new forms, however momentary, which Huffer (xvii) calls the "generous" mode (see also Freud [1920] 1964), and which cannot be equated with the biopolitical understanding of life as that which must be optimized at the expense of those deemed unworthy of life. As theorists from Deleuze and Guattari (1988) through Elizabeth Grosz (2004), Jasbir Puar (2007), and Tim Dean (2000, 2009) have clarified in different ways, biological reproduction need not be the telos of the life drive: its point is to mix substances, to coalesce with others, to self-extend and thus retroactively transform the self, to renew living on different terms and in ways that need not culminate in the schemes of personhood we know today but may pass through styles of affiliation that we can learn from. And of course the generous mode can equally discombobulate the status quo as long as its practitioners remain ironic enough not to let the social forms they generate petrify and become inevitable.

Returning to Harney and Moten: they insist on a social imaginary that focuses on "reroutings" rather than on negation. This idea of rerouting may have been lost in queer theory's handing off of the baton of queer antirelationality from Bersani to Edelman, for one distinct strand of Bersani's thinking involves the way that art and sex alike, in shattering the forms through which we perceive ourselves and the world, open up the potential for new connections among psyches, bodies, and environments—new relays for connectivity. Bersani actually has a very lush social imagination, for he posits new relationships based on aesthetics, even on design—on the visual rhymes of body parts in anonymous sex acts, or on what he calls (in Dean et al. 1997, 6) a "correspondence of forms" that extends the self toward others in relations of partial sameness, ringing changes on the couple-centeredness of sociality itself. But this, too, is a spatial and effectively visual formulation, however useful I have found it. The hypersocial, by contrast, is not just excess sociability but sociability felt and manifested along axes and wavelengths beyond the discursive and the visual—and even beyond the haptic, for the synchronization of bodies does not require their physical touch, but rather a simultaneity of movement in which the several become one. In theorizing sense-methods as a means toward and a way of thinking queer hypersociability, then, I lean on the prefix "hyper" meaning not only over, above, beyond, in excess, but also (in its more present-tense, truncated usage) a suggestion of excessive motion, as "hyper" is slang for "hyperactive."

Furthermore, the forms of sociability afforded by alignments and re-alignments in and through time are not just synchronous—they also hop the timeline in ways that the term "hyperlink" invokes. In this book, then, I also want to draw out an aspect of an older, Marxist materialism, which sees history not as a congealed past but as the continual making and re-making of the social field—of the relations among people, including between the living and the dead as well as the not-yet-born, as in Walter Benjamin's ([1950] 1968, 260) reminder that the working class, figured as the redeemer of future generations, forgot a hatred "nourished by the image of enslaved ancestors rather than that of liberated grandchildren." But even this is too linear and too aligned with genealogical descent. Meanwhile, Deleuzian assemblages are often theorized as taking place within a particular time period (usually the present), rather than vertically, across eras in ways that blur the boundaries between now and then, and in doing so change social possibilities in the present. My concept of sense-methods, on the other hand, intersects with an underdiscussed element in Foucault (1990a, 143), his idea of biohistory, or the process in which the history that humans make, their organization of power, intervenes in what seem like immutable laws of biology, changing the physical constitution of the human. Foucault (143) describes biohistory as "the pressure through which the movements of life [i.e., what would seem to be merely biological] and the processes of history [i.e., collective human activity] interfere with one another." While *Beside You in Time* does not track the biological per se, it does explore how physiological acts and social formations intersect with and reconstitute one another across time as well as within particular spaces. I take up, therefore, not only the rhythms of discipline but also another mode of subjectification, engroupment, and self-dissolution that is connected to the invention of race: the rise of historical feeling, or the sensation of being connected to and derived from non-kin ancestors or prior to non-kin progeny, which partially contributed to the periodizing of populations that Stoler (1995) describes but is not reducible to that function. Among denizens of the late eighteenth and nineteenth centuries and beyond, the feeling of belonging to and extending into time from out of a particular past was inculcated through reading secondary histories, historical fiction, and anthropological treatises about the development of humanity's various cultures. Historical feeling also took shape through physical practices that involved the temporal recalibrations of bodies and subjects: rituals of patriotism, grief, and other shared emotions; heritage activities such as collecting and tourism; and especially the historical reenactments that became popular beginning with eighteenth-century *tableaux vivants*—all tuned the body to other epochs, just as discipline tuned it to new rhythms.[12] In this book, I contend that sense-methods can rearrange the relations between past and present, linking contemporary bodies to those from other times in reformulations of ancestry and lineage.

Finally, the idea that the sensory register can organize what belongs together, what can be brought together, and how that "bringing" happens, also influences the way I read and think in this book, which I am not sure boils down to a method I can formulate for transfer to students and colleagues or a gambit in the current method wars. But let us call it, too, a sense-method. I begin, always, with finely grained close readings of imaginative and documentary texts, whose "reroutings" of bodies, relationships, and perceptual possibilities take patience to apprehend. Part of that apprehension includes a kind of ingathering of a critical and historical archive whose contours I don't have in mind in advance, as the primary work begins to speak outward, to incline me toward material that further illuminates it or that it suddenly casts in a different light. I've always described my method to students as slow, blind, groping in the dark, but that seems an especially apt metaphor for a book on embodied ways of knowing that are at a temporal slant to official knowledge. As disability studies has taught us, slowness and blindness are not lesser forms of understanding but merely alternative ones. And groping, despite its bad reputation as a sex act, is just a mode of sensory improvisation. All of this is to align my method with, itself, a promiscuous hypersociability of approach of the sort that will be recognizable to anyone trained in cultural studies, in which we cannot know in advance with what materials our objects will demand proximity. My hypersocial method may also resonate with some current discussions of surface reading as a "mutual pedagogy of erotics" (Cheng 2009, 102) between text and critic, text and contexts, text and other texts, rather than as a hermeneutic aimed toward the recovery of unconscious material or hidden historical causes—though I cannot lay claim to never reading symptomatically.

It might be more modest, and more honest, to claim both the methods of mutual attunement and resonance that I track between bodies in *Beside You in Time* and the methods I use to reorganize literary texts in relation to one another and to other materials, as feminine, feminist, or even lesbian-femme, with an emphasis on the critic's, and even the textual object's, receptivity and susceptibility to various "outside" materials.[13] In fact, queer hypersociability is not tuned to the drama of the antisocial thesis, a theory developed in urgent response to the early AIDS crisis in which gay white men were portrayed as forces of death and to the rise of a gay movement insistent upon normativity, but responds instead to the erosions of everyday life that have perennially characterized female, non-white, lesbian, poor, disabled, and other less privileged existences. My touchstone thinker, then, is not the Freud of the death drive but Audre Lorde, whose 1978 paper "The Uses of the Erotic" advocated the feeling body, in common pursuit with others, as a source of knowledge and power.[14] Lorde writes, "In the way my body stretches to music and opens into response, hearkening to its deepest rhythms, so every level upon which I sense also opens to the erotically satisfying experience, whether it is dancing, building a bookcase, writing a poem, examining an idea" (Lorde [1978] 2007, 341). She links the mutual timing of bodies, which she calls "self-connection shared" (341) and satisfying "our erotic needs in concert with others" (342) to a political demand for structures based on human need rather than on profit. The stakes for sense-methods and for queer hypersociability, then, are both contemporary insofar as they address the twentieth and twenty-first centuries' acceleration of ordinary modes of debilitation, and specific to the long nineteenth century insofar as they address the historically specific role of time in maximizing the force of the human body, wearing it down, and countering its reterritorialization as endlessly useful for state and market interests.

To clarify my argument once more: this book claims that the sense of time is instrumental to becoming social in an expansive mode I call a queer hypersociability, and that time is itself a mode of engroupment for both dominant and subordinated human energies. I track queer hypersociability through dance in chapter 1. In chapter 2, I explore a form of this drive to combine with both the dead and the living in African American performances of playing dead. In chapter 3, I investigate queer hypersociability across time in amateur historiography. In chapter 4, I show how the use of chronic time expands queer relationality. And in chapter 5, I connect queer hypersociability back to the sacramental and incarnational. To see the very long nineteenth century in terms of sense-methods, then, is to see the overlapping and shifting powers of discipline and sexuality, the ordering force of time in the production of bodies and collectivities, and the racialization of time in places within, alongside, or instead of the official political state. The scenes in which sense-methods do their work, as the chapters to come will show, are variously rhythmic, historical, and/or divine, and they expand not only the boundaries of the human body but also those of the nineteenth century itself.

On the Archive and the Period

My archive of very long nineteenth-century texts is perhaps most notable for what is not in it: much of the gay white male corpus of the period that has been foundational to queer nineteenth-century American literary studies. For Thoreau, Whitman, most of Melville (though I do nod to "Bartleby, the Scrivener"), Charles Warren Stoddard, Henry James, and others, I've substituted the celibate Shakers, ex-slave writers who are ambivalent about the family, the ostensibly heterosexual Mark Twain and Pauline Elizabeth Hopkins, and the Sapphic modernists Gertrude Stein and Djuna Barnes. These are all artists whose chief aims seem to be an expansive vision of sociability rather than a drive toward identity or even queer sex practices. I'm not convinced that the white male archive, especially that of the nineteenth century, leads inexorably to homosexuality or to the antisocial thesis, and indeed, Peter Coviello (2013) has made a persuasive argument, in *Tomorrow's Parties,* that much of that archive— Whitman, Thoreau, and Melville in particular—elegiacally preserves forms of sociability that would become illegible under the regime of sexuality. I feel greatly indebted to Coviello's project. But I do think that my alternative constellations of texts have brought me to the idea that the time-sense produces forms of collectivity and association that "sexuality" and even Coviello's more diffuse erotics may not fully contain.[15]

Even given this shift in archival materials, though, it may seem incongruous to make an argument about the uses of the timed body through analyses of linguistic texts, as this book does. To this I would argue that the sense-world of the past is available to us only at one remove, through representation. Nonrepresentational sound recordings can give us back the sonic past, but only a very specific slice of it—a single performance, a particular ambient soundscape. Old smells, also indexical rather than representational, can body forth the remains of the past, as when an opened grave smells of rot, but these smells are not composed of the original object's molecules, because if they are, then the object that they emanate from still exists in some form in the present. Similarly, we can touch or taste objects *from* the past, but not *in* their past. We can "feel" the past only through a second-order representation of it, in a visual or linguistic medium that evokes other senses, or through a physical reenactment that, given the new context in which it takes place, can never be a perfect capture. But even reenactment cannot recreate the way that performances worked in their own moment to recruit beholders into their scene. We can see the horizontal process of recruitment, of belonging, mapped out *as process* only in second-order presentations whose participants, witnesses, and commentators—as narrators and characters—appear on the same historical plane as the activity itself.

Of the various media through which representation takes place, only the durational ones—the ones that unfold over a stretch of time rather than being apprehensible all at once, like a painting—can capture the process of coordinating, gathering, transmitting, and otherwise transferring energies from one body to another. Thus the works explored in this book are almost all prose (some supplemented by images), precisely because prose takes place through linear time, establishing relations of cause and effect and highlighting process. The works I take up are also predominantly *narrative* prose, because seeing the processual nature of sensory engroupment depends, in part, on the narratorial commentary surrounding it. And they are predominantly but not entirely fictional because characters too can comment on the recruiting process and thus offer a glimpse of how sense-methods worked in their own moment. Therefore, many of the texts I discuss in this book depict performances, among them song and dance, stage shows, and liturgical acts; many of them include commentary and other reactions by witnesses who are, or resist being, pulled into the scene of performance. I examine anti-Shaker tracts whose polemic is supported by lurid descriptions of the Shakers as well as lithographs of their performances in chapter 1; narratives of former slaves as well as folk tales, stage performances, and illustrations in chapter 2; newspaper accounts of performances in both chapters 1 and 2; Mark Twain's short essays and speeches in chapter 3; and short stories and novels in all five chapters, including fiction by Catharine Maria Sedgwick, Sutton E. Griggs, Pauline Elizabeth Hopkins, Mark Twain, Herman Melville, Gertrude Stein, and Djuna Barnes. In all of them, we can see historically specific bodies at work in and through time in ways that would otherwise be difficult to take hold of.

The span of these works, from the late 1700s to the mid-1930s, is unwieldy only according to traditional nation/period demarcations. *Beside You in Time* tells a story about the power of the timed body during the very long nineteenth century, a period that I first understood as a period at all through the history of sexuality. This period is bookended by the consolidation of discipline in Europe and its colonies on one side in the late eighteenth century, and on the other, the somewhat belated consolidation of sexual identity in the United States after European sexological texts were translated and made available here—a consolidation not complete, if it ever was, until after the first third of the twentieth century (see Chauncey 1995 and Kahan 2017). Or, to put it more simply, I am interested in the period bounded on one end by the European prison/factory/hospital in Foucault's *Discipline and Punish* and refracted in the experience of the Shakers that I discuss in chapter 1, and on the other end by the American gay bar that glimmers through the first volume of *The History of Sexuality* (Foucault 1990a) and Foucault's essay "Friendship as a Way of Life" ([1981] 1984) and that shows up in Djuna Barnes's *Nightwood* ([1936] 2006), the subject of my final chapter. But I am less interested in these as spaces than as temporal orders.

Another way to look at the very long nineteenth century, then, might be in terms of shifts in the lived experience of temporality. On the one hand, by the late eighteenth century, Europe and the United States had seen an intense solidification of the power of clock time (Sherman 1997; O'Malley 1990) and work discipline (Thompson 1967), the temporal motors of Foucault's prison/factory/hospital complex. By the mid-nineteenth century, these interrelated phenomena had dispersed over new domains such as slavery (see M. M. Smith 1997) and, as Catharine Beecher's *A Treatise on Domestic Economy* (1841) makes clear, housework. At the apex of discipline's regime, we can presume, time began to seem immutable and unmalleable both because it was orchestrated by institutions large and small, and because it was seen to emanate from the individual body's very gestures—though, as I will go on to argue, these orchestrations could be turned into forces that countered institutional modes of temporality. But during the latter half of the nineteenth century through the period before World War II, new technologies such as the railroad, photography, the cinema, and air travel made time seem suddenly pliable, such that the ordinary rhythms of things sped up or slowed down, events could be made to run backward, or a juxtaposition of disparate moments could invoke change over time (see Schivelbusch [1977] 1986 and Doane 2002). A multiplicity of possible times, and interventions in the systematized time of capitalism, opened up during the latter part of the long nineteenth century, emblematized by the wanderings and flaneurship that comprised life for the denizens of urbanized spaces such as Wall Street in "Bartleby, the Scrivener," which I explore in chapter 4, and Djuna Barnes's Paris in *Nightwood,* which I explore in chapter 5. Rather than tracking a teleological history of time as it moved from discipline to flaneurship, though, this book names and locates some of the prevailing temporal regimes of the period I describe in the United States, and places some alternate sense-methods in relation to them. To put it yet another way, I track the timed body across several proximate and entangled regimes—religion and secularity, race, historiography, health, and sexuality—a body that acts in various and varying relation to the most legible imperatives of those regimes.

Chapter Breakdown

The modes of bodily control I explore in this book are also specific, though not always unique, to the United States and its empire. The first of these I explore, in chapter 1, is the order of secularity, otherwise known as mainline Protestantism, which demoted cultures that were seemingly too dependent on bodily means of worship to the status of savages racialized as Native American or, less often, automatons or machines racialized as black. The United Society of Believers, or Shakers, is a case study for the way that rhythmic alterity, when seen as countervailing the norms of gender and sex, could racialize people who in other ways seemed thoroughly white, for the Shakers were New England Protestants hailing from the mother country itself. But the dominant forms of Protestantism emerging in the late eighteenth century, in keeping with Puritan ideals and as a way of distinguishing themselves from ecstatic worship, subordinated the liturgical body to the word—to scriptural exegesis, verbal confession, and homiletics. Protestantism became less and less apprehensible as a system that, itself, temporally ordered bodies and life trajectories as it took shape in negative reaction to communities such as the Shakers, who used explicitly somatic, rhythmic modes of belonging to counter heteromarital hegemony and to express their ideal of celibacy. The Shakers' method of worship, I argue, was simply too corporeal, even when Shaker elders reordered it into highly disciplined, patterned dances. In fact, as I demonstrate, the Shakers' reformed dance style doubly racialized them as so overly regulated that they hyperbolized whiteness into a form of deathliness associated with blackness and enslavement.

Following up on this association of blackness and death, the second order of timing that I explore, in chapter 2, is the one that regulated chattel slavery in the United States. This was not primarily the proto-Taylorization of plantation work, as the latter was influenced by the factory system, even if the reordering of plantation time was a second-order way of making slave bodies docile (M. M. Smith 1997). More fundamental to the system of slavery was the fact that slave owners had absolute power to wrest enslaved people from genealogical time, and to shorten or terminate slaves' lives—to effect what Orlando Patterson (1982) calls the "social death" of enslaved people as a prelude to and rehearsal of an actual death imposed from without as a matter of murder or enforced deterioration. The sense-method that emerged in response to this condition was a performance of death that I call *chronothanatopolitics,* or playing dead, reenacting social death so as to both refuse the consolations of a liberal, white humanism that depends on antiblackness for its meaning, and gesture at other forms of sociality. As my archive for this chapter—several African American folk tales; the ex-slave narratives of Harriet Jacobs ([1861] 1987), Henry Bibb ([1850] 2001), and Henry Box Brown ([1851] 2008); and Sutton E. Griggs's novel *Imperium in Imperio* ([1899] 2003)—clarifies, playing dead is a performance, but not a mode of performativity dependent on resignification in the idiom of queer theory. Rather, what it has in common with queer theory is an asocial, though not entirely antisocial, mode of relationality counter to marriage, kinship, and reproduction—saturated as these latter forms are with the temporalities denied to people of African descent.

The concept of social death is also precisely what allows the temporality of slavery to be understood as enduring beyond the period in which white Americans legally owned black ones. It ruptures any easy periodization of before and after 1865—the dominant periodization for scholars of American literature and culture. Related to slavery, then, is a third form of temporal control that congealed in the long nineteenth century, that of academic history. The dominant historiography of the nineteenth century was made up of firm boundaries between then and now, between bodies categorized as modern and those cast as savage or primitive, and between bodies of different eras: in other words, historical writing was a way of ordering time in and for a nineteenth-century present tense deeply invested in hierarchical differentiations between bodies. In chapter 3, I explore how two fin de siècle authors, Mark Twain and Pauline Hopkins, burst these temporal boundaries to write histories that, as fictional versions of historical reenactment, thrust then-contemporary bodies into much earlier times in ways that contested and still contest both the periodization of US history and the rigid categories of gender, race, and sexuality. In Twain's *A Connecticut Yankee in King Arthur's Court* ([1889] 1982), a white traveler to medieval Camelot fails to see, though Twain's readers are set up to recognize, how medieval forms of power and violence persist in the wake of US chattel slavery, particularly in post-Reconstruction America. In Hopkins's *Of One Blood* ([1903] 1988), a traveler to the ancient seat of Ethiopia finds it preserved underground as if time has stopped, and discovers that Western culture derives from African people's inventions and ideas: the novel effectively rewrites global history. Importantly, these ruptures of historical periodization are also ways of reconstituting erotic life, as if writing or experiencing history otherwise might be a form of sex. Twain's main character "abuses" history as a mode of "self-abuse," masturbating his way out of linear-historical time and clarifying how a sexual disorder is understood as a temporal one, and how "bad," amateur historiography is linked to aberrant sexuality. Hopkins's main character literally marries his way back into a dynastic Afrocentric history on a somewhat more conservative note, but the trope of reincarnation that animates *Of One Blood* moves beyond the genitality of masturbation in Twain to suggest a form of reproduction and cross-temporal contact that supersedes marriage and dynasty.

As Twain and Hopkins show, nineteenth-century American history proper—both the writing and the making of dominant history—was linked, in turn, to the production of normative bodies, those understood to lead the project of nation building and hence modernity. Early in the very long nineteenth century, disciplinary techniques such as those Foucault describes were used to hone the militaries that fought in the name of American independence (see von Steuben 1779), and these remained fairly stable through the War of 1812, a battle that defined US nationhood. As weapons technology developed, infantry tactics followed in a variety of manuals pertinent to each US war (see *Military Field Manuals, 1782–1899,* 2007). And reenactments of wars and battles were a mode of masculine self-fashioning (see Schneider 2011). But drills and exercises with a nationalist horizon were not just the purview of the military and its civilian imitators. The rise of the Boy Scouts, the physical culture movement, and organized sports involved ordinary people in projects understood to contribute to the destiny of the United States. By the late 1800s and into the first quarter of the twentieth century, imperial might was idealized in the figure of the white, able-bodied, sporting man (Bederman 1995; R. Dyer 1997; Green 1986). Concomitantly, after the failure of Reconstruction, proponents of racial uplift envisioned the future of black people in terms of middle-class norms of sexual propriety, domesticity, and heteronormative gender roles (Carby 1987), terms that framed particular routines and rhythms of work, leisure, and home life as vital to the future of that particular population and to humanity as a whole. Both imperial white masculinity and black racial uplift were framed in eugenic terms. By the early twentieth century, the idea of "human resources" was born to address the problem of national vitality and, in particular, the role of chronic maladies in sapping it: chronic time, we might say, had become a national problem precisely insofar as the state and the market fostered an almost machinic productivity. This is the context I use in chapter 4 to explore Gertrude Stein's novella "Melanctha" ([1909] 2000), which pits the time of the chronic, embodied in the eponymous female protagonist, against racial uplift's discipline of "regularity," embodied in her lover, Dr. Jeff Campbell. Reading "Melanctha" alongside of Melville's short story "Bartleby, the Scrivener" ([1853] 1979), which in many ways anticipates it, allows us to see chronic illness, recalcitrance, and lack of will as forms of resistance to the temporally disciplined bodies that supposedly make history national, and make national history.

In chapter 4, I describe how chronic time, grammatically inflecting "Bartleby" and elaborated both as plot and as style in "Melanctha," also opens bodies to new forms of connection with the world and with others by slowing them down, dilating, and intensifying them. Chronic time decalcifies and disaggregates "sexuality" thought in terms of objectchoice, bringing us back, conceptually, to the way that discipline reassembles individual and social bodies, opening them to one another in new ways. But as experienced by those left out of the times of empire and uplift, chronic time does not always produce a mass that can be managed as a population, nor does it necessarily work in service of projects that serve the state or capitalism. As "Melanctha" clarifies, the connections that chronic time forges are micrological, temporary, and uninevitable. Surprisingly, Stein characterizes these moments of connectivity and assemblage as religious, which hearkens back to my analysis of Shaker worship practices. While sacred ritual can directly serve dominant institutions of power, the religious feelings Stein conjures up are rooted in bodily experience in ways that recall an American history of dissident, enthusiastic, emphatically minor sects. My final chapter, then, turns back to a stigmatized and especially visceral religion in the United States, Catholicism, and its incarnational doctrine of the sacraments. The sacraments, I argue, are in many ways a consummate sense-method, for they involve contact between the body and material understood to bring participants closer to God and to one another through the body of Christ. Baptism, for example, uses water—by sprinkling, pouring, or even complete immersion—to transform the baptismal candidate into a Christian and bring him or her into the spiritual kinship of Christianity, as well as to renew the baptismal vows of observers who have pledged to support the candidate's life as a Christian. Even as the sacraments bring people together horizontally with one another and with the divine in earthly form, they also enfold Catholics and their Anglican counterparts into a vertical form of history and descent, as with the laying on of hands that accompanies ordination and folds the ordinant into a history of apostles, or as with the chrism (anointing oil) that is part of the sacrament of extreme unction, which signifies that the dead person is now part of a genealogical line of saints. I locate a sacramental mentality, which I call a *sacra/mentality*, in a counterintuitive place: Djuna Barnes's high modernist novel *Nightwood* ([1936] 2006). In the teeth of a homosexual identity that has by the time of *Nightwood*'s first publication begun to consolidate, the novel offers up the sacraments as an alternative route to human connectivity and lineage. It does so with deep irony, of course, for in *Nightwood* baptism, the laying on of hands, and especially the Eucharist are modes of linking together those who are—by Christian and state standards—damned, including the lesbian Nora Flood, the cross-dresser Matthew Dante O'Connor, and the androgyne Robin Vote. Detached from the institutional Church, the sacramental becomes this book's final vision of queer hypersociability.

I finish with a coda that brings *Beside You in Time* into the twentieth century, via Amiri Baraka's short-short story "Rhythm Travel" ([1995] 2009), which turns rhythmic entrainment toward both reparations for slavery and an Afrofuturist horizon. Here, the time-sense connects the narrator to others in a way that no timetable could contain, queering affiliation and succession far beyond the work of Foucauldian discipline. "Rhythm Travel" reminds us that, as slaves and their African forbears understood, timing allows bodies to find one another in ways that have the capacity to reformulate social life as we know it.

1 SHAKE IT OFF

The Physiopolitics of Shaker Dance, 1774–1856

A *New Yorker* cartoon from 1999 shows a little boy in contemporary clothes staring up at a tall man wearing a broad-brimmed hat and an apron. The man stands before a large table, building a smaller table with old-fashioned tools, including a mallet, an awl, a hand-held planer, and a small handsaw. Behind him on pegs are two ladder-backed chairs. The man says to the boy, "No, lad, we aren't movers. We're just Shakers" (figure 1.1).

Playing on the phrase "movers and shakers," the joke is simple enough: Shakers, caught hopelessly behind in their artisanal ways, are not at the forefront of modern business or culture. There's also a gentle pun on "movers" as in "carriers"; Shakers may make furniture, but someone else transports it out into the world. And finally, the cartoon clinches the image of Shakers as apolitical. Not being "movers," they can hardly be thought of in terms of movement politics, and their "shaking" is merely quaint, with no critical thrust whatsoever. This cartoon is a good

"No, lad, we aren't movers. We're just Shakers."

1.1 "No, lad, we aren't movers. We're just Shakers." Mick Stevens, *The New Yorker* Collection/The Cartoon Bank, 1999.

take on how the Shakers are remembered by contemporary Americans, if at all: as a gentle people uninterested in social change though vaguely pacifist; notable only for their old-fashioned clothes and lovely hand-made objects; fossilized in a style of furniture that remains popular; but otherwise, immobile—not least because most of the Shakers are now dead (Blakemore 2017).

Yet the Shakers were originally a radical sect, akin to the American Mormons and upstate New York's Oneida Community in their experi-mental kinship system, and descended from the British Methodists in the way that they put the feeling body at the center of their religious cere-monies. Indeed, the Shakers had a kind of moving, kinesthetic politics—or politics of movement—in which their liturgical dance performed and embodied a radically gender-egalitarian, asexually generative, and eventually communitarian society. For the Shakers, dance was a method through which to arrive not only at spiritual enlightenment but also at a way of living that contested the hegemony of domestic-marital couple-hood under industrial capitalism. I begin this book with them because their history, particularly as it is reflected in the anti-Shaker and apos-tate literature that emerged almost immediately on their arrival in the

United States, offers an archive of coordinated physical activity, however mediated, of reactions to that activity, and of changes to it over time. In the early Shaker and especially the anti-Shaker archive, we can see a late eighteenth- and early nineteenth-century embodied sense-method in the flesh, through descriptions of their dances and their eventual adjustment of these dances to what they understood as Anglo-European norms.

Breaking away from the Quakers in England in the late eighteenth century as the Quakers subdued their ecstatic forms of worship, the "Shaking Quakers," or the United Society of Believers in Christ's Second Appearing, as they called themselves, arrived in the United States from Liverpool, England, in early August 1774 with their future leader, Ann Lee (S. J. Stein 1992, 7). Theologically, the Shakers parted ways with other English Protestants by—among other things—insisting on the equality of the female principle in the godhead (they understood Ann Lee as a female Christ), requiring that their members be celibate as a means of controlling worldly temptations and the flesh, and, paradoxically, claiming that worship ought to include the body because God would not disallow, as a means of professing faith, any facility given to man ("W." 1873).

While their theology was radical, it is the Shakers' literal, bodily actions that I wish to focus on in this chapter—locomotions that were neither reproductive nor forward-moving. The celibate Shakers used song and dance as a way of "shaking off" carnal temptations and as an expression of being filled with the Holy Spirit. In a sense, they danced their way out of genital sex and into embodied, holy communion with one another and with God. Originally, this involved erratic and spontaneous movements and dissonant singing: the earliest Shakers danced, sang, and chanted in groups, but each dancer moved according to individual whim, creating what looked to outsiders like chaos. Within roughly a decade of their arrival in the American colonies and after much approbation, the Shakers formalized their songs and dances, about which more below—but this did not garner approval from the rest of the Anglo-American population either.

The history of the early American Shakers, then, is a story of how between their arrival to the North American colonies in 1774 and their reforms in 1787, a small group of people used agitated, discontinuous bodily tempos to mark out their difference from the rest of the world, with the predictable result of being stigmatized. Yet it also eventually becomes a story of how, even though in 1787 and beyond the Shakers imposed on themselves a more orderly rhythm, the terms rather than the degree of their stigmatization changed. My central claims for this chapter are as follows: first, the Shakers make vivid how a particular sense-method, rhythmic dance, "timed" bodies into structures of belonging that both reflected and contested the dominant ones of the era, casting light on the role of timing in the political management of both extant eighteenth-century groups (religions and "civilizations") and emerging nineteenth-century populations (nations, races, genders, and sexualities). Second, when the Shakers responded to racializing and sexualizing stigmas against them by tightly regulating their liturgical movements, they were not accorded the status of whiteness after all; the metaphors by which they were stigmatized and the racial group with which they were affiliated simply shifted. All this ultimately suggests that long-nineteenth-century whiteness itself *was* a sense-method, one intimately bound up with time.

The Racial and Sexual Politics of Tempo: The "Back" Style

The history of sensibility and sentiment offers the clearest account of how denizens of the late eighteenth and nineteenth centuries were accorded differential abilities to sense, or physically apprehend, their environment and the objects and people in it according to the principle of empiricism, and then to take the time to order those senses into proper emotions, modes of understanding, and forms of affiliation (Schuller 2017). This process was, profoundly, a matter of proper timing. Seventeenth-century debates among Protestant theologians, for example, sought to distinguish the subjects of true Christian feeling and experience from "formalists" who mimicked the outward trappings of religion, and—more importantly for our purposes here—from "enthusiasts" who were dupes of their own response systems, variously troped as imagination, animal spirits, or nerves (Taves 1999, 16). The problem with religious enthusiasm, in a nutshell, was that it failed to subordinate the passions to reason, a process that took time. As Jordy Rosenberg points out, John Locke's critique of religious enthusiasm centered on its claims to immediate knowledge based on sensory input: in Locke's view, according to Rosenberg, enthusiasm "lacks the necessary reflexivity and commitment to duration that is integral to the empirical process" (Rosenberg 2011, 37).

Here, the problem with enthusiasm is less the lack of authorized religious interlocutors—mediators—in the transaction between God and believers, and more the alacrity—immediacy—with which input makes claims on the understanding. Rosenberg goes on to claim that Hegel too dismissed enthusiasm as incompatible with the slower tempo of true scientific knowledge, and cites enthusiasm as the eighteenth-century sense that foregrounded "the intersection of knowledge with time" (38). Shakers, along with other ecstatic worshippers, were dismissed by many of their detractors as "enthusiasts" insofar as they represented the danger not only of overly *embodied* responses to stimuli but also of overly *quick* ones, of pure reaction-formation and impulse. The stigmatization of enthusiasts clarifies the way that secularism emerged, in part, as a particular temporal regime that demanded pause and deliberation.

The capacity to respond in an ordered and timely way to sensory input distinguished not only proper religious experience and scientific knowledge from enthusiasm but also, by the mid-nineteenth century, "civilized" from "uncivilized" populations. Kyla Schuller's *The Biopolitics of Feeling* (2017) makes a compelling case that the nineteenth century's ideas about inheritance, evolution, and civilization centered on the body's capacity to receive impressions and to respond to them methodically. First, properly "civilized" subjects would coordinate impressions into considered and meaningful patterns of adhesion with other bodies under the sign of a sympathy coterminous with white subjectivity. Second, according to the Lamarckian theory prevalent at the time, impressions would accumulate over timescales that exceeded the human lifespan under the sign of a development coterminous with white racial health. The proper response to impression, the one that produced sympathy and human evolution, was, like Locke's and Hegel's scientific knowledge, a matter of timing: lesser races were cast as, on the one hand, impulsive, grasping, and overly reactive to impression, and on the other, torpid, sluggish, and impervious to it. Schuller's (2017, 58) trenchant formulation that "biopolitics entails the racialization of temporality" reflects not only the familiar notion that some races are cast as the past of humankind and others the future but also the idea that some bodies emerge as improperly calibrated, temporally speaking, to what touches them, responding too soon or not soon enough. Biopolitics, then, is not only a matter of binding individual bodies into populations with a state-sanctioned past and destiny—the famous Foucauldian formulation that biopolitics involves the state letting some populations flourish at the expense of others, and that "race" is the mechanism for doing so. It is also a matter of binding bodies to their immediate milieux, to one another, and to the future in ways neither too immediate nor too delayed, and of anathemizing those who are out of step. The early Shakers made this binding process literal in their dances but, try as they might, remained at odds with the normative biopolitical timing of individual and collective bodies.

In fact, the earliest Shakers in the United States were immediately identified as metrically awry. The first anti-Shaker pamphlet published in the United States, the Shaker apostate Valentine Rathbun's *An Account of the Matter, Form, and Manner of a Strange New Religion* (1781), emphasizes the rhythmic aspect of Shaker worship in ways that became typical in the literature denouncing Shakers, much of which drew directly from Rathbun's account:

> They begin by sitting down, and shaking their heads, in a violent manner, turning their heads half round, so that their face looks over each shoulder, their eyes being shut; while they are thus shaking, one will begin to sing some odd tune, without words or rule; after a while another will strike in; then another; and after a while they all fall in, and make a strange charm:—some singing without words, and some with an unknown tongue or mutter; some in a mixture of English: the mother, so called, minds to strike such notes as make a concord, and so form the charm. When they leave off singing, they drop off, one by one, as oddly as they come on; in the best part of their worship, everyone acts for himself, and almost everyone different from the other. (V. Rathbun 1781, 7)

What seems to have disturbed Rathbun so thoroughly was the lack of harmonic or rhythmic convergence, of "rule," in much of the ritual. He recoiled from the Shakers' reliance on an improvised but incomplete "concord" with "everyone act[ing] for himself." Here we see a process of (mis)timing that fails to produce proper adhesion between people, multiplying difference rather than consolidating sameness as proper sympathy would.

Rathbun's grandson Caleb, who remained a Shaker for some time, along with his father, Valentine Rathbun, Jr., would expand on the senior

Rathbun's account in 1796, describing the Shakers abusing their young male charges: "They were jirked [*sic*] each by one leg and one arm, from side to side, across the floor, and violently jammed against the wal [*sic*], they were next stripped quite naked, and tied with their hands above their heads, and there slapped with a stick, like a pudding stick, for near half an hour; and finally they were loosened in this naked situation, and set to jumping about, the Elders in the mean time running round among them and pushing them over" (C. Rathbun [1796] 2013, 4). Here, the punishment echoes Rathbun Sr.'s descriptions of Shaker dance as a matter of jumping, stripping, and nudity. This correlation between Shaker worship and physical cruelty is especially ironic given that a major point of contention between Shakers and the world's people was their pacifism, especially their refusal to fight in the American Revolution (S. J. Stein 1992, 13–14). But it separates them definitively from the civilized, for whom the sympathetic mutual attunement of bodies was understood to mitigate *against* violence, marking Shakers' physical responses to one another as destructive to rather than constructive of sociability. And rather than an inheritance consisting of impressions passed from body to body across generations, this remark depicts a scene of intergenerational jerking, jamming, slapping, jumping, running around, and pushing that fails to bind the elders to the future of the young, and, by extension, to the destiny of even their own people. It is a literalization of the damage that Shaker celibacy was understood to inflict on the nation.

The Shakers' violence, then, is also an aspect of their lack of a specifically national belonging. Rathbun Sr. writes, "It is impossible to point out any exact form, for they vary and differ and seldom act the same form exactly over again. They chuse to do so, to be singular, lest, as they say, they should be connected with Babylon" (V. Rathbun 1781, 8). At first glance, this "singularity" reiterates Rathbun Sr.'s claim that every Shaker dancer acted for himself, and references the Shaker prohibition of marriage. But it also indexes the early Shaker distrust of rhythmic and harmonic simultaneity. The negative invocation of "Babylon," where humans originally spoke one language, suggests that the early Shakers linked synchrony to evil. A combination of mimesis and repetition, synchrony depends on sameness of sound and regularity of the gaps between sounds, a resolution of acoustic dissonance and temporal disorder into unisonance—a euphony of voices speaking simultaneously. Unisonance, in turn, underlies the fantasy of the nation itself as a bounded and bound population of fellow readers, prayers, and chanters. Indeed, for Benedict Anderson (1982), the nation-form is distinguished precisely by synchrony, by the "meanwhile" time of print culture, specifically newspapers and novels, which are not only read in tandem by citizens but also exhibit multiple storylines taking place simultaneously.

Early Shaker distrust of synchrony is also connected to their refusal of the print culture that, Anderson argues, bound national subjects to one another by fostering a sense of mutual activity across distant spaces. Shakers declined to reproduce their theology and services into materials that could be apprehended by readers who could keep a safe distance from Shaker meetings, which were originally open to the public and understood as recruiting events. Indeed, Shakers mistrusted literacy in general, preferring a pedagogy of musical and rhythmic entrainment. As Etta Madden (1998, 33) has argued, since Ann Lee was not conventionally literate, her predominant mode of "reading" was her interpretation of visions, "people's minds, hearts, and bodies," and the Scripture delivered orally. An apostate writing in 1795 described how Ann Lee "would walk around [worshippers], smile upon them, lay her hand upon their heart, then take their hand and press it upon her own bosom. She would stroke their arms, lay her hand on their heads, and many other things . . . all the while she would be singing and chanting forth a strange bewitching kind of incantation, until the person was wrought into a perfect maze" (Anonymous 1795, quoted in Wergland 2011, 18).

Here, liturgical dance and seduction are one and the same: the "perfect maze" expresses the way that Ann Lee's singing, dancing, and gestures ensnare the worshippers both physically and affectively. As in many enthusiastic religions, Lee's sense of what it meant to embody and to reach a constituency was in dramatic opposition to Enlightenment modes of abstract citizenship, wherein the citizen checked his bodily particularities at the door of the public sphere, and spoke, ideally in print, as a generic national subject (see Warner 1990b). In response to Lee's oral, pictorial, and physical recruitment techniques as well as to Shaker celibacy, anti-Shaker writing was adamant about the unfitness of Shakers for national belonging: as anti-Shaker writer James Smith ([1810] 2013, 14) saw it, "Let Shakerism predominate, and it will extirpate Christianity, destroy marriage and also our present free government, and finally depopulate America."

The most surprising stigma against the Shakers, however, was not their status as suspect Christians, nor their lack of "civilization," nor even their anti-Babylonian refusal of nation-making synchrony. It appears in Rathbun's passing description of Shakers singing "in an Indian tone"; in Peter Youmans's (C. Rathbun [1826] 2013, 311) claim that Shakers "scream, shout, and holloo like Indians"; in Absolem H. Blackburn's ([1812] 2013, 238) claims about Shaker "[g]esticulations, of which the savages themselves, never would have dreamed of at a war dance"; in Horatio Stone's ([1846] 2013, 153–54) description of the Shakers' "wild savage revelries"; and in an anonymous writer's ([1847] 2013, 167) denouncement of Shaker rituals as "similar . . . to the blind and superstitious orgies of untutored savages." All of these representations of Shaker dance suggest that the Shakers' lack of adherence to European forms of song and dance made them available to racial stigma.

The Shakers did not bar people of color from their communities or worship, and several Shaker songs dated 1830 and thereafter are self-consciously "Indian" and "Negro" (their words) in ways that embarrass modern readers but did leave Shakers open to being conflated with Native and African Americans.[1] More broadly, though, early Shakers were racialized in and through the idiom of time, first as Native Americans. First, their mode of worship was embodied and immediately responsive to the perception of a holy spirit. In fact, a Shaker missionary wrote in 1807 of a visit to the "Shawnee prophet Tecumsah" that the prophet "sensibly spake by the power of God" (Andrews 1972, 120), and John Mac Kilgore (2016, 105) suggests that that visit enabled the Shakers and indigenous Americans to recognize that they had in common "immediate inspiration, ecstatic dancing, a message of reform and renunciation, and a kind of folk communism." Second, like Native Americans, the celibate Shakers' kinship patterns did not follow the middle-class Anglo-American norm of the monogamous nuclear household but relied on adoption and cohabitation. Putting these two things together, we might say that the timing of Shaker songs and dances, like those of Native Americans to which apostates analogized them, refused the heteroreproductive temporal order of late eighteenth- and nineteenth-century America.[2] Thus, the anti-Shaker tracts that I quoted from above that figure Shaker worship as "Indian" or "savage" link the harmonic and rhythmic irregularities of two cultures imagined as temporally sexually aberrant, as if the sexual aberrance caused the musical/metrical irregularity or vice versa. If the Shakers did not become a race, precisely, they were figured in terms that barred them from the temporal and sensory qualities of whiteness, for whiteness entailed physical responses and bodily synchronies that indexed and fostered sympathy, and a conception of the future understood in terms of reproductive inheritance and racial development.

The Shakers' distance from whiteness, in their conflation with Native Americans, had to do not only with the nonmarital, "promiscuous" modes of affiliation expressed in their dance but also with their method of reproducing themselves via recruitment. Tellingly, in his initial description of a Shaker dance, Rathbun Sr. genders female the power to coordinate or decoordinate musical notes and movements: he notes that the "mother," or eldress at the head of the ceremony, provides some harmonic confluence with the notes she "strikes" (whether this means singing or playing a percussive melodic instrument such as the triangle is unclear in this account), and these moments of harmony are what draw viewers and participants further into the ritual. By equating these fleeting euphonies with a "charm," Rathbone suggests that the Shakers conform to ordinary European expectations about harmonics only briefly, in order to draw unsuspecting witnesses in. Also pointing to the power of female recruitment, an anonymous writer protesting Ann Lee declares that "her religious performances were so very clamorous, her rites so gymnastic and subversive of the peace of families . . . the sect was deemed a public nuisance by the people, and was suppressed by the civil authority" (1795, 82). The writer's statement that Shaker rites threaten "the peace of families" suggests that more was at stake than quiet enjoyment of the neighborhoods in which Shakers resided. Rather, Shaker dancing itself seems to have been understood as something that could break up families by seducing people into leaving their natal homes to join Ann Lee's sect.

These worries about a woman "charming" unrelated people into a new form of sociability clarify just what was so threatening about the Shakers and why both their dances and their celibacy were so often described in terms of promiscuity: in a sense, Shaker celibates had sex without having sex, engendering new kinds of subjects, bodies, and families. They put into stark relief the way that rhythmic dance, like rhythm in general, is asexually generative. Writing about how humans achieve consciousness of and through rhythm, the psychoanalyst Nicholas Abraham (1995, 70) argues that rhythm manifests as "bodily movement that feels like it triggers the next manifestation"; in other words, perceiving rhythm is generally a matter of moving in response to it, however subtly. That movement then literally incorporates rhythm, making the body seem like its motor, like the origin of the rhythm itself—which in a sense it is, insofar as rhythm does not preexist its perception or, more specifically, its proprioception. Within rhythmic activity, the perceiver, in Abraham's (75) words, "becomes a rhythmic object." The boundaries between perceiver and perceived dissolve, and bodies reassemble into larger units of action that seem to share a subjectivity: an assemblage that does not reflect the marital-reproductive family. Moreover, rhythm itself gives rise to futurity in the form of an asexual bodily feeling that another "manifestation" is coming.

Shaker rhythms were also asexually generative in ways that directly flouted the timing of sex itself during the period. According to Henry Abelove's (2003, 23) speculations, by the late eighteenth century, when the Shakers moved across the Atlantic, sex had been, at least in England, reorganized according to the rhythms of capitalist production, with everything that was not "cross-sex genital intercourse" recategorized as what we would now call foreplay—a prelude to the main event.[3] Abelove reads the increase in English population during the long eighteenth century as evidence for an increase in heterosexual intercourse that corresponds, in turn, with a rise in productivity in general. And, concomitant with the ideology of production, he suggests, came a new understanding that sex could be divided into unproductive and productive aspects, and that the former should be, at best, a lead-in to the latter. The sexual body was, it seems, newly paced and ordered; heterosexual intercourse became a sense-method for intuiting and performing the demands of industrial capitalism, a method that no doubt crossed the Atlantic toward a new republic that needed, above all, productivity and reproduction. While the story of how heteronormativity was "timed" into being is an incomplete one, Abelove's analysis provides a lens through which to look at Shaker dance. As ordinary eighteenth-century sex practice consolidated around cross-sex genital intercourse, with other bodily activities becoming foreplay, sex assumed a kind of linearity and couple-centricity that Shaker dance and Shaker celibacy eschewed. The linking of this refusal to Native Americans, again, suggests that the sense-methods of whiteness include not only sympathy and reprofuturity but also a proper sequencing of courtship, foreplay, and intercourse.

Shaker bodily practices, by contrast with those of dominant Anglo-America, departed from the centralization of sex around intercourse: their dancing was a diffuse physical exertion that, in keeping with their celibacy, led to no climax, sexual or otherwise. The Shakers drew their authority to dance in worship from Old Testament descriptions of Israelites dancing to the Lord in gratitude (2 Samuel 6:14–21). In that story, David dances before God in a skimpy garment, and Michal, the daughter of Saul, chides him for it; David defends his actions, saying that the Lord has chosen him as prince of Israel over Saul, and he is allowed to make merry, play, or celebrate before the Lord. In a Shaker service reconstructed by a group of religious studies scholars (Davies, Van Zyl, and Young 1984), the exegesis compares the Shakers to these Israelites, and one early nineteenth-century defender of the Shakers wrote, "Sacred dancing would not appear in so debased a light, had it not been perverted by the wicked generally for the purpose of nocturnal recreation" (T. Brown 1812, 85). In other words, Shaker dance protested the secularization of dancing into a mode of romantic courtship or sexual foreplay. But it also spiritualized dancing into a mode of religious and social reorganization.

Shaker dances, then, repudiated couple-centered eroticism. But they also performed new arrangements of gender and sexuality. For example, the reconstructed Shaker service includes a brief list of theological concepts and justifications taken from Shaker writings, including the statement "Such dancing allows for the recognition and consecration of natural aptitudes and skills" (Davies, Van Zyl, and Young 1984, 2). In other words, rather than fostering couplehood, Shaker dance manifested individual and collective talents that could contribute to the community. The early style in which each person moved independently of others engaged in simultaneous but different movements can also be fruitfully understood in terms of Roland Barthes's (2013, 6) concept of *ideorrhythmy,* a mode of rhythmic togetherness in daily life that does not preclude individual retreats and improvisations, and thus balances community and singularity.

In addition, the Shakers' movements expressed and enacted their antagonism to the world's people, whose gender and sexual hierarchies as well as liturgical practices Shakers opposed: the second half of the sentence from the reconstructed Shaker service quoted above is "and it [Shaker dance] affirms the equality of the sexes" (Davies, Van Zyl, and Young 1984, 2). Avoiding the rules that governed secular dance, which usually focused on partnering men and women, Shaker dance could serve to critique gender inequality and what might be called not just compulsory heterosexuality but compulsory sexuality. Shaker dance was not a lead-in to romantic love or sexual intercourse but, in its conglomeration of singularities, a mode of collective expression and, itself, an expression of collectivity. We can read Shaker dance, then, as a foil for what would eventually be the Foucauldian "regime of sexuality," whereby the meaning of irregular bodily movements, alone or in groups, could only be concupiscence (see Foucault 1990a). Shakers' bodily agitations simply did not add up to the secret of sexuality.

Changing It Up: The Laboring Dances

Relatively swiftly, the Shakers responded to the accusations that they were oversexed, disorderly savages who threatened the nation by introducing the rhythmic regularity for which they are now best known. After the death of Ann Lee and her brother William Lee in 1784, and that of their successor, James Whittaker, in 1787, Joseph Meacham emerged as the leading elder. Meacham introduced and codified a system of communal living and mutual ownership of land and goods, organized the celibates into sex-segregated families according to age and spiritual ability, fixed a daily schedule and standards for the products Shakers made, and imposed schedules and activities for worship. Post-1787 Shakers lived in large communal "families" separated by sex, whose members were not biologically related: children were separated from parents and raised in separate collective houses by elders; those who had married before joining the Shakers were not allowed to interact with their spouses. This novel kinship arrangement, again, expressed as well as fostered the celibacy that was at the center of Shaker theology and reform. But most importantly for our purposes, Meacham made dancing orderly and collective so as to reflect this new order, introducing what the Shakers called "laboring" dances in which men and women, still separated, moved in tandem rather than individually (S. J. Stein 1992, 32–46).

The first order of business was to straighten out the body; laboring was supposed to be performed with, according to one song, "body right erect with ev'ry joint unbound" (Andrews [1963] 2011, 103), as opposed to the whirling, jerking motions described by early apostates. The two main dance steps, solidified between 1787 and 1790, were a shuffle, with knees bent and feet strongly hitting the ground in a step-close-step motion, and a skip used for movement forward and backward. Men and women stood in separate groups, facing a singer, and alternated skipping advances and retreats toward one another and/or the singer, punctuated by shuffles and turns in place (D. W. Patterson 1979, 102). At no point did the groupings intermingle the sexes, nor did individual dancers ever pair off into male/female couples. The stamping shuffles kept the beat like a drum, and dancers held their forearms outstretched, palms downward, with their hands gently flapping in time to the music, imitating a motion of shaking off water from the skin. While Shaker dance is difficult to picture (the shuffle especially), the Wooster Group dance company has reconstructed, reinterpreted, and performed some of the dances, setting them to the tunes of an LP made in 1976 by the Sisters of the United Society of Shakers at Sabbathday Lake, Maine. The rehearsal videos (see Wooster Group 2015) show just how unusual these dances must have looked to Americans who were used to rural American and cosmopolitan European dance forms.

In the 1820s, additions to the dances included circle-within-circle formations, with men and woman moving in opposite directions; new hand motions, such as waving the hands over the head and pantomiming to the lyrics; and sprightly marching steps, a new kind of shuffle adapted for an aging population (Davies, Van Zyl, and Young 1984, 6; D. W. Patterson 1979, 247). The marching steps evolved into a separate dance form resembling military drills, called "marches." In 1837, a period of spiritualist activity in Shaker communities began, understood by those who claimed to be possessed by spirits as a revival of Mother Ann's work. Many of these visionaries saw new dances and brought them forth to their communities; these innovations included some meeting of couples within the dance (bowing and changing places, though still not touching), as in traditional American folk dances. Those who claimed to be visited by Native

Americans sometimes danced solo, in the manner of the early Shakers, but alone with an audience instead of all together (D. W. Patterson 1979, 378). The spiritualist era passed, but its legacy was yet another alignment of dance patterns with doctrinal concepts, as in, for example, breaking out into four circles symbolizing the four great "dispensations" of Shaker theology (Adam to Abraham, Abraham to Jesus, Jesus to Mother Ann, and Mother Ann to the community) (Robinson 1893, 116, cited in D. W. Patterson 1979, 387). Dances also slowed to a dignified pace, again to accommodate the elderly.

Earlier, I suggested that Shaker dance was stigmatized even after it became more orderly, but that the terms changed. As I'll demonstrate below, from the 1830s onward, some important anti-Shaker literature stigmatized Shaker worship by focusing on the tedious uniformity of their culture. The trope of oversimilarity that governed responses to the new dances had very different racializing implications than the violence and promiscuity associated with Native Americans: it made the Shakers figuratively black. This racialization did not replace the association of Shakers and Native Americans but overlapped with it and then took on a life of its own, focused less on their "wild" gyrations and more on their threatening oversynchronization.

I have argued thus far, following several critics, that late eighteenth- and early nineteenth-century whiteness, as a sense-method, involved the following: finely calibrated delays between receiving a sensation and responding to it (Rosenberg 2011 and Schuller 2017); understanding stimuli as cumulative and heritable over time (Schuller 2017); and sequencing intercourse properly (Abelove 2003). I have also suggested that the failure to achieve whiteness involved a certain sluggishness and/ or impulsivity, or being too slow or too fast in relation to one's surroundings, as well as dissonance and too much rhythmic differentiation and too much or too little sex. But blackness, in particular, is often figured as a simple excess of repetition, leading to an inability to achieve rhythmic intention and thus to enter the flow of time. For instance, Abraham (1995, 72) describes rhythm as "the expectation of what has just been constituted"—a stretching toward a future that will yield up a representation of the past in the form of a repetition. But he denies such temporal complexity to people of African descent. He writes that "most African tribes" use a monotonous rhythm in their drumming, a "succession that *does not advance*" (84; emphasis in source). He continues, "[In drumming,] the same cycle is constantly repeated, and duration—the very environment of conscious acts—marches in place" (84). Abraham goes on to attribute to Africans "a fascinated consciousness, subjected to an inevitable, horizonless future" (84). In other words, "African" rhythm, because it does not necessarily resolve into European measures, cannot be productive of retrospective-anticipatory time, the time of humanity and of history alike. Rather than being made into rhythmic "objects" in a way that promisingly liquidates subjectivity, as Abraham's unmarked white subjects are in the first material I discussed from his book, his "Africans" are "fascinated" and "subjected," figuratively enslaved by their percussive patterns, their minds bound to a future over which they have no control and cannot see. Abraham goes on to posit that "the absence of a revalorization of the past as a constitutive process clearly reflects the total axiological passivity of the individual before the imperatives of the group. Entirely in the present, extended toward the future that is imposed on us, we no longer have to face the past" (84).

In other words, in the case of Africa, rhythm becomes evidence not of the ordering capacities of the human mind but of the incapacity for temporal order. There are echoes here of the discourse of enthusiasm as lacking the capacity to receive a stimulus and narrate how it came into being, that is, as lacking a historical sense. Abraham's "we" is spuriously inclusive, too, as it implicitly links African polyrhythms, misrecognized as monorhythm, with modern totalitarianism ("the passivity of the individual before the imperatives of the group"). He is, of course, tapping into a long history of understanding nonwhite cultures as without proper differentiation, rhythmically and otherwise: perhaps the paradigmatic example is the fictional Marabar Caves in E. M. Forster's *A Passage to India* whose echo is a "monotonous noise," an "ou-boum" that is "entirely devoid of distinction" (Forster [1924] 2005, 137). This racialized echo of India is also sexually aberrant, for it predicts and contributes to the assault that Adela Quested claims to have undergone in the cave. And it stops time even outside the cave, the ringing in her head a figure for an India she cannot escape.

To see the Shakers moving toward racialization as black, we must begin with the nineteenth-century material that figures them as repetitive. Writing in 1842 about a visit to the Shaker village of New Lebanon, for example, Charles Dickens focuses on precisely this deadly quality of rhythmic repetition. He calls the Shakers "wooden men," and describes "a grim room, where several grim hats were hanging on grim pegs, and the time was grimly told by a grim clock which uttered every tick with a kind of struggle, as if it broke the grim silence reluctantly, and under protest" (Dickens [1842] 2001, 236). Dickens's term "grim" tolls like a funeral bell over and over again, as if to mimic the movement of the ticking clock, but also overtakes it. The repetition of "grim" and the image of worldly time in the figure of the clock, struggling against the "grim silence" of Shaker eternal time, suggest that observers saw the Shakers as overly regulated, their insistence on measured time as productive of a deathly sameness, a time stoppage.

This is nowhere more floridly described than in Catharine Maria Sedgwick's novel *Redwood* ([1824] 1969). Centered on a power struggle between Caroline Redwood, a Southern belle, and Ellen Bruce, who epitomizes New England womanhood, *Redwood* also contains a subplot about a young girl, Emily Allen, who is held captive by a Shaker community. The novel's marriage plot—which culminates in the union between Ellen and a young man whom Caroline has previously claimed as her own—unfolds in contradistinction to Shaker celibacy. In *Redwood,* the sexual promiscuity that marks the earliest criticisms of the Shakers is gendered entirely male. Early in the Emily Allen subplot, a villainous Shaker elder, Reuben Harrington, sings "a shaker tune, at all times sufficiently dissonant, [which] . . . sounded like the howl of an infernal," and "to this music he shuffle[s] and whirl[s] in the manner which the sect call dancing and labour worship" (1:96). Sedgwick seems to have blended the early and the reformed styles in her depiction of Shaker dance, but Harrington's sounds and rhythms accord with his predatory nature as he sets out to seduce Emily. We glimpse, again, the correlation of Shakers with Native Americans as Emily's aunt Debby shouts to this dancing Shaker, "Stop your dumb pow-wow!" (1: 96). True to his "infernal" howl, erratic body movements, and "Indian" dancing, Harrington turns out to be a libertine, a kidnapper, and a rapist—and indeed, his accomplice in this abduction is none other than one of the era's stereotypically drunken Indians. Thus we can still see, in this post-1787 text, what I have been calling the racialization of the early Shakers via their harmonic and rhythmic styles, which align them with Native Americans.

But the major shortcoming of Shaker society is, in *Redwood's* terms, "monotony," and this turns the critique in a much different direction. The narrator of Redwood speaks of "the uniform habits and monotonous occupations" of the Shakers, which "have a strong tendency to check every irregular feeling, and to intercept every vagrant desire" (Sedgwick [1824] 1969, 2:18). Harrington's desire is out of control because he sings and dances in the early style. But in the narrator's description of Emily's captivity among the Shakers, the post-Meacham style dominates, and uniformity and monotony present a very different kind of threat. In fact *Redwood,* like Dickens's *Notes,* signals the undifferentiated rhythms of Shaker society with the image of a clock: "Emily had paused at the staircase from extreme weakness; the loud ticking of the clock had arrested her attention; this sound, always the same, seems like the natural voice of this monotonous solitude. 'Oh,' said Emily, unconsciously uttering audibly her thoughts, 'to what purpose is time measured here? There is no pleasure to come—there is none past that I dare to remember'" (2:23–24).

Here we see an echo of Abraham's contention that African rhythms do not produce a past or an intentional future. As a non-Shaker, too, Sedgwick apparently cannot imagine Shakerism as a form of sociability but only as solitude. The clock that "voices" this solitude with a "tick," notably like the clock in Dickens, has no "tock," no redeeming difference that encompasses pleasure past or future. Cast as Emily's unbearable loneliness, "monotony" comes to signify a lack of differentiation both sexual and rhythmic. It is as if the difference that resolves sameness into complementarity, and isolation into sociability, like the "tock" that would turn two "ticks" into a pair, is the "pleasure" of proper heterosexual desire itself: in other words, *heterosexuality is redeemed as the difference that makes time possible.* Without the differentiation emblematized by heterosexual desire, there is no "purpose" to measuring time; thus Shakers are outside of time by virtue of their celibacy. They are not simply outside of the rhythms and pacings of heterosexual courtship and sexuality; they are absolutely atemporal.

Redwood depicts Shaker dance in much the same terms. The narrator describes Emily's sisters and brethren moving "with a uniform shuffling step, as if it was composed of so many automatons, their arms rising and falling mechanically; and their monotonous movements, solemn melancholy or stupid aspects, contrasting ludicrously with the festive throngs which are usually seen stepping on 'light fantastic toe' through the mazy dance" (Sedgwick [1824] 1969, 2:43). The terms "uniform," "automatons," "mechanically," "monotonous," and "stupid" work together to portray Shaker dancing as so undifferentiated as to be inhuman. Whether together like the dancers or alone like Emily, Shakers are so overregulated by time that they are no longer in it, and so uniform that what they do is no longer legibly social.

This takes on racial characteristics in the equation of Shakerism with enslavement, and Shaker dance as a means of expressing and promulgating slavery. For instance, in 1810 James Smith wrote, "It is said, if those under the Shakers are in bondage, they are *voluntary* slaves. They are just such voluntary slaves as the ten kings and their subjects were under the Pope, they were artfully led into it . . . they are objects of pity, seduced, bewildered and lost; under strong delusion, kept in bondage, by the fear of hell or the terror of the whip" (Smith [1810] 2013, 185). Here, anti-Catholicism merges with anti-Shakerism and racism in the suggestion that Shakers lack the psychological capacity for independence. In an example that more directly correlates Shaker enslavement with their dance, Christopher Clark's long anti-Shaker treatise, *A Shock to Shakerism* ([1812] 2013, 10), equates Shaker rhythms of work and worship with a mental slavery akin to the bondage of African Americans, declaring that "it is easier to gain white Negroes in America, to work, and dance all their days, than to obtain money to purchase black ones." Clark goes on to racialize and equate Catholics and Shakers for giving confessions to intermediaries rather than directly to God: "God would just as soon damn for their sins, a Pope or Shaker confessor; as he would a Hottentot, or a Guinea Negro" (18). Finally, beginning in the 1840s, Shakers performed their songs and dances in costume in traveling shows such as the one advertised as a "Great Moral Curiosity! Shaker Concert!" in the *Maine Cultivator and Hallowell Gazette* on March 27, 1847. These shows no doubt competed with and complemented the minstrel shows also popular during the 1830s and 1840s, putting the Shakers, as historian Christian Goodwillie (2013, 1:xxxii) writes, "on equal footing with the most vulgar public entertainment," and further racializing them.

The most widely circulated image of the Shakers as "white Negroes," a lithograph published in 1831 by Anthony Imbert, "Shakers near Lebanon

1.2 "Shakers near Lebanon, State of New York," 1831. Library of Congress, Prints and Photographs Division, LC-USZ62-13659.

State of New York," (figure 1.2), follows the tradition of equating uniformity with people of color, and Africans and people of African descent with a lack of rhythmic differentiation.

In this print, a group of men dance toward a group of women, with a fashionable "Gentile" woman watching. All the dancers have their arms out, palms down, in the traditional manner; the women appear to be stepping backward while the men step forward (though in reality, the dancers would be more likely to be facing a singer). The women are almost completely uniform in appearance, their faces lit to the same degree of bright whiteness, with only variations in age and facial expression distinguishing them from one another. But the men are much more individuated and grotesque, for they appear to be prancing with their buttocks pushed outward, and wear a variety of unhappy, somewhat leering faces. Five figures stand out from the crowd of men: in the front and third row foreground are two men with large-nosed, sharp profiles, who are in some versions of the lithograph clearly dark-skinned; in the second row an incongruously short, fat, bald man dances next to a tall, gaunt man in a white wig. In the very back row is an African American man whose profile echoes that of the short bald man, but this time drawn with the low forehead, flat nose, round buttocks, and protruding lips typical of racist stereotypes of the era, which refract back onto the bald man and racialize him as black, or at least off-white. Next to the first African American man, in silhouette, is another apparently African American man. While the Imbert lithograph might be signaling "amalgamation," or simple race mixing, the gender segregation, and the ways that the bodies of the white men echo those of the black men within an image of synchrony and uniformity, suggest a certain asexual "contagion" of blackness, such that blackness can be spread through the overly uniform dancing.

This lithograph bears instructive comparison to a much more Shaker-sympathetic watercolor done by Benson John Lossing in 1856 (perhaps Lossing even had the earlier lithograph in mind). In this piece, men and women dance in the same direction in the front three rows, men behind women, with the back rows dancing in the opposite direction (figure 1.3). Both men and women have their elbows bent, forearms extended, and palms up. The women are uniformly dressed in white with sheer, dark-trimmed bonnets, heads bowed.

The men all have on blue vests, and either white or blue-grey pants. All have dark hair cut short in front, longer in back, or light hair in a modified "bowl" cut. The men all wear a neutral or slightly pleasant expression, and all are fair-skinned. Again, the men are more differentiated than the women by color, but this time blue rather than black, and not differentiated through racial caricature, as all the dancers are white.

While there were, indeed, African American Shakers, most famously Rebecca Cox Jackson, in the Imbert lithograph the most clearly black men bring up the rear of the dance, and iconographically, the way they hold their bodies adds to the lithograph's presentation of Shaker men as grotesque, insofar as all the men take up the postures of stereotypically racist images of African Americans. As a whole, too, Imbert's men are literally blacker than Lossing's—their backs are cast in shadow, they wear dark vests, and only two heads of light or white hair appear among the dozen male figures. The lithograph precedes the post-Emancipation period in which black men were sexualized; rather than being cast as lechers, Imbert's Shaker men appear to be feminized in their imitation of the women's dancing, and fools in their taking on the poses of black caricatures. But read alongside the Lossing watercolor, Dickens's *Notes*, Sedgwick's *Redwood*, and the Smith and Clark anti-Shaker tracts especially,

1.3 Benson John Lossing, "The Dance," 1825. Watercolor, 4 1/2 in. × 6 1/2 in. Dated "Saturday, 16 August 1856." MssLS 1-289. The Huntington Library, San Marino, California.

the Imbert lithograph suggests that the overordering of Shaker worship, including its tandem movements and physical separation of the sexes, is not just deathly to dancers in terms of its connection with a gender-nonnormative and sexually aberrant refusal to reproduce. The Shaker rage for order, as caricatured here, is also related to—though importantly not coterminous with—the status of social death accorded to slaves (O. Patterson 1982), and by extension to Native and African American people on the Eastern seaboard of the United States. Like slaves, Shakers were socially dead insofar as their kinship forms were legally meaningless, though Shakers as a whole did not suffer the destruction of these forms in the way that slaves did. Like Native and African American people, Shakers were seen as inhuman precisely insofar as their physical movements were read as either excessive or overly mechanical (see Ngai 2005, 89–125).

Taken together, the Imbert lithograph and the literary texts I have explored here suggest that the problem with Shakers was a surrender of European norms—sexual, gendered, *and* racialized—that added up to their being literally out of step with America. This "America," a white one, demanded proper reaction times, a heterosexuality marked by a reproductive stance toward the future, a correct sequencing of sex, and a right balance of synchrony and rhythmic differentiation. As the Imbert lithograph especially clarifies, to seek out alternate tempos and movements in concert was to risk, paradoxically, both the hyperwhite deathliness of the women pictured, and (relatedly) the suspect blackening of the men. Neither was a proper form of whiteness.

From the Shaker point of view, though, their bodies were metronomes keeping time with something more divine than capitalism, the nation, heteronormativity, or whiteness. *Redwood* clarifies this with an unexpectedly Shaker-sympathetic passage. Back in the stairway scene, Emily's Shaker aunt, Susan, who is primarily responsible for preventing Emily from leaving the Shaker settlement, offers a Shaker calibration of time: "'Do you ask to what purpose [time is measured]?' said Susan . . . '—Oh, have you already forgotten when every stroke of that clock was as a holy monitor to you, arousing you to redeem the time . . . when the stroke of every hour carried with it the record of your innocence?" (Sedgwick [1824] 1969, 2:24). Susan does not see clock time as undifferentiated without the saving aspect of heterosexual love: for her, rhythm inheres in the relation between the "tick" of the earthly clock and an unspoken "tock" of religious arousal, a fullness of time differentiated not from itself but from the world, and not through heterosexuality but through the redeeming aspect of sexual "innocence," or celibacy tuned to a "holy monitor." Here, the plenitude of time, and the celibacy it indexes, is a new form of sociability, a union with God.[4]

And while *Redwood* does not, in the end, endorse Susan's philosophy of rhythm as a form of asexual religious ecstasy, a counterpoint to the novel's general dismissal of Shaker time as undifferentiated emerges in the epigraph to the chapter that follows the exchange between Emily and Susan. The epigraph is from the French educational philosopher Madame de Genlis: "Le bonheur se compose d'une suite d'actions et de sensations continuellement répétées et renouvellées; simplicité et monotonie voilà en général ce qui le form et le constitue." (Happiness consists of a combination of actions and sensations continually repeated and renewed; simplicity and monotony are generally the form it takes and what constitute it) (Sedgwick [1824] 1969, 2:35; translation mine).

Here, repetition is renewal, and not death, which is somewhat in keeping with the value put on pausing in eighteenth-century discourses of enthusiasm, and with Abraham's conception of European rhythm as anticipatory and history making. But surprisingly, monotony itself is a form of regeneration—again, not reproduction. This sounds remarkably like Foucauldian discipline and like a tempered version of the ecstatic togetherness that William H. McNeill (1997) attributes to keeping together in time. Tellingly, Sedgwick leaves untranslated this seemingly pro-Shaker vision of "monotony" as renewal by repetition. Though Susan's figure of "redeeming the time" is a form of asexual "happiness" that strongly counters Emily's vision of heterosexualized "pleasure," the novel does not pick up on the radical implication that rhythm does not kill, but queers—by which I mean here, offers a vision of a life outside of white temporality and not centered in marriage and family. In this sense, Shaker rhythms were, precisely, both queer and sacred, for they lifted the Shakers out of various earthly tempos and united them with one another in a spiritual form of belonging that might be thought of as not only akin to queer world making but also truly, radically Christian, if we remember that Jesus instructed his followers to abandon their biological families: "If any man come to me, and hate not his father, and mother, and wife, and children, and brethren, and sisters, yea, and his own life also, he cannot be my disciple" (Luke 14:26; see also Shell 1995).

Still with Us

The Shakers, it might be said, eventually stilled themselves. With a population in continual decline after about 1850 due to their inability to recruit and retain members, the remaining Shakers simply aged and died. By the 1900s, the elderly Shakers had ceased their dancing, and by the 1940s even marching had died out. What remained was what we might quaintly call their "moveables," their furniture and other artifacts. No longer shaking, Shakers moved into the mainstream through an aesthetic of symmetry, simplicity, and craftsmanship. As the definitive history of Shaker life in America (S. J. Stein 1992, 423) puts it, "Once feared, hated, and persecuted, now the Shakers are the darlings of American popular culture." Major museums, including the Whitney and the Corcoran, have mounted exhibits of Shaker objects; there are Shaker "living museums" staffed by actors at Hancock, Lebanon, and other formerly occupied Shaker villages; "Shakerana" is mass-produced; and Americans seem to prefer the Shakers as designers rather than as agitators for celibacy, communitarianism, and asceticism. Their rhythms may have ground to a halt, but it is important to remember that the Shakers were, in their day, both literal and political movers indeed.

The scene of social death that anti-Shaker literature only hinted at is the topic of my next chapter, which focuses not on the so-called monotonies of African-derived culture but on repetitions, testing, and even play in the face of overwhelming social death. Its archive is a set of nineteenth-century texts in which ex-slaves or freedmen repeatedly return to the scene of their own status as slaves by feigning death. Their repetitions and returns to the scene of social and actual death are anything but dancelike, though they are certainly performances of a sort. And the "players" face not rhetorical stigmatization but, variously, reenslavement, live burial, and lynching. Yet their activities are ways of negotiating another over-arching temporal regime of the very long nineteenth century: the status of slaves and eventually free black people as avatars of chronopolitical nonbeing.

2   THE GIFT OF CONSTANT ESCAPE

Playing Dead in African American Literature,
1849–1900

Black studies' concern with what it is to own one's dispossession,
to mine what is held in having been possessed, makes it more
possible to embrace the underprivilege of being sentenced to the
gift of constant escape.

FRED MOTEN, "Black Op"

If antebellum anti-Shaker literature linked monotony
and repetition to death and, by implication, to blackness, nineteenth-century African American literature
tells a somewhat different story. Postbellum narrative
fiction such as Pauline Hopkins's *Of One Blood* ([1903]
1988) and Charles Chesnutt's late nineteenth-century
tales, collected as *The Conjure Stories* (2011), often mo-
bilizes the trope of the *living* dead. Hopkins's novel, discussed in the next chapter, contains African American
ghosts and an ancient Ethiopian civilization buried
in a crypt. The short stories collected as *The Conjure
Stories* include "The Goophered Grapevine" (1887), a
tale about enchanted grapes that cause their enslaved
eaters to age prematurely and then return to youth, foiling the lifespan and the binary between dying and living.
A tale published the following year, "Po Sandy," tells of
a slave who turns into an immobile but living tree await-
ing the return of his sold-off wife. Sandy gets cut down

and made into lumber, and then haunts the narrator and other characters through the walls of buildings made from the lumber. As several critics have argued, the most immediate sense-methods of African American literature of the late nineteenth century might be melancholia, haunting, and encryption—sensations that at once capture the horror of the Middle Passage, slavery, and the failure of Reconstruction, and that allow black writers to preserve and remobilize the histories erased by white supremacist revisionism.[1] These sensations are neither monotonous, as in the racist depictions of African (and Shaker) rhythms, because they elicit fear and wonder, nor are they strictly repetitive, because they are matters of return and surrogation with a difference.[2]

Instead of signaling a thralldom to monorhythm, these African American figurations of blackness as living death register the legacy of what Orlando Patterson has famously described as the complete, unremitting social death imposed by slavery. According to Patterson (1982, 13), slavery is *the permanent, violent domination of natally alienated and generally dishonored persons*" (emphasis in source). As a substitution for death, the "natal alienation" of slavery imposes living death, or what Achille Mbembe (2003, 21) calls "death-in-life." This is effected by complete isolation from the legally recognized social ties that comprise kinship and human belonging, a position on which Hortense Spillers (1987) and Saidiya Hartman (2008) have elaborated extensively. Furthermore, to be outside of recognized structures of belonging that include ancestry and descent as part of their meanings is to be not only outside of the horizontal relations of gender and kinship, as Spillers in particular argues, but also outside of generational time and "lifetime," birth-to-death time. Frank B. Wilderson III (2010, 279–80), then, has extended Hartman's and Spillers's work to reconceptualize social death as the foreclosure of temporal capacity, of the enslaved person and his/her descendants' ability to meaningfully shape the past, present, and future. This foreclosure of slaves' generationality and temporality is only hinted at in Patterson (1982, 38), but made explicit when he cites Claude Meillassoux's (1975, 20–21) statement "[The slave] can never be brought to life again as such since, in spite of some specious examples (themselves most instructive) of fictive rebirth, the slave will remain forever an unborn being."

This chapter complicates Meillassoux's characterization of slaves as "unborn" and/or unremittingly dead-in-life by focusing on how actual slaves and their descendants, some fictional and some historical, exorbitantly and often repeatedly *mimed* death. While I do not mean to dismiss or overwrite the powerful theorizations of African American time in terms of melancholia, haunting, and encryption, I also want to claim that the experience of slavery and its aftermath, and modes of protesting and recalibrating that experience, involved an investment in rhythmic movements—not just song and dance, but a kind of shuttling toward and away from (social) death without reanimation, resurrection, or reincarnation. Playing dead is a sense-method insofar as it involves the body touching death and/or becoming temporarily dead. It is a kind of *fort-da* for confronting the (a)temporalities of slavery and its aftermath, particularly the static time of social death—for accepting neither the permanence of social death nor the consolations of white humanism and the latter's commitment to what it designates as a life. In part, this means considering the queer potential of slaves' and their descendants' voided kinship ties and resultant temporal suspension, focusing on the possibilities and limitations for critical race theory of queer theory's "antisocial thesis," or the claim that queers ought to exploit and mobilize our position as avatars of death and reproductive sterility (see Bersani 1987; Edelman 2004; and Caserio et al. 2006). In part, it means seeing the movement toward and away from death in various narratives and performances as rhythmic, and rhythm as a mode of dealing with durational time, the unremitting time of antiblackness. Finally, it means understanding African American writers' and performers' elaborate movements toward and away from death as occupations, in the political sense of that term, of social death. I call both the regime of slave timelessness and African American stylizations of it a *chronothanatopolitics*—about which more below. I counterpose state-sponsored chronothanatopolitics as bio/necro-politics, to African Americans' individual and collective recapture of chronothanatopolitics. In what follows, I trace this recapture, via the sense-method of playing dead, through three ex-slave narratives (the fictionalized autobiography of Harriet Jacobs and the life stories of Henry Bibb and Henry Box Brown), one set of performances (Brown's lectures and panorama), and one work of post-Reconstruction narrative fiction (Sutton E. Griggs's novel *Imperium in Imperio*), framing them with two Br'er Rabbit trickster tales, and linking the motif of playing dead in these works to the current-day protest performances of Black Lives Matter.

Chronothanatopolitics: Br'er Rabbit

The equation of enslavement with unremitting death is belied by some of the most foundational African American stories, the trickster tales deriving from African folklore and recalibrated to address slavery—examples one could hardly call "specious," *pace* Meillassoux, and that differ from postbellum fiction's backward-looking figures of melancholia and haunting. In these folktales, "fictive rebirths" foreground the movement of slaves and their descendants in and out, toward and away from, death. The slave may be unborn in these stories, but he or she is not, for that, dead. Instead, the slave *plays* dead, using feigned death to engage in what Jared Sexton (2011) has called "the social life of social death," or the forms of relationality, available within a state of natal alienation and dishonor, that do not simply replicate the modalities of white supremacy: nation, family, citizenship, love.

In African-derived folktales about playing dead twice in the road, then, death is a game. A trickster—Anansi the Spider in West African versions of the tale, Boukee in a Bahamas version, Br'er Rabbit in Joel Chandler Harris's (1881a) famous reworkings of slave tales—lies down in the road, playing dead.[3] Let us call him Br'er Rabbit, for familiarity's sake. His straight man—Br'er Fox in Joel Chandler Harris's retelling— has been hunting, and is bringing home a heavy load of game. Br'er Fox sees Br'er Rabbit "dead" in the road and says to himself that he will leave this delicious-looking dead rabbit and go on to see if there is another one in the road further on, and if so, he will turn back to get the first one. This enables Br'er Rabbit to hop up, outrun Br'er Fox, and play dead in the road a second time. Seeing this, Br'er Fox determines to put his load of food down and go back for the first dead rabbit, planning to come back and pick up his food and the "second" dead rabbit on his way home. However, Br'er Rabbit makes off with his food, and Br'er Fox arrives home empty-handed, with neither his original load nor a rabbit for dinner.

While he may, indeed, never have been "born" except in his famous briar patch, Br'er Rabbit plays dead as opposed to hiding and stealing the food, scaring Br'er Fox into dropping it, or some other possible ruse. He does so twice. And he gets enormous pleasure out of being *reborn,* or, if slaves are never properly born into recognized kinship forms, secondarily born without an origin and without any resulting kinship ties. His performance of death makes possible a birth that undermines the position of birth as a primary event that automatically connects the born person to a web of legibly human relations. At the heart of the tale are the theatricalized pleasures of repetition without reproduction, incarnation without resurrection, death without prior life. There's a certain glorious excess in this story, along the lines of Georges Bataille's (1986) formulation of death as a form of proliferation and hence of life: feigned death begets, over and over again, new Br'er Rabbits—reborn outside of marriage and reproduction, not as freemen but as slaves who have temporarily and momentarily escaped.

What I wish to focus on here, though, is less the coming-back-to-life aspect of the Br'er Rabbit tale and the texts that I will argue are its successors, but the complexity of playing dead, especially multiple times. Playing dead certainly evokes Mbembe's (2003) concept of necropolitics, or the way that the state and its auxiliary powers create "death-worlds" filled with the "living dead" (Mbembe 2003, 40). For Mbembe, necropolitics is countermanded by those who turn their bodies into weapons in service of both eternal life and an unrealized future. But Mbembe focuses on the relation between the necropolitics employed by the United States in the Middle East, and its strategic recalibration as Muslim martyrdom, dodging the fact that slaves, by definition, were denied the subjectivity that martyrdom assumes. Even Jasbir Puar's (2007) powerful reworking of Mbembe's work on suicide bombers claims the latter as queer because they dissolve bodily and temporal boundaries of the sort fundamentally denied to slaves. By contrast, playing dead twice requires no subject: it is like squaring death, or cubing it. Playing dead does not allegorize physical death as a redemptive release from social death, nor does it portray physical death as a redundant confirmation of social death, nor does it claim a bodily coherence or stable subject that it then goes on to deconstruct. Instead, it trades on an exorbitance of death beyond death, death beside death, death within death. Finally, playing dead also does not turn back upon death, or the system that produces social death, to destroy them in the name of life or even of continuation in a radically new mode.

More useful for my purposes than necropolitics is Dana Luciano's (2007) idea of a *chronobiopolitics,* which foregrounds time. Drawing from Foucault's ([1978–79] 2008, 1990a) conception of biopolitics, Luciano adds the prefix *chronos* to describe cultural and political arrangements of time that not only designate some lives as long, coherent, and meaningful while cutting others short and/or relegating them to atemporal meaninglessness but also focus on the feeling body as the key to nonlinear temporalities: most importantly, her term emphasizes temporality as an affective technique of necro/biopower. In place of *necros/bios,* though, my term "chronothanatopolitics" references Thanatos, Greek mythology's personification of death, of whom an Orphic hymn (circa 3rd century BC–2nd century AD; Orpheus 1792, 224) declared, "On thee, the portion of our time depends, whose absence lengthens life, whose presence ends." This description of Thanatos imagines the god flickering between absence and presence: unlike bio/necropolitics, it does not oppose life and death to one another but coils the line separating them. Here, life is dependent on and constituted by death.

Thus the hymn foregrounds the way that life, rather than being the opposite of death, is the opposite of the *presence* of death—merely a temporary "disappearing" of death and a counterperformance of it that does not negate it. The hymn allows us to conceptualize tricks such as Br'er Rabbit's as a staging and involution of the life/death binary rather than just a commitment to life or an unchanging black deathliness. *Thanatos,* of course, also references Freud ([1920] 1964), who, in "Beyond the Pleasure Principle," transformed its meaning in his conception of the death drive to emphasize the organism's psychic impulse to return to an originary, quiescent, atemporal state. Again, the death drive confounds any easy opposition between life and death, as the very pulsation of the drive toward death is entailed in living. But chronothanatopolitics is neither a purely psychic drive nor a universal phenomenon; instead, it is a production of deathliness and nonbeing by historical forces external to the subjectivity it creates for nonblack people, and forecloses for people of African descent: one might call it a sociopolitical death drive enacted by white supremacy.[4] And as the example of Br'er Rabbit shows, chronothanatopolitics can also be counterperformed as a kind of dancing on the edge of death or a shuttling movement between life and death, and in this it is different from both bio-/necropolitics and chronobiopolitics.[5]

The Politics of Nonresurrection: Harriet Jacobs

Why not simply claim that miming death is fundamentally Christian, derived from a theology of (re)incarnation and life after death? For in literature about slaves and even sometimes by ex-slaves, symbolic resistance to social death and a commitment to (re)birth often include a rhetorical commitment to the Christian trope of resurrection—a life-in-death in which they are not chattel (Genovese [1974] 1976, 164). Harriet Beecher Stowe's *Uncle Tom's Cabin* (1852, 273) offers a vivid fictional example of this when Tom says to Legree, "*I can die*" and then suggests that his troubles will be over when Legree kills him, whereas Legree will end up in hell. The problem here, as so many critics have noted, is that the Christian model of resurrection offers no succor in the here and now: it was, in fact, a tool that slaveholders used to encourage enslaved people to seek their reward only in the afterlife.[6] In contrast to *Uncle Tom's Cabin*, many narratives written by former slaves use the trope of resurrection to figure freedom in *this* life: for example, Frederick Douglass ([1845] 1982, 113) famously writes, after the incident in which he fights back against his owner Covey, "I felt as I had never felt before. It was a glorious resurrection from the tomb of slavery, to the heaven of freedom." Indeed, resurrectional and insurrectional rhetoric were often intertwined in the versions of Black Christianity that centered on Jesus. Crucified by power but returning to life to redeem his people, Jesus offered a powerful vision of resistance and symbolized a master with greater authority than that of slave owners (Genovese [1974] 1976, 165). But of course Douglass is not legally emancipated after this incident, and this points to a problem with even black Christian reworkings of resurrection: the permanent freedom granted in the afterlife has yet to be won by living black people on any lasting basis. Hence the trope of approaching and escaping death, dying and being reborn and then dying again, and, especially, willfully playing dead, figures the precarity of black existence both before and after slavery.

This is clarified in Harriet Jacobs's autobiography, *Incidents in the Life of a Slave Girl* ([1861] 1987). Jacobs's protagonist, Linda Brent, inters herself in an attic for seven years to ensure that her children are freed, and thus the narrative is often read as a tale of heroic motherhood—or, to use Lee Edelman's (2004) term, of *reprofuturity*, a coinage naming the conflation of the future with the production and care of children.

For example, Georgia Kreiger (2008) has read Brent as someone who "plays dead," but argues that the death is a linear journey into the underworld symbolized by Brent's confinement in the attic, which metaphorically cleanses her from the sexualized sin of choosing to be a white man's mistress to avoid her rapacious male owner, and makes her legible through the matrifocal lens of white female sentimental discourse. But Brent's escape from confinement is no resurrection: as Jacobs makes clear, Brent's victory is equivocal both insofar as a patron eventually buys her freedom, confirming her status as property, and insofar as she must tell her tale under the dominant terms of domesticity even as she is denied full access to it.[7] The fact that this (deferred) domesticity itself was troped by Jacobs's white contemporaries as "the Angel in the House," as Barbara Welter (1976) reminds us, suggests that domesticity is not utterly disconnected from death, even if, following Patterson (1982), it seems the opposite of social death. For not only does domesticity wrest women out of history and into a changeless, if exalted, eternal time somewhat akin to the nontemporality of slavery, it also—akin to but not equivalent to social death—depends on the alienation of a people ("free" women) from birth name and property. My aim here is not to analogize domesticity and slavery, which were indeed extremely different and often-counterposed forms of subjugation in that domesticity and its privileges were entirely denied slaves. It is to point out that Brent's symbolic death threatens to bring her not life, but another, however more velvet and attenuated, form of death via the genre of sentimental fiction. This may be why Jacobs so insistently avoids the ending that the latter genre demands, writing in the voice of Brent, "Reader, my story ends with freedom; not in the usual way, with marriage" (Jacobs [1861] 1987, 201), citing *Jane Eyre* only to reverse that novel's terms. Jacobs may have to occupy the genre of sentimental domestic fiction in order to be heard, but her protagonist will not entirely yield to its rules, nor organize her own life in accordance with them.[8] Yet Brent does wish for a "hearthstone of my own" (Jacobs [1861] 1987, 201), especially for her children, which suggests the possibility that physical well-being—shelter, warmth—and domestic ideology might be separable. In other words, if the genre that entraps Jacobs repeats death in a different, whiter key, Brent's refusal of marriage and pragmatic wish for a hearth provide one more, decidedly not resurrectional, escape from death.

To my eye, Brent's compounding, antiresurrectional (or at least non-resurrectional) relation to death—her movement from social death toward and away from the threat of domestic death, from death to death and then out again, as it were—is analogous to the Br'er Rabbit story.[9] This relation to death is dramatized rhetorically by Jacobs's refusal to cast Brent as a virtuous married woman and by her attempt to pry the fact of sanctuary away from the ideology of domesticity. In Br'er Rabbit, it is effected with the flesh, mutely, as it were, repeating but not redeeming the violence enacted on black flesh, so often left to die or rot in the road.[10] As we shall see, that relation to death is recapitulated, albeit sometimes in metaphorical form, in several African American texts of the nineteenth century: the ex-slave Henry Bibb's autobiography ([1850] 2001); the performances of the ex-slave Henry Box Brown from 1851 through the late nineteenth century; and a somewhat Gothic scene in Sutton E. Griggs's *Imperium in Imperio* ([1899] 2003). Finally, it finds its most dramatic expression in what may be the paradigmatic African American trickster tale, the story of the Tar-Baby.

The Family as Social Death: Henry Bibb, Queer Theory, Afropessimism

Henry Bibb's *Narrative of the Life and Adventures of Henry Bibb* ([1850] 2001) focuses specifically on the natal alienation of the slave, but not by arguing, along the lines of Harriet Beecher Stowe, that slavery's profoundest injury is the destruction of family ties—nor even, following Spillers (1987), that the negation of African kinship ties in the Middle Passage is fundamental to the reduction of black slaves to agendered, asexualized nonhumanity. Instead, the *Life and Adventures* clarifies how even the resistant, extralegal family ties fostered by slaves could compound rather than ameliorate social death. The title of Bibb's narrative alone signals the disjunction played out in the text: this is not just "the life" of an ex-slave, expressed as a teleological movement from birth to marriage and to freedom or death and resurrection. The text also narrates his "adventures," his periodic detours from that journey and, by extension, from narrative itself, using a term that connotes play. While Bibb does not literally play dead to escape, there is an element of the ludic in his "adventures" off the plantation, which he captures by describing how from the age of ten onward he practiced "the art of running away" (Bibb [1850] 2001, 15), and by figuring one of his later escapes as "a tramp" (135). Nevertheless, escaping is a deadly game for him, not only because each time he runs away (a total of five times in his adult life) he risks being either killed or remanded back to the state of social death, but also because Bibb, like Br'er Rabbit, must stage his escapes over and over. Remarkably, he runs away to a free state, Ohio, no less than three times out of his five escapes from slavery. But instead of staying there or going on to Canada, each time he goes back to his wife and child in Kentucky, pretending to have returned permanently while plotting to free them. We might say that rather than playing literally dead like Br'er Rabbit or Linda Brent, Bibb plays socially dead, repeatedly enacting the role of an obedient and submissive returned slave.

Because Bibb's repetitions and returns are an effect of his family ties, his narrative might also be readable in terms of queer theory's "antisocial thesis." Within a strain of queer theory embodied by gay white men, namely Leo Bersani (1986, 1987) and Lee Edelman (2004), the antisocial thesis is shorthand for an insistence that queers are cast as the negation of sociability, much as, according to Spillers (1987), slaves were cast as the negation of humanity through the annihilation of African kinship ties and the misrecognition and destruction of African American ones. But whereas Spillers (1984) first suggests that black women's sexual vernacular theorizes black desire and belonging otherwise, and then later (Spillers 1987) advocates a kind of radical black androgyny as a position from which to dismantle white patriarchy, Bersani and Edelman cling to an unmarked whiteness to link queerness with the Freudian death drive. For Bersani (1987), the sex practice most imbued with the threat of death, anal sex, is a figure for the queer practice of rupturing the boundaries of the life-affirming, imaginarily whole, dominating ego—an ego that is, of course, not granted black subjects, as even a cursory reading of Frantz Fanon ([1952] 1994) makes clear.[11] Edelman advocates embracing the homosexual's structural place as an avatar of death, as this positionality refuses everything to do with the production of the political future, which he argues is inevitably constructed in the name of life, and especially of children—a position that does not acknowledge eugenic projects that aimed to curtail people of color's reproductive futures. Nevertheless, in light of Bersani and Edelman, Bibb's repeated movements back toward social death might also look like futile, self-deceiving movements back toward the "life" indexed (in heteronormative terms) by his wife and children.

But Bibb's family is actually, *itself*, a site of social death: far from redeeming Bibb back into social life along the lines suggested by Edelman especially, Bibb's family ties intensify his deadness. Early in the narrative, for instance, he describes his courtship of and marriage to his wife Malinda as another form of oppression: "I suffered myself to be turned aside by the fascinating charms of a female, who gradually won my attention from an object so high as liberty" (Bibb [1850] 2001, 33). While this sounds simply misogynistic, it also acknowledges that much of Bibb's "social" life is actually inseparable from death, as slave owners cemented family relations among slaves only to the exact extent that these relations would generate more slaves and keep slaves from running away. Marital- and repro-futurity, then, are almost the literal death of Bibb, and as my epigraph from Fred Moten's "Black Op" (2008a) suggests, they sentence him to "the gift of constant escape," since he must repeatedly undo his escape in order to attend to his family: "I must forsake friends and neighbors, wife and child," he writes, "or consent to live and die a slave" (Bibb [1850] 2001, 47). Significantly, Bibb refers to his wife as "dead to me" (189) once he finds out that her male owner has taken her on as a concubine. On the one hand, his dismissal of her as dead to him on hearing the news reflects his apparent inability to understand that Malinda's adultery is impossible to conceive of as such under the condition of captivity, which forecloses a consent that entails ownership of the self. On the other, following Spillers and Hartman, we might read Bibb as, by the end of the narrative, having bought a semblance of freedom through the multiply vectored social death of his wife, which involves not only her natal alienation and dishonor but also the negation of her humanity through a specifically sexual violence.

In any case, because slaves' family ties were used by owners to enmesh them further into captivity rather than to bestow liveliness and humanity on them, the antisocial thesis is a suggestive but incomplete way to understand Bibb's repeated, doomed returns to a slave state, and to the state of slavery. In order to fully comprehend Bibb's movements, we must consider the African American philosophical formation sometimes referred to as Afropessimism, to which I have alluded in citing Patterson,

Spillers and Hartman (who have been taken up by Afropessimism but differ from its main theorists in some important ways), and Wilderson. I understand the term "Afropessimism" to comprise two developments: first, it is an extension of Patterson's theory of slavery as social death that understands emancipation as an incomplete project, and antiblackness as both the foundation and the contemporary aftermath of slavery. Second, "Afropessimism" is an ironic détournement of the original term—which indexed the idea that sub-Saharan Africa was too damaged to ever "achieve" democracy and modernization—toward the work of, in particular, Fanon, especially *Black Skin, White Masks* ([1952] 1994).[12] Critical Afropessimism takes as axiomatic that modern definitions of "humanity" and "the human" were forged against people of African descent; indeed, these formulations can be found in—at the very least—Kant's *Critique of Pure Reason* (Kant, Weigelt, and Müller [1871] 2007; see also Judy 1991), Thomas Jefferson's *Notes on the State of Virginia* ([1785] 1998), and Hegel's *Lectures on the Philosophy of World History* ([1837] 1981). Antiblackness is, in Afropessimist terms, the bedrock of humanism, a white-supremacist formation under which the black person is the aporia, the negative, of modern consciousness and historical becoming: as Fanon writes, "[The Negro] has no culture, no civilization, no 'long historical past'" (Fanon [1952] 1994, 34). According to David Marriott (2011, 60), who also draws from Fanon, racism is thus "a discourse of time" because—as Nicolas Abraham's formulations in the previous chapter also reflect—it posits blackness as ahistorical.[13]

In this sense, then, chronothanatopolitics is originally a tool of racialization, not only because it involved the state's investment in black death but also because theories of human beings as temporal and historical emerged in contradistinction to the construction of blackness as atemporal and ahistorical. While Wilderson focuses on time, Marriott (2011) turns toward the discipline and concept of history, claiming that it emerged to explain the progress (or lack thereof) of "the race," or of various races, such that black life as "event," as living possibility, is inconceivable within history's terms of progress and realization.

Given all this, in Afropessimist thought it is not possible to intervene on antiblackness using discourses of humanity, family, history, civility, national belonging, and so on, insofar as each of these discourses of progress figures the black person as its constitutive outside.[14] There is something of a resonance, then, between Afropessimism's refusal of humanist futurity and queer theory's antisocial thesis. Both recognize their objects, black and queer people respectively, as being outside of time as it is conceived in Western humanist terms: reproductive and genealogical time, historical time, the time of progress. Furthermore, both refuse the central turn in queer theory, performativity, as a solution to the problem of being always-already deathly. The antisocial theorists refuse performativity because their models for intervention are not invested in linguistic or semiotic resignification so much as in designification and the dissolution of certain psychic structures (though the antisocial thesis springs from the same deconstructionist roots as performativity theory). And some Afropessimists refuse performativity because it relies on a legibly gendered body that must be denaturalized through performance, whereas they see blackness as the foreclosure of meaningful embodiment and the reduction of the black person to ungendered flesh. To put it more simply, both the queer antisocial thesis and Afropessimism are invested in the sociostructural position of the oppressed, rather than in a historical sedimentation of identity that might be denaturalized. They are both, one might say, productively ahistorical.

But there is also a key difference between the queer antisocial thesis and Afropessimism: within the terms of white supremacy, black people are antisocial not because they do not reproduce but because they have been defined within the terms of the social as not human; even their reproduction has been cast in terms of animality or property relations. Queers may be rhetorically aligned with the inhuman, the unnatural, the sterile, and the deathly, but it is a stretch of the imagination to think that modern humanity—as opposed, say, to salvation or sinlessness—has been conceptualized as such against sexual aberrance itself. Indeed, as Foucault (1990a, 127) has shown, sexuality, "originally bourgeois," is arguably the core of a modern-secular humanity understood in terms of an interiority secretly motored by erotic desire: it is a sign of the human within humanism, if an unruly one sometimes attributed to animality. As Wilderson (2010, 290) might describe it, queers are structurally "alive" insofar as the concept of sexuality itself presumes the capacity to narrate and the possession of an interior, whether soul or psyche. This is why black people have been cast as having no desire, as in the sexless Uncle Tom or Mammy stereotypes originally promulgated by minstrelsy, or, conversely, as having sexual urges in excess of human desire, as in the rhetoric of accused black rapists as animals and monsters.[15] As Fanon ([1952] 1994, 134–35) describes this absence of desire and superabundance of sex-without-sexuality, "the black consciousness is held out as an absolute density, as filled with itself, a state preceding any invasion, any abolition of the ego by desire." Bersani's (1987) model of anal sex as the paradigm of the ego abolished by desire and penetration clearly does not apply here. And Fanon's spatial language of density also infers a particular time, a time without difference, without the movement even of the drives that comprise desire, contradicting Edelman's model of queerness as always negatingly mobile despite its antifutural aims.

Black antisociability or antirelationality is thus not quite the same kind of political option as white queer antisociability or antirelationality, even as Afropessimism thoroughly vexes the question of relationality: as Wilderson (2010, 18) puts it, "*African,* or more precisely *Blackness,* refers to an individual who is always already void of relationality" (emphasis in source). Note that he does not say that blackness means being "devoid," but "void," as in "voided," or canceled by whites from the Middle Passage onward, and as in "originarily bereft," or as unintelligible in humanist terms—rather than, as with queer relationality, intelligible as the pathological inverse of normative sociality. Queers are, it might be said, not entirely void of relationality insofar as even the most damning rhetoric about queerness understands it as a relation to other people, as desire for the same sex must be by definition. Furthermore, in Bersani and Edelman, embracing the death drive is a kind of opt-out, a hygienic practice to cleanse the psyche of ego for Bersani, and for Edelman the basis of a(n anti)political stance operating as a force that deconstructs and destructs all pastoral notions of the good life: *there is something in the first place, however much a fiction it is, to give up or lose.* But the death drive in Afropessimist terms is less an internal, psychic mechanism than it is an external, well-oiled machine ensuring that black people have died sooner and in greater numbers proportional to their population than others for centuries—we might call it a death drive appearing as the state itself.[16]

Black sociability, a black life drive, black hope: these models of a nonhumanist futurity that is not the same as antifuturity seem on the face of it imperative. This is the gist of, for example, José Muñoz's *Cruising Utopia* (2009), which is among several works that theorize queer of color world making through performance and performativity, which offer glimpses of the future in the present.[17] And yet Afropessimism offers a perhaps productive impasse for critical race and queer theory, even for queer of color critique. For as Wilderson (in Hartman 2003, 120) remarks in an interview with Saidiya Hartman, "performance cannot reconcile this gap between the place of slaves and the places of all others." Stylization is not, in and of itself, liberation. Or as Sexton (2011, 34) puts it, following Wilderson, performativity theory "remains insufficiently elaborated" if it cannot grapple with the condition of social death, which is, for Afropessimism, unending.

The queer antisocial thesis relies on a certain hyperbolic repetition of a social order in which queers represent death, a repetition reminiscent of if not coterminous with performativity—the self-shattering of anal sex for Bersani, for Edelman the *sythomosexual* who undermines and destroys formal and ideological coherence. There is, then, a fundamental temporal contradiction between Afro-pessimism and the way that white queer performativity theory has depended on (re)iterability to formulate the possibility of change. I have written elsewhere (see Freeman 2010) of the temporal seductions of queer performativity theory, at least as it is represented by Judith Butler: briefly, performativity undoes the fantasy of an original through denaturalizing the repetitions that consolidate a social identity; these repetitions "with a difference" (the difference of slowness, perhaps, or of gender nonconformity, race, even time period) clarify that there is no anterior "there" there to imitate. Interestingly, in queer performativity theory, an essentially rhythmic semiotic practice deconstructs a fantasmatic past, somewhat in the way that repeating the word "duck" a dozen times empties the term's historically sedimented meanings and turns it into defamiliarized sound, available for other semantic possibilities. Within black critical theory, especially as it intersects with performance studies, these repetitions are what Henry Louis Gates (1988) calls "signifying" and Afro-optimist Fred Moten calls "the break," the interruption that makes another performance possible.[18]

Sexton and other Afropessimists, on the other hand, posit no break in antiblackness: they posit blackness, insofar as slavery has not ended but only mutated, as a continuation of social death. Sexton (2011, 6) poses the crucial question: "But how, then, does one mark time and think historicity, how does one engage the iterability of the performative, if nothing ends? How to orient or make sense of lived experience, the lived experience of the black no less, without break or interval or punctuation in the fact of (anti)blackness?" Antiblackness is more than repetition, even without a difference, if such a thing is possible; it is simply, duration, ongoingness without even the promise of the break that allows for repetition. We might even say that social death is death without a drive, without the constant and teleological movement toward inanimacy that renders the death drive destructive and thereby, however inadvertently, productive of the new. How, then, can there be repetition within a condition of unending death, or a repetition of unending death?

Bibb's repetitions—not precisely rhythmic, but certainly understandable as a kind of regressive, death-doubling "punctuation" of what would otherwise be a linear journey from death to life, from enslavement to resurrection—echo Sexton's (2011, 28) contention that "nothing in [A]fro-pessimism suggests that there is no black (social) life, only that black life is not social life in the universe formed by the codes of state and civil society, of citizen and subject, of nation and culture, of people and place, of history and heritage." It is precisely when Bibb moves toward his own approximations of the civilizational codes of informal marriage and extralegal descent that he becomes entangled back into the social death that is slavery. The aspect of black social life under slavery most uncongenial to the queer antisocial thesis is precisely that black family relations are not at all sacralized; they are themselves a negative, if psychically ameliorative, force, a set of shackles binding the slave to death and timelessness instead of promising life and futurity.[19] Henry Bibb, like Harriet Jacobs, clearly casts himself in terms of family but also acknowledges that the discourse of family is in no way separable from the institution of slavery, that family, too, is entangled with death. Thus in both Jacobs and Bibb, a return to family is also a return to death, an embrace of death or a play with death in the form of interment for Jacobs and temporary reenslavement for Bibb. Neither has an alternative to this interlacement of the social and social death; both of their protagonists, instead, hyperbolize and repeat death itself with no promise of its capacity for destruction of the status quo. Bibb's and Brent's seizing of death in this way, their willingness to mime it and then to escape it in ways that each recognizes as temporary or contingent, is a critical chronothanatopolitics—a kind of horizontal and repetitive movement between states of being rather than, as with haunting and melancholia, a vertical movement backward in time.

However, Sexton also reminds us that though black life may not adhere to the codes of past and present indexed by the civilizational, it is not, for that, antirelational. In this he differs from Wilderson, who argues that blackness is always already void of relationality. The latter is true only if relationality is reduced to its sanctioned forms or their approximation. If family, friendship, and community all take place within the terms of a humanness from which slaves and their descendants have been barred, how to conceive of black relationality? And must relationality be human-to-human? The story of Henry Box Brown uses the sensemethod of playing dead to stage the same kind of question.

Rhythm in and as Relationality: Henry Box Brown

Henry Box Brown's retellings and reenactments of his escape are eventually directly intertextual with Bibb's narrative. The first of these retellings was the *Narrative of Henry Box Brown, Who Escaped from Slavery, Enclosed in a Box 3 Feet Long and 2 Wide, Written from a Statement of Facts Made by Himself, with Remarks upon the Remedy for Slavery, by Charles Stearns* (Stearns 1849).[20] This text was considerably revised in 1851, republished as *Narrative of Henry Box Brown, Written by Himself* (Brown [1851] 2008), and performed in parts onstage in Brown's lectures and "African Panorama," about which more below.

According to historian Jeffrey Ruggles (2003) as well as Brown's two narratives, the slave Henry Brown enclosed himself in a custom-built wooden box and paid a sympathizer to mail the box to the Abolitionist Society in Philadelphia. Having been nearly suffocated, forced to travel hours while standing on his head, deprived of food and all but a little water, and tossed out of the train car that bore him, Brown was "unboxed" around 6 AM on Saturday, March 24, 1849, which liberation his narrative rather typically calls "my resurrection from the grave of slavery" (Brown [1851] 2008, 87). He fainted before being helped out of the box, whereupon according to him and his witnesses, he awoke and sang a hymn of thanksgiving. Shortly thereafter he joined the abolitionist lecture circuit as Henry Box Brown, penned a song about his escape, and eventually turned his lectures into a self-narrated panorama of scenes from American slavery of which his escape was a climax. Toward the end of his career, Brown reinvented himself yet again, as an "African Prince" who specialized in mesmerism, spiritualism, and, finally, magic (see Ruggles 2003; Brooks 2006; Rusert 2017).

As several critics have noticed, Brown's *Narratives* are permeated by images of interment, and the box itself is a kind of traveling coffin.[21] His confinement is, too, more than literal, for as John Ernest (2007) demonstrates, early on his books and lectures were constrained by the rhetorical confines of the abolitionist sentimental style, just as Harriet Jacobs's narrative seems at first glance entombed in the discourse of sentimental domesticity. And just as Jacobs broke with sentimentalism by explicitly portraying her protagonist's refusal to marry, Brown eventually broke with it by adopting the gestures and tenets of spiritualism in his performances as the African prince (Brooks 2006; Rusert 2017). But most important for the purposes of my analysis here is the fact that just as Henry Bibb returned or was returned again and again to slavery, Henry Box Brown continually returned, or was returned, to his box. In the latter's case, this return to a symbolic live burial reflected not just the social death of slavery but also the extension of social death in the Compromise of 1850, whose Fugitive Slave Law dictated that officials and residents of free states were required to aid in the return of runaway slaves and thus created what performance theorist Daphne Brooks (2006, 66) calls an "age of anxious escape."

The first manifestation of Brown's dialectic of return was the flurry of visual representations of that container, the earliest extant example of which was a rendering of the box over the lyrics to the improvised hymn that Brown claimed to have sung when he came back to consciousness and realized he was free (figure 2.1).[22]

Here, Brown is completely interred, the box figuring much more powerfully than his escape. At the same time, the hymn itself is based on Psalm 40, but incorporates repetition, presumably a call-and-response structure, in a way that blends the form of a psalm and African music—signaling, perhaps, the importance of repetition to Brown's performances.

This illustration also appeared on a song sheet featuring Brown's rewriting of the minstrelsy song "Uncle Ned," but this time the lyrics feature Brown entering his box over and over. The chorus, repeated six times, proclaims that

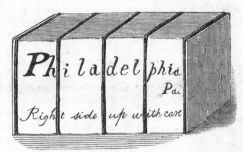

Engraving of the Box in which HENRY BOX BROWN escaped from slavery in Richmond, Va.

SONG,

Sung by Mr. Brown on being removed from the box.

I waited patiently for the Lord ;—
And he, in kindness to me, heard my calling—
And he hath put a new song into my mouth—
Even thanksgiving—even thanksgiving—
  Unto our God !

Blessed—blessed is the man
That has set his hope, his hope in the Lord !
O Lord ! my God ! great, great is the wondrous work
  Which thou hast done !

If I should declare them—and speak of them—
They would be more than I am able to express.
I have not kept back thy love, and kindness, and truth,
  From the great congregation !

Withdraw not thou thy mercies from me,
Let thy love, and kindness, and thy truth, alway preserve me—
Let all those that seek thee be joyful and glad !
  Be joyful and glad !

And let such as love thy salvation—
Say always—say always—
The Lord be praised !
  The Lord be praised !

Laing's Steam Press, 1 1-2 Water Street, Boston.

2.1 "Engraving of the Box in which HENRY BOX BROWN escaped from slavery in Richmond, Va." and "Song, Sung by Mr. Brown on being removed from the box." Laing's Steam Press, Boston, c. 1850. Library of Congress, Rare Books and Special Collections Division.

Brown laid down the shovel and the hoe,
Down in the box he did go,
No more slave work for Henry Box Brown,
In the box by Express he did go. (Ruggles 2003, 58)

Even within this four-line chorus, Brown goes "in the box" twice. In temporal counterpoint to these repetitive lines within a repeated chorus, the lyrics narrate Brown's story in linear fashion, describing how "they stole all [his] rights," how his box went on a car to a steamboat north, where he was turned on his head and then righted by passengers who used his box as a seat, then tossed in the train yard, then carried on a wagon to his friends, who rapped and asked if he was alright, and opened the box and "set [him] free from his pain." But the chorus keeps putting him back into that box, over and over again.

This, in fact, was what kept happening to Brown—what he in many ways chose, and what was also thrust upon him. First, the Boston abolitionists who took him in after his arrival in Philadelphia rechristened him "Henry Box Brown," making him and his box inseparable, figuratively inserting the box into him, even casting him *as* a box, a form of property. Second, he began to lecture about his escape, renarrating his entrance into and emergence from the box for audience after audience and distributing the aforementioned song sheets with their representation of the box. By the summer of 1849, Stearns and Brown had produced the book that tells of the escape, whose last page is a "Representation of the Box," with the same illustration used on the song sheets (Ruggles 2003, 62). Thus the narrative of Brown's escape ends on the note of visually stuffing him back into his box. As Brooks (2006, 77) puts it, "A (re-) boxed Henry Brown at text's end overturns the critical notion that 'once the protagonist achieves his freedom, the nineteenth-century slave narrative terminates'" (quoting Hedin 1982, 27). In other words, this image of the box reminds us that freedom is incomplete. But so, Brown's reemergences suggest, is social death.

The same year that Brown published the first version of his narrative, a children's book appeared with the first illustration of him actually emerging from his box (figure 2.2). *Cousin Ann's Stories for Children* (Preston 1849) told the story of Brown's escape in five pages, and included an illustration in which Brown stands in an open box incorrectly addressed

2.2 Henry Box Brown illustration (DAMS 1250). From Ann Preston, *Cousin Ann's Stories for Children* (Philadelphia, PA: J. M. McKim, 1849). Call number: Am 1849 Pre Wy 7627. Historical Society of Pennsylvania.

to "Thomas Wilson," presumably to protect the identity of the actual recipient. Brown extends his hand to a white man holding a small axe. Here, the gesture of equality between two men suggests Brown's complete liberation, but the facts that he has not yet stepped out of the box, and that the hand he extends to his patron is white, belie that possibility somewhat. Though the whitened hand is probably intended to indicate that Brown is holding his palm outward, it has the effect of suggesting that liberation occurs on white people's terms or "whitens" Brown, while the submersion of Brown's lower third in the box suggests that he is not yet fully free.

In 1850, Brown began to offer copies of a new print during his lectures and prior to the publication of his revised narrative. This print, titled "The Resurrection of Henry Box Brown at Philadelphia" and attributed by Ruggles (2003) to the artist Samuel W. Rowse, shows three white men and a black man gathered around a box (figure 2.3).

This time, the black man holds the axe, and one of the white men holds a hammer. The black man and one of the white men are holding

THE RESURRECTION OF HENRY BOX BROWN AT PHILADELPHIA.
Who escaped from Richmond Va. in a Box 3 feet long 2½ ft. deep and 2 ft. wide.

2.3 "The Resurrection of Henry Box Brown at Philadelphia, Who escaped from Richmond, Va in a Box 3 feet long 2 1/2 ft. deep and 2 ft. wide." Deposited for copyright in Boston on January 10, 1850. Library of Congress, Prints and Photographs Division, LC-USZ62, 1283.

the lid aloft, and Brown is shown only a third of the way out of the box, crouching and holding on to its side as his head, shoulders, neck, one elbow, and upper torso emerge. While the caption word "resurrection" alludes to the aforementioned trope of total freedom, and along with the axe clarifies that Brown is arriving, the focal point of the picture could as easily be read as the boxing *in* of Brown, the packaging of him rather than the unpackaging. There is something about this image, in which the box lid could be coming up or going down, in which Brown crouches and clings to the box rather than standing and shaking hands, that captures his jack-in-the-box performances of symbolically going into a coffin, then symbolically leaving it, and then returning, and so on, with each performance. As with Br'er Rabbit, there is an exorbitance to the way he revisits his own symbolic deathbed that cannot be equated with a final resurrection. His performance expresses both momentary escape and the continuity of death-in-life.[23]

The rhythmic movement of playing dead and then undead that this lithograph suggests is, in fact, the one that animated Brown's career subsequent to the publication of his first narrative. According to Ruggles (2003), by the end of 1849 Brown had conceived of and begun to execute a moving panorama, *The Mirror of Slavery*. The panorama, a newly popular media form, consisted of a long scroll unfurling horizontally, on which were painted various scenes. A precursor to the cinema, the panorama gave the illusion of a moving, changing background in front of which a narrator told and occasionally acted out whatever story was keyed to the panel behind him. A kind of visual travelogue, the panorama was also a mode of historiography, a repetitive if not precisely circular one, as the scroll was rewound and began again for each new performance (Ruggles 2003, 77; see also Brooks 2006, 80–81). As Ruggles (2003, 88) writes, Brown's panorama premiered in Boston on April 11, 1850, and included scenes of a "Nubian family" before their enslavement, during capture, in the Middle Passage, at auction, and at the moment of final separation. Ruggles speculates that the scenes then shifted to more general depictions of chain gangs, prisons, punishments, workhouses, plantations, and escapes. Included among the latter was Brown's own escape, from boxing up to release, and the escape of the aforementioned Henry Bibb, drawn from Bibb's own narrative and its illustration of Bibb with his family facing a wolf in the swamp (figure 2.4).

Both protagonists were, in this performance, liberated and then, in preparation for the next performance, symbolically unliberated when the scroll was rolled back up and the scenes reenfolded into one another. Brooks (2006) clarifies how Brown's panorama both mimicked the unfurling motion and progressive temporality of US imperialism and, with its repetition of scenes of slavery, undermined it, much as, I am arguing here, the visual and performative repetitions of Brown's interment undermined both the smooth narrative of progress toward freedom and the finality of social death.

Brown's performance in front of the screen was yet another doubling of his movement in and out of symbolic death. For at least one advertisement for the panorama promised that "the box may be seen, and Mr. Brown in it, after each exhibition" (Ruggles 2003, 105). The scholarship on Brown offers no visual or textual record of what this looked like, but it is possible that he posed halfway out of the box in imitation of

2.4 "The Escape." From *Narrative of the Life and Adventures of Henry Bibb, an American Slave, Written by Himself* (New York: published by the author, 1850). Image reproduction courtesy University of California, Davis, Special Collections.

the lithograph, in the manner of a tableau vivant, or that he restaged his actual emergence from the box in a more kinetic performance. An engraving from the period of his performances, for example, shows Brown in an upright box, chest and shoulders out, shaking hands with a white man with one hand while gripping the side of his box with the other (figure 2.5).

All four men surrounding the box are white, and Brown's face is indistinct. This is more likely a representation of the escape itself than of the performance after the panorama, but it does invoke the scene that panorama audiences were promised in some of the advertisements. In any case, the panorama performance was the most insistent way that Brown played dead, entering and exiting his box at least once per show, going toward death one more time, every time, and then rewinding the historical narrative in ways that echo Marriott's contention that racism casts black people out of progressive time.

Ironically and terribly, the year that Brown's panorama and this performance debuted, the US Senate extended the reach of social death yet further by passing the Fugitive Slave Act of 1850, which called for federal officers to enforce the 1793 Fugitive Slave Act remanding runaway slaves to their owners. Whereas the 1793 law had been mostly unenforced, the

HENRY BOX BROWN.

2.5 Engraving from *The Liberty Almanac for 1851*. Published by the American and Foreign Anti-Slavery Society. Division of Rare and Manuscript Collections, Cornell University Library.

new law compelled citizens to abet the process of slave capture by levying a one-thousand-dollar fine and six months in jail if they aided a runaway slave; it also denied fugitives the right to a jury trial. Claimants had merely to assert ownership over a runaway rather than providing evidence for it, as they had under the old law. The constant possibility of freedom's undoing, of a literal return to social death, was now cemented into American law. Surely black audiences for Brown's performance could read his reentering his box as a figure for the possibility that his freedom was precarious at best. And indeed, Brown, like many former slaves, fled to England for the next twenty-five years to avoid recapture.

What kind of temporality, though, and what kind of relationality are at play in Brown's consistent movement back into his box? I have offered "rhythmic" as one possibility for thinking the temporality of Brown's existence, attending to the pattern of repetition and recapitulation in his performances and the literature and images surrounding them. Under these terms, rhythm is useful analytically in that it offers no necessary break from the status quo; it can cohabit with duration and endlessness while giving those conditions some shape. Indeed, the African polyrhythms incorporated into slave music—surely in this new context even more connected to life and survival than they might have been before—modulated the work rhythms of slavery, texturing and giving form to, rather than rupturing, the extended duration of the workday.[24]

Thought as a mode of relationality, rhythm can, as I showed in the previous chapter, enable forms of engroupment that do not depend on subjectivity or the identity markers proper to humanity. Here, though, it is difficult to conceptualize Brown's stage work in terms of engroupment: perhaps he catalyzed some forms of community, perhaps not. Perhaps he felt connected to the captured Africans who endured the Middle Passage when he traveled in his box and then went back into it over and over again, perhaps not. Rather than signaling a connection to other black people, I would suggest, Brown's performances mark a relationality with his box, and thus with death itself—most insistently with the negation of humanness, the void that is, in Afropessimist terms, blackness itself, or within Patterson's more historically located terms, the social death of slavery. Brooks (2006, 122) calls Brown's performances a "cheat[ing of] of social death in slavery," but I am not sure that the cheating is complete or permanent. Instead, Brown's chronothanatopolitical returns to the box are equally well read as concession to the incomplete status of freedom itself, to the duration of social death, even as they punctuate and texture that condition in ways that acknowledge that social death is a historical phenomenon with the potential to change form and even potentially end, rather than an ontology. They are, one might say, a form of relation to nonrelationality. I will return to this in the coda, but want to turn first to an instance of playing dead that registers the only form of relationality concretely posited in Afropessimism, one that is both prefigured by Brown's connection to his box, and commensurate with the gratuitous violence that defines slavery and its afterlife: putting the living out of the picture.

To Put the Living Out of the Picture: *Imperium in Imperio*

In Sutton Griggs's *Imperium in Imperio* ([1899] 2003), the main black character, Belton, finds himself on a dissecting table presumed dead, with the villainous white Dr. Zackland preparing him for dissection. Zackland leaves the dissecting knife near Belton, and goes to get a pail of water. When he returns, Belton attacks: ". . . he now raised himself up, seized the knife that was near his feet, and at a bound was at the doctor's side. The doctor turned around and was in dread alarm at the sight of the dead man returned to life. At that instant he was too terrified to act or scream, and before he could recover his self-possession Belton plunged the knife through his throat. Seizing the dying man he laid him on the dissecting board and covered him over with a sheet" (Griggs [1899] 2003, 107). Belton then forges a note to the other doctors for whom Zackland was preparing the dissection, buying time to escape by requesting that they not touch the body until Zackland's return.

While typical of the melodramatic style of much of *Imperium in Imperio*, this scene also recapitulates some of the Br'er Rabbit story, namely its figure of doubling death, of feigned literal death under social death, this time the social death of the post-Reconstruction period—during which, as Hartman (1997) and others have argued, slavery did not so much end as transmogrify. The scene also clarifies, in figures that echo Afropessimism's claims about the endurance of social death, why the trope of playing dead is so powerful. For it appears within a chapter that condenses many of the ways that slavery continued under other names: Jim Crow, imprisonment without due process, the spectacularization of black bodies, the demotion of free black people to manual labor, disenfranchisement, lynching, and the use of black people as subjects in medical experiments without their consent. The chapter begins with a survey of Jim Crow law: at the beginning of the chapter, Belton is hired to replace the white college president who has had to resign in the face of laws forbidding whites to teach in schools for "Negroes." Recapitulating *Plessy v. Ferguson*, Belton travels to the college in the first-class coach of a train that, unbeknownst to him, passes into territory in which black people are not allowed to ride in the same coach as whites. The white passengers physically toss him off the train—much as Brown in his box was tossed—and into the mud. As he resumes his journey, he is refused seating at a lunch counter, and refuses in turn to pay for his to-go meal. The owner calls the police, who jail him, fine him, and exile him from the city. Then the chapter turns to the spectacularization of black bodies: on the next train we meet Dr. Zackland, whose eyes "follow [Belton] cadaverously" and who finds him "the finest lookin' darkey I ever put my eye on" (Griggs [1899] 2003, 100). As if to double the "cadaverous" expression of his eyes, Zackland states his wish to dissect Belton. Next we see the remanding of black bodies to manual labor: apparently following Booker T. Washington's Tuskegee plan for educating his fellow black people, Belton adds an industrial wing to his college, but the black people whom he hires to erect the building are overrun by whites, who steal their jobs and demote the black men to hod carriers and other servant roles. The chapter then moves rapidly to disenfranchisement: when Belton lectures his students on the importance of voting, a sympathetic black man warns him of the consequences of trying to foil the white-dominated political system, so he stops. Finally, the chapter culminates in a lynching: after politely showing a white woman in church where she can find her place in the hymnal, Belton is beset by a mob. Zackland asks the mob to keep the corpse pretty, and Belton is shot and hanged. He miraculously survives by feigning his own death, and ends up on Zackland's dissecting table, whereupon he comes "back" to life and stabs Zackland. It is as if Griggs is somehow staging African American playing dead as a response to the entire history of US post-Emancipation terrorism against black people.

With Belton's return from death to kill the doctor, the chapter also invokes the racialized myth of zombies, who do not feign death but come back from it to eat and thus zombify the living.[25] However, as Wilderson (2010) reminds us, the project of black liberation cannot be to bring the dead to life. Instead, Wilderson writes,

> If, when caught between the pincers of the imperative to meditate on Black dispossession and Black political agency, we do not dissemble, but instead allow our minds to reflect on the murderous ontology of chattel slavery's gratuitous violence—seven hundred years ago, five hundred years ago, two hundred years ago, last year, and today, then maybe, just maybe, we will be able to think Blackness and agency together in an ethical manner. This is not an Afrocentric question. *It is a question through which the dead ask themselves how to put the living out of the picture.* (43; emphasis mine)

Wilderson here seems to mean that slavery's violent death world ought to negate any humanist pretense to agency thought in terms of life. But Belton acts this out literally, returning the homicidal impulses of the passengers on the train, the cruelty of Jim Crow law, Zackland's blood-thirsty gaze, the violence of menial labor and disenfranchisement, and the murderous drive of the lynching posse to Zackland's body itself, putting it out of the picture by covering it and leaving it to remain, potentially for hours, before being discovered.

Yet as much as Belton achieves a form of freedom by bringing the living to death as Wilderson figures it, his freedom too is bought with the price of black death, a death that figuratively substitutes for his own. The chapter after Belton's murder of Zackland focuses on Belgrave, the other protagonist of the novel, who convinces a jury to acquit Belton and then proposes to his (Belgrave's) lover, Viola. In this Belgrave seems to want to match his (false) resurrection of Belton through the civil structure with an equally false rescue of Viola into the humanity conferred by marriage. But Viola tells Belgrave that she cannot marry him, and will explain why at 10 AM the next morning. When Belgrave arrives at her house, he discovers that she has committed suicide and left a note explaining that as a child, she read a book called "White Supremacy and Negro Subordination," which argued that the white race intended to subjugate the black race by racial admixture: "It demonstrated that the fourth generation of the children born of intermarrying mulattoes were invariably sterile or woefully lacking in vital force" (Griggs [1899] 2003, 118). But this inter-marriage, she writes, had no such effect on whites because they cast their "half-breeds" back into the "Negro" pool, polluting it with white blood but not accepting any black blood into their own. In any case, Viola has pledged to refuse participation in this project of exterminating the black race, and thus cannot marry Belgrave because he is a "mulatto." In the two chapters concerning Viola, then, even freely chosen familial relationships unshackled from slavery are construed as death-bearing and geno-cidal. The twist is that it is whiteness, and not blackness, that confers this deathly inheritance.

Viola's death cannot be read as a feint; she is well and truly, permanently dead. As with Bibb, Belgrave's freedom is finally achieved by redoubling the black woman's social death, rather than by dying himself: instead of including sexual liberation in his platform for black freedom, Belgrave pledges to continue her mission against miscegenation. He realizes his pledge when Belton reappears, summoning him to become president of a black separatist state, the underground "imperium in imperio" of the novel's title, which is eventually betrayed to the United States whose mirror image it is. By contrast to this liaison with the state, Belton's moment on the dissecting table is a way of seizing not only social death and its nontemporality but also the living, life itself, by killing it. His murder does not depart from death by looking to the nation-form for resurrection, as Belton and Belgrave's society does; instead, Belton transfers death from his own body to a white one—prefiguring, as it happens, Bigger Thomas's statement in *Native Son* (Wright [1940] 2005, 429) that "what I killed for, I *am*."

Playing dead, then—whether by the side of the road as in the Br'er Rabbit tale, or via Henry Bibb's daring reentries back into slave territory to rescue his family, or through Henry Box Brown's multiply-mediated performances, or in Belton's exchanging his status as a corpse for another's— cannot be read merely as a trick for gain or an escape strategy, though these may be its immediate functions, and of course it is intimately connected to what Moten calls, in the epigraph that begins this chapter, "the gift of constant escape." Rather, playing dead is expressive of the "life" and "afterlife" (or we might say, "afterdeath") of slavery itself, of a state of social death that changes form but does not abate, and that *includes* marriage and reproduction rather than just severing the slave from those privileges. In these texts and in Afropessimism, there is no détournement wherein death itself becomes destructive of the system that produces it, as there is in the queer antisocial thesis: only mass acts of counterviolence rather than the individual acts of men like Belton could produce this. And there is none of queer antisociality's hygienic renunciation of the social field or social ties either, since under slavery these were the owner's prerogative anyway, and after slavery they became the province of the courts, lynch mobs, drug cartels, and the police. Instead, in these texts death extends its reach, proliferates, and mutates, and the response is what Kreiger (2008) calls "thanatomimesis," a kind of willed inanimacy. In African American literature, then, only thanatomimesis fully indexes chronothanatopolitics.

The psychoanalytic literature on thanatomimesis is instructive here, as well, for at base, it describes the would-be subject's response to temporal incapacity. Clinical research on infants has shown that they respond very positively to feedback that they themselves control: kicking to make a bell ring, and so on. Psychologist Sally Moskowitz (2005) hypothesizes that the infant takes similar pleasure in and sustenance from caregivers' responses to its cries, gestures, and facial expressions. She hypothesizes that this experience is crucial to the formation of a bodily ego—that Freudian sense of the self as a bounded shape with receptive surfaces— and enables infants to modulate themselves in relation to an increasingly less nurturing world. I would add that this ego is also temporal, in the sense that the infant's bodily coherence also depends on immediate responses that aggregate over time to allow it to survive the caregiver's absences. But when that immediate feedback is withdrawn too early, and their activities no longer get a response, infants "suddenly lie motionless, breathe with sleeplike respiration, and stare into space with nonconverging eyes" (907–8). Similarly, presented with an adult face that is still, motionless, and inexpressive, infants try at first to elicit a reaction, and when they cannot, they "become somber, avert their eyes, and slump over nonresponsively" (908). This infant defense, Moskowitz suggests, is a kind of playing dead.

Set against Frantz Fanon's work, this research offers one possible explanation for the trope of playing dead in African American literature and culture. Fanon ([1952] 1994) famously describes the bodily ego of the black person as socioculturally mediated, as, indeed, a shattering produced by being responded to as an object: "Look, a Negro!" The subject is first "sealed into . . . crushing objecthood," a coherent form, but not one that whose shape or timing he has control over. Then, Fanon describes a profound scene of nonrecognition: "I turned beseechingly to others. Their attention was a liberation, running over my body suddenly abraded into nonbeing, endowing me once more with an agility that I had thought lost, and by taking me out of the world, restoring me into it. But just as I reached the other side, I stumbled, and the movements, the attitudes, the glances of the other fixed me there, in the sense in which a chemical solution is fixed by a dye. I was indignant; I demanded an explanation. Nothing happened. I burst apart" (109). Fanon's scene exactly recapitulates the experience of nonresponsiveness, or negative responsiveness, and its bodily results: the experience, within the family, that bodily integrity and competence can be endowed by another, then in public, the shattering rescinding of this endowment, the blank gaze of the other—in the face of which the narrator freezes and then bursts apart. Later he echoes this rhetoric: "Then, assailed at various points, the corporeal schema crumbled, its place taken by a racial epidermal schema" (112). Here, the externalization of the self, the making of the self into an object, is not the achievement of somatic coherence but "an amputation, an excision, a hemorrhage that splattered my whole body with black blood" (112). Fanon's ego is, like Freud's, first a bodily ego, but also second, a bodily ego, insofar as it remains utterly epidermal: the black person is read by his or her skin and experiences the white gaze as a physical undoing. The black ego is also denied temporal capacity: Fanon's narrator describes attention "running over" his body and making him agile, then being withdrawn so that he "stumbles," losing rhythmic control over his body, and then being "fixed" in both space and time, denied what both Moskowitz (2005, 898) and Wilderson (2010, 250) describe as an essentially *formal* coherence. This form, as Fanon's rhetoric of stumbling and being "fixed" clarifies, is not only spatial but temporal.

The literature that Moskowitz reviews suggests that an infancy characterized by a lack of caregiver response can lead to later behaviors coded by psychoanalysis as "masochistic"—anorexia, cutting, and other kinds of self-administered pain—which she understands, quoting Kerry Kelly Novick and Jack Novick (1987, 374), as efforts to "stabiliz[e] the representational world," to give the body and its context boundaries and form. But unlike cutting or anorexia—or, to glance back at Bersani, anal sex—playing dead is a strategy that does not depend on a conception of agency or will, or even of selfhood expressed through violence to the self. Instead, it breaks through the need for recognition, as it is autogenerated, autoauthorized (note that I do not say "self-"). Under social conditions characterized by nonresponse—that is, a country's consistent turning away from its black people—playing dead is, itself, a way of stabilizing the representational world. It is a response to an environment that is not so much chaotic and formless as distorted like a fun-house mirror, and bifurcated in the way that W. E. B. Du Bois ([1903] 1997) describes in his model of double-consciousness, in which black subjects must experience themselves to be objects as the very condition of their subjectivity. Playing dead is a mode of asocial (in Jared Sexton's [2008] sense), if not antisocial, quasiautonomy. If playing dead marks the perdurance of antiblackness, of social death under and beyond slavery, it does so in black—with black, as black on (anti)black. That this mark is not total transformation or liberation is its very point.

One final figure for playing dead in the nineteenth century offers a model of this asociality, this lack of social relations "in the structural sense," as Wilderson (2010, 250) puts it. African American folklore's Tar-Baby is inanimate: silent, resistant, and black if not quite of African descent, figured in Joel Chandler Harris's (1881b, 24) retelling by the refrain "Tar-Baby, she ain't sayin' nuthin.'" Br'er Fox, susceptible though he is to Br'er Rabbit's performance of playing dead in the previous tale I discussed, creates this figure as a way to entrap Br'er Rabbit. Br'er Rabbit rails against the Tar-Baby's lack of recognition, and finally punches the effigy in an attempt to reanimate this inert matter. Of course his hand sticks, as does the other hand, and then his feet when he kicks, and finally, when he tries to butt the Tar-Baby, his head. On the one hand, his body is entangled and deformed, much as Fanon's narrator describes his own body in his first encounter with racism. On the other, his enmeshment with the Tar-Baby is a form of relationality that depends not on repudiating death but on figuratively embracing it. Br'er Rabbit is well and truly stuck in and with blackness, with death social and otherwise. In some versions of the story he outwits Br'er Fox in the end, convincing Br'er Fox that an apt punishment for Br'er Rabbit's crimes is being thrown back into the bramble bush that is his home. In others, though, Br'er Rabbit is left stuck to the Tar-Baby, with Br'er Fox promising to "take dinner" with him: either eat with him or, more likely, eat him. Suspended in the time between life and death, Br'er Rabbit can only hold on to his own deathly avatar.

Coda: Playing Dead in the Twenty-First Century

In 2012, after Trayvon Martin was shot and killed by a vigilante neighborhood watchperson, the Black Lives Matter movement was catalyzed. Black Lives Matter focuses on what Saidiya Hartman (2008, 45) calls "the afterlife of slavery," the ways that the random violence enacted on black bodies has, since slavery, shifted modes but not diminished: the owner's whip has been replaced by what Black Lives Matter, in its guiding principles, calls a system "where Black lives are systematically and intentionally targeted for demise," including but not limited to extrajudicial police and vigilante violence and the prison system (Black Lives Matter, n.d.). Black Lives Matter leashes the power of the social media meme and

Twitter hashtag, as well as more traditional modes of protest and counter-cultural experiments in living.

Certainly, Black Lives Matter could be read as gesturing toward what Afropessimists might view as the unviable value-form of the "life." But the pun on "matter" complicates this, as it invokes not only importance but also the "fleshliness" that Hortense Spillers (1987) describes as the end-point of the Middle Passage. As a verb, "mattering" implies both coming to importance and becoming-inert-substance, giving the phrase a positive and negative valence (see Butler 2011). More to the point, a "matter" is an event or situation, the sort of thing-in-time that some Afropessimists argue is foreclosed by blackness as a structural position. In its shimmering between negativity and becoming, "mattering" implies an equivocal stance toward the enforced temporal incapacity that defines blackness in Afropessimist terms. And indeed, Black Lives Matter has directly confronted time: the times of shortened lifespans and slow death, the times of instantaneous violent responses and of stubborn nonresponse to black people, the times of posthumous condemnations (Trayvon Martin's reputation ruined after his death) and agonizing suspensions of closure (Michael Brown's body left in the road for four hours, just as slave "transgressors" were left dangling from nooses, placed at crossroads to terrorize would-be insurrectionists, and so on). As Nicholas Mirzoeff (2015) succinctly puts it, "All #BlackLivesMatter protest memes call attention to time and duration." He goes on to cite the chant "Hands Up Don't Shoot": "performed with raised hands, [it] repeats a version of what activists believe were Michael Brown's last words. It freezes time in that crucial moment before he died and defies the imaginary police to shoot" (Mirzoeff 2015). In other words, this performance turns toward rather than away from the timelessness accorded to Africans and their descendants.

And of course, Black Lives Matter has revived the die-in, a particularly stark example of thanatomimesis enacted by the AIDS Coalition to Unleash Power (ACT UP) before it, and by the anti-war movement before ACT UP. Mirzoeff describes variations on the die-in that are specific to Black Lives Matter and that enact temporal conjoinments with death rather than resurrections from it: "A participant might count out 'I can't breathe' 11 times, as Eric Garner did. Or the die-in might be timed to last four-and-a-half minutes to symbolize the four-and-a-half hours that Michael Brown's body lay in the street." Miming death and temporal incapacity rather than seizing life and temporal capacity, Black Lives Matter thus far has eschewed a literal version of Wilderson's suggestion that the only response to being cast as always-already dead is to bring the living closer to death: murder is not on their agenda. But in their dying on the streets, playing dead in the road over and over again, Black Lives Matter activists commit to an (a)social life within death even as they fight for an end to the annihilation of blackness.

3 FEELING HISTORICISMS

Libidinal History in Twain and Hopkins

The *four untimely essays* are altogether warlike. They demonstrate that I was no 'Jack 'o' Dreams,' that I derive pleasure from drawing the sword—also, perhaps, that I have a dangerously supple wrist.

FRIEDRICH NIETZSCHE, *Ecce Homo*

Cast out of humanity by European Americans, enslaved African Americans were also cast out of what counted as history. As discussed in the previous chapter, some nineteenth-century slaves and freed people used their bodies to stage a direct encounter with death in a rhythmic play not so much with specific *historical* events and eras, as with a *structural* position as the deathly, inhuman, unchanging void for which the Middle Passage and the social death of slavery are paradigmatic, and against which humanism shaped its ideals and history was understood to unfold. But this intervention has the effect of deemphasizing change over time, paradoxically reiterating the ahistoricity of blackness. The Afropessimistic account with which I framed the sense-method of playing dead is less concerned than is black performance studies with what Dana Luciano (2003, 152; emphasis mine) calls "a stylized and *historically informed* blackness," or Daphne Brooks (2006, 290; emphasis mine) calls "*historically thick* black identity formation." In other words, the structuralist logic of Afropessimism can sometimes downplay the way that African American subjects have lived and performed not only a temporal position outside of linear progress but also a historical position of becoming and changing outside of the dominant record.

One way that nineteenth-century black historians countered dominant accounts of the past was simply to write their own collective histories, beginning with William Cooper Nell's *Services of Colored Americans in the Wars of 1776 and 1812* (1851) and *The Colored Patriots of the American Revolution* (1855), and culminating with George Washington Williams's two-volume *History of the Negro Race in America from 1619 to 1880* (1883), a history of African Americans that accorded with the professional historical standards of the era (see Bruce 1984a, 1984b). Like their white counterparts, postbellum black historians aimed for "scientific" historiographical conventions, along the lines of Ranke and Humboldt, which purported to rigorously separate fact from fiction, narrated events "objectively" in the third person to distinguish the writing of history from genres such as poetry and travel writing, and focused on the interpretation of primary documentary sources (see Lorenz 2009; B. G. Smith 1998, 70–156). Another mode of writing history was fiction. Though the historical romances from which professional historians attempted to distance themselves freely borrowed dramatic, poetic, and novelistic conventions and time schemes, like documentary history they also invoked prior events and aimed to give a sense of earlier times, sometimes even incorporating historical allusions and documentary sources.

But within disciplinary history and the historical romance alike—the two nineteenth-century forms of narrative most distinctly engaged with collectively experienced events of the past—there was, for most of the century, no analogue for the bodily breaching of life and death that we see in the thanatomimetic theme I've traced in folk tales, ex-slave narratives, and Sutton E. Griggs's *Imperium in Imperio*—even in the work of Charles Chesnutt, this kind of movement was relegated to dreams, hallucinations, superstition, and magic. Nor in white fiction did the theme of direct contact with a historically specific era (as opposed to with death or with a personal past) appear in the form of a novel until William Morris's *A Dream of John Ball* (1888), though the latter was preceded by the anonymously published short story "Missing One's Coach: An Anachronism" (1838)—and these texts, too, figured time travel as a hallucination or dream. In American fiction, the historiographical equivalent of thanatomimesis, or corporeal context not with death but with a particular past, would initially appear with Mark Twain's *A Connecticut Yankee in King Arthur's Court* (1889), considered the first time travel novel in the English language (Collins 1986, 102).[1] And in African American fiction, the literal encounter between a contemporary person and bygone times emerged with Pauline Elizabeth Hopkins's extraordinary *Of One Blood, Or, The Hidden Self,* published serially in *The Colored American Magazine* between 1902 and 1903. Taken together, these two novels posit a mode of writing and enacting history in which, as with dance and thanatomimesis in the previous chapters, the sensate body is itself a method of knowledge and transformation.

Twain's and Hopkins's novels, in fact, might be read as literary versions of historical reenactment, a popular practice of amateur historiography that began in the eighteenth century with *tableaux vivants* (see Holmström 1967) and the mock battles that were part of military drills (see During 2010, 192–93). These novels precede the invention of Civil War reenactment in 1913 (Schneider 2011, 8), but they partake in reenactment's fantasy that bodies can repeat events from the past, and in repeating them transform them. Reenactment wagers that participants can feel themselves into other eras rather than becoming surrogates for or descendants of specific historical characters; it generally traffics in the fantasy of ordinary people becoming historical as they dissolve into an event, a persona, and/or an environment, in what performance theorist Rebecca Schneider's contemporary Civil War–reenacting informants call a "wargasm" (35). But rather than staging bodies seamlessly reentering historical events, *Connecticut Yankee* and *Of One Blood* depict present-tense bodies encountering past environments. And these novels depend on the shock of misalignment between contemporary sensibilities and past ones, late nineteenth-century ways of having and feeling a body and prior ones.

Elsewhere, I have described the imagination and performance of enfleshed encounters with the past as "erotohistoriography": a carnal and pleasurable encounter with history (Freeman 2010). What this term implies, which I will develop more fully in this chapter, is that the writing of history, the feeling of oneself and one's community as "historical" or embedded in collective endeavors with meaning for the future, and the encounter with relics from the past all have a libidinal logic, one that mixes political desire with sensory encounter. Though historicizing projects and processes cannot be understood as universal and biological drives, as Freud understood the libido, they are matters of desire; they also engage the body. They are shaped by the kind of body that undertakes them and in turn they engage and shape those bodies. "Erotohistoriography," in my earlier work, privileged sexual, often genital, pleasure because queer criticism and theory had so insistently turned toward melancholia, shame, and loss, and toward the psyche rather than toward sex practice. But here, I also wish to claim, as part of erotohistoriography, sensory experiences are not always recognizable as sex, and not always pleasurable. I will begin, then, with the more obviously erotohistoriographical novel *A Connecticut Yankee in King Arthur's Court,* moving toward a broader account of libidinal historiography as a sense-method in *Of One Blood.*

Historical Hankerings: *A Connecticut Yankee in King Arthur's Court*

Versed in the academic historical works that were canonical in his time, as well as engaged with the question of how to write a historical novel that did not repeat the romanticizing offenses of Sir Walter Scott, Mark Twain set many of his novels in previous periods.[2] These included fifteenth-century France in *Personal Recollections of Joan of Arc* (1896) and the same Austrian era in *No. 44, the Mysterious Stranger* (1902–8). Twain also wrote of sixteenth-century England in *The Prince and the Pauper* (1881) and of the early eighteenth century in *The Chronicle of Young Satan* (1897–1900). He explored the antebellum United States with *The Adventures of Tom Sawyer* (1876), *Adventures of Huckleberry Finn* (1884), and *Pudd'nhead Wilson* (1894). But it is *A Connecticut Yankee in King Arthur's Court* (1889), set in sixth-century Camelot, that most self-consciously and metacritically takes on the problem of how to make history—both how to make a distant past immediate to readers and how to influence the course of events in time.

In this novel, Twain uses the body of his protagonist, Hank Morgan, as a wrench in the works of stadial, evolutionary history. In 1879, Hank's malcontent factory hand Hercules clonks him over the head with an iron bar and sends him back to the year 528. There, Hank decides to fast-forward the modernization of England by 1300 years, but his underlings rise against him, and he kills them en masse. This counterfactual, tongue-in-cheek history asks, as science fiction writers such as Castello Holford, H. G. Wells, and Robert Heinlein would do after Twain, whether bygone events might have happened otherwise—though Twain stops short of imagining the resulting, transformed present or future. Instead, following nineteenth-century, female, amateur historians' emphasis on everyday life and the immediate experience of people of the past, Twain depicts Hank as a sensory receptacle for the medieval period (see B. G. Smith 1998, 159). Hank variously sweats, itches, lusts, and starves his way through Arthurian England: his corporeal discomforts hint at the dangers of acutely sensing the past. *A Connecticut Yankee* also revels in the trope of a contemporary man modernizing the premodern, and reminds us that this is generally the figure that imperialist and colonialist ventures used to justify themselves. It suggests that these ventures acted directly on both the bodies of the colonized, whose indigenous gender and sexual norms were overwritten and reshaped by their oppressors, and the bodies of the colonizers, whose gender and sexual norms were made relative and often influenced by the people over whom they ruled.[3] Hank Morgan's sensory immersion in history, then, is inextricable from his erotic designs on the inhabitants of another time and place and, as I'll elaborate below, on himself.

If Hank's eventual destruction of Camelot figures the idea of forcing one's body too insistently into the course of human events, it may also stand in for Clemens's single moment of putting his own body on the line in the service of official national history, and his only military exercise. One intertext for *A Connecticut Yankee* may be Twain's humorous essay "The Private History of a Campaign That Failed," published in *Century Magazine* in December 1885, in which Twain reveals that he is, technically, a deserter of the Confederate army. In 1861, Clemens's home state of Missouri was attacked by Northern forces, and the governor called for a militia of fifty thousand to defend the state. Young Clemens and several friends in Marion County got together and formed a military company, the Marion Rangers, of which Clemens was made second lieutenant. The essay foreshadows *Connecticut Yankee*'s contempt for medieval knight-errantry and for the French (about both of which more below), for Twain relates that the boy who proposes the name Marion Rangers for the group is "full of romance, and given to reading chivalric novels"

(Twain 1885, 194). The young man's name is Dunlap, but Twain claims he changes it to "D'Un Lap," or "of a stone," or "Peterson" (194) and later refers to him as "the ass with the French name" (195). But Peterson is not the only Ranger given to theatricality, for the hapless group finds out that war is predominantly boring and uncomfortable. After bumbling about the countryside, falling down a hill, being attacked by farmers' dogs, and variously responding to and sleeping through false alarms, Clemens's company sees a man on horseback outside of their barn. In an overzealous display of firepower akin to *Connecticut Yankee*'s famous final Battle of the Sandbelt, the young men shoot the stranger five times only to find that his corpse is in civilian clothes and unarmed. Dismayed, Clemens vows to leave the war effort; Twain writes, "It seemed to me that I was not rightly equipped for this awful business; that war was intended for men, and I for a child's nurse. I resolved to retire from this avocation of sham soldiership while I could save some remnant of my self-respect" (203). And there, feminized by Twain in the figure of a child's nurse, young Samuel Clemens exits the masculine-historical stage.

Connecticut Yankee, likewise, tells the history of a masculine-imperial campaign that fails. Attempting to modernize sixth-century England according to the technological and ideological developments of the nineteenth century, Hank Morgan crowns himself "Sir Boss," arrogating military and managerial powers. When his subjects eventually rebel, he builds an electric fence, deserts by escaping from the battle into a cave, and from there watches the fence electrocute the whole of the Camelot army. The wizard Merlin casts a spell on him that lasts thirteen hundred years, until he awakens, grizzled and old, and hangs around Warwick Castle telling his tale to strangers, one of whom is the narrator in the novel's frame tale. The Twain of "The Private History" ends his narrative by ruefully noting, "I could have become a soldier myself, if I had waited. I had got part of it learned; I knew more about retreating than the man that invented retreating" (Twain 1885, 204). Hank Morgan, likewise, ends his life in complete retreat, mumbling and fading away in a bedroom in the castle, with no trace of his heroic adventures left except a bullet hole in a suit of armor (which the castle's docent suggests was introduced in Cromwell's era) and the manuscript he has handed over to the narrator, which makes up the bulk of the tale. And of course Hank's entire journey backward to the sixth century can be read as a retreat from the complexities of the nineteenth, specifically from the failure of the Reconstruction, after 1877, to liberate African Americans from de facto, if not de jure, slavery. In both of Twain's texts, then, the protagonist's attempt to make his body into an instrument of radical historical change—of secession in "The Private History" and of revolutionary modernization in *A Connecticut Yankee*—results in depletion: effeminization in the first, enfeeblement in the second.

Connecticut Yankee's literal deflation of the historically agentive body points to another piece of Twain ephemera that could serve as one of the novel's intertexts: Twain's satirical speech against masturbation for a gathering of the Stomach Club in 1879, "Some Thoughts on the Science of Onanism" (Twain [1879] 1976). In this speech, Twain admonishes his listeners, "When you feel a revolutionary uprising in your system, get your Vendôme Column down some other way—don't jerk it down" (25). Here, he directly associates masturbation with political activity, analogizing onanism not to the priapic monument honoring Napoleon Bonaparte but to the Paris Commune that "jerked" it down in 1871. Twain compares masturbation to the sort of historical action that aimed to upset the supposedly smooth movement of monarchical and electoral succession and the invisible hand of the market, and to the radical working class—indeed, it is notable that 1879 marks the year of both his speech to the Stomach Club and the fictional Hercules's uprising against the factory boss Hank Morgan. It would be too literal to say that Hank masturbates his way into Camelot, but as we shall see, the novel does go on to correlate his political overreachings with the kind of failed masculinity that masturbation indexed in the nineteenth century. In other words, "The Private History of a Campaign That Failed," "Some Thoughts on the Science of Onanism," and *Connecticut Yankee* align gender and sexual aberrance with flawed interventions into history.

Hank Morgan is certainly a figure for capitalism as the motor of history. Aligned with American robber barons, he is named after the nineteenth-century capitalist J. Pierpont Morgan and was drawn by illustrator Dan Beard in the first edition of the novel with the head of American financier Jay Gould. But Hank is not just a metaphorical American robber baron. He becomes a slave across several chapters, when he and the king are wandering Camelot to get a feel for the plight of the common man and are captured by a slave driver. Parallels between

Hank and French revolutionaries of various eras also appear in his opposition to the Catholic Church, and in the destruction of his own Vendôme Column in the form of Merlin's tower, which he blows up. Finally, Hank is a kind of closeted Napoleon. Critics have traced the very worst of Camelot's debauchery in *Connecticut Yankee* to descriptions of the revolutionary masses in Carlyle's *The French Revolution* (see, e.g., Fulton 2000). It is thus tempting to read the fictional events of 1879 in *Connecticut Yankee* as Twain's commentary on the events of 1789 and after, as if he slyly reversed some digits and the whole novel makes a mockery of the French Revolution. This makes some sense of Twain's invented device of traveling backward in history, since one of the notable accomplishments of the revolutionaries was a form of time travel—a new calendar instantiated on October 5, 1793, but beginning analeptically on September 22, 1793 (and, it might be noted, picked up again by the Paris Commune of 1871). The year Hank gets brained by his factory hand, 1879, also marks the year Twain traveled to France and received a lukewarm welcome from the French people, as well as finding himself "appalled by French sexual standards" (Britton 1992, 197). Like his mockery of "D'Un Lap" in "The Private History," both his joke about the Vendôme Column in the Stomach Club speech and *Connecticut Yankee* draw on his reputed hatred of all things French, especially French sexual mores. Most important, in Twain's complex scrambling of French revolutionary moments, historical actors of both 1789 and 1871 seemed to possess the capacity both to deform sex and to turn back time, the latter only the most literal of their many deformations of stadial, developmental history.

But in *Connecticut Yankee,* the Camelot peasants' uprising against the freedom that Hank supposedly offers them is not, like the French revolutions, a rational response to his increasingly autocratic rule or to their economic subservience to him as Sir Boss; rather, it is an outgrowth of their bawdy, infantile worldview, congruent with their civilizationally underdeveloped status. Indeed, Twain portrays the peasants in ways typical of nineteenth-century representations of not only medieval folk, black people, and the colonized but also the white and multiethnic working class: like Hercules, the brawny Greek factory hand who attacks Hank with a phallic tool, the people of Camelot are sexually excessive, physically strong, and given to childish pursuits. Thus *Connecticut Yankee* is haunted by a sexual specter less visible and perhaps more powerful than simple working-class unrest.

The Arthurian peasants seem, on the face of it, to be foils to the ostensibly democratic, modern, masculine Hank Morgan. But throughout his visit to Camelot, Hank himself acts something of the reactionary fop, nostalgic for the homosociality inherent in chivalry, overly invested in nudity and little children, uninterested in the ramblings of the medieval wife he takes, and too fond of theatrical "effects" to pass as completely heteromasculine. Finally, he fails most prominently at a sexual self-mastery for which his limitations as a historical actor and a historian are symptomatic—and this correlation of deviant history making and improper sex acts suggests the pleasures and dangers of amateur historiography as a sense-method, especially for the white man.

Bonnie G. Smith (1998), Mike Goode (2009), and Carolyn Dinshaw (2012) have each demonstrated that the amateur historian, of whom Hank is a stereotype, was a sexually charged figure in the eighteenth and nineteenth centuries as disciplinary history took shape. Bonnie G. Smith (1998, 18) claims Germaine de Staël as an early amateur historian for whom opium use was a relay to historical genius, a corporeal knowledge practice that Smith calls "narcohistory." De Staël, Smith argues, inspired a whole line of female amateur historians for whom excitement, eroticism, and trauma formed the basis of historical knowledge (67), in contradistinction to the growing scientism of documentary, seminar-based, professional history (103–7). Thus amateur historiography has been coded as feminine. Goode demonstrates that as disciplinary history took shape in the late eighteenth and nineteenth centuries, antiquarianism in particular was correlated with aberrant masculinity, reproductive sterility, and perverse sexual practices such as fondling statues. Dinshaw links the amateur historian, especially the contemporary reenactor of medieval times, to queer sexuality through the trope of temporality: in her analysis, the amateur refuses progressive and reproductive time for an immersive, tactile relationship to the past. In all of these accounts, amateur historians are feminized, linked to suspect bodily states and practices, and queered.

Perhaps unsurprisingly, then, *Connecticut Yankee,* a novel written by the amateur historian Twain, framed by the amateur historian who reads Hank's manuscript, and taking up the aberrant historical practice of time travel, is rife with perversions. As "Sir Boss," Hank may aspire to capitalist manhood, but he continually lapses into the voyeurism, homophilia, pedophilia, and flamboyance that marked the poor, people of color, and the revolutionary French in Twain's and other nineteenth-century European and American stereotypes of them. These sexual aberrations also characterized the late nineteenth-century sexual "deviant" of the white leisure classes. They are most clearly condensed in Hank's relationship with his medieval sidekick, Amyas "Clarence" Le Poulet, who appears to him at first sight as "an airy slim boy in shrimp-colored tights that make him look like a forked carrot" (Twain [1889] 1982, 15), and whom illustrator Beard drew with the head of the French actress Sarah Bernhardt. Shortly after, both doubling Clarence and for the first time exposing his own nakedness, Hank finds himself stripped of his supposedly enchanted clothes by the king's men, and thus "naked as a pair of tongs!" (26). Part of Hank's failure as a historian is that he mistakes historically specific difference for infancy, hewing to a linear model in which earlier times stand for the childhood of the human race. His relationship with Clarence brings out the erotic aspect of this misapprehension: at a banquet, responding to tall tales of Sir Kay the Seneschal's military prowess, Clarence whispers to Hank, "Oh, call me pet names, dearest, call me a marine!" (20), and then "nestle[s] upon [Hank's] shoulder and pretend[s] to go to sleep" (23). Clarence's real name, "Amyas le Poulet," is perhaps an anachronistic pun on the Puritan Sir Amyas Poulet but most definitely translatable, too, as "love the chicken."[4] That Twain was aware of the sexual innuendo is confirmed by Hank's later reference to the deadly and beautiful Morgan le Fay as "fresh and young as a Vassar pullet" (99). In other words, Hank Morgan likes a twink.

But of all the perversions coded into *A Connecticut Yankee,* the most suspicious one is Hank's status as a masturbator. At the end of the novel, he expires in a suspiciously onanistic pose: at the closing of the novel's nineteenth-century frame, he dies in bed, glassy-eyed, pale, and delirious, "mutter[ing] and ejaculat[ing]" endlessly while "pick[ing] busily at the coverlet," the very picture of the solitary vice (Twain [1889] 1982, 258). This is a fitting end for him. Over the years, as Hank conquers the Arthurians with nineteenth-century technology disguised as magic, Clarence becomes Hank's "head executive [and] right hand . . . a darling" (52), recalling again Twain's speech to the Stomach Club, in which he prefaces his admonition about the Vendôme Column with the winking warning,

"If you must gamble with your sexuality, don't play a Lone Hand too much" (Twain [1879] 1976, 25). In fact, it is Hank and not right-hand-man Clarence who becomes the ultimate Lone Hand, playing the part of a "lone" ranch "hand" with a lasso in a jousting competition.

As well, Hank's last name "Morgan" may suggest his capitalist agenda, and his full name, Henry Morgan, after the famous seventeenth-century Welsh pirate, may imply that his program is another form of robbery—but his nicknames add an erotic fillip or two. In calling Hank a "Yankee of the Yankees," Twain ostensibly suggests that Hank was a solidly white New Englander, as per the most popular etymological explanation for the term "Yankee," a North American Indian approximation of the word "English" (*yengee*).[5] More recently, though, Henry Abelove (2008) has also traced the word "yankee" to the slang term "yankum," or masturbatory act, rereading the song "Yankee Doodle Dandy" as a bawdy commentary on masturbation. As Abelove suggests, "doodle" was eighteenth-century slang for "penis," and "dandy" carried its current meaning of a fashionable fop; so, in Abelove's words, "a yankee doodle dandy is a primping penis puller" (Abelove 2008, 14). The figure of a "Yankee of the Yankees," then, conjures up two things: first, it evokes the kind of extreme whiteness associated with both racial purity and the pallor incurred by self-abuse, and second, it figures a yanker yanking other yankers in an endless circle jerk. Indeed, the novel's most literally shocking event, the mass electrocution of the knights of Camelot, is, precisely, a yanking Yankees' circuit of bodies electric. During the final battle between medieval peasants and modernization, twenty-five thousand English knights in armor die as they hit a high-voltage fence that Hank has built. In a grotesque parody of democratic fraternity and spiritual magnetic attraction alike, the current is passed, man to man, until Hank and his army of fifty-two men are surrounded by an enclosure of corpses.

Even Hank's all-American nickname is not safe from ribald punning: an obsolete meaning for "hank" is "a propensity; an evil habit," from which it's possible we get the verb "to hanker." But it is also "a . . . curbing hold; a power of check or restraint," the psychological equivalent of reins or a noose.[6] A hank embodies both dissolution and restraint, the very dynamic that organized the meanings of both white middle-class selfhood in US industrial capitalism, and masturbation in transatlantic medical and popular literature (Castronovo 2000, 198). It was not an accident that the American literature against masturbation was directed toward white people, even toward Yankees: as Kyla Tompkins (2014, 253) argues, anti-onanistic discourse was part of a "project of national embodiment . . . linked to the consolidation of whiteness as the dominant racial position." Hank the Yank(er) exemplifies what could go terribly wrong with that project.

In sum, then, *Connecticut Yankee* and its Twainian intertexts make several suggestions about nineteenth-century historical sense-methods. The first is that the seemingly incommensurable domains of historical consciousness and eroticism might have to do with one another, as Schneider's (2011, 35) informants' phrase "wargasm" reminds us. Twain also suggests that to be out of tune with one's own historical moment—a less directly political feeling than, say, radical opposition to a particular regime or system of oppression, but one on a continuum with it—might be a somatic feeling. In *A Connecticut Yankee,* being out of time is visceral, akin to being clonked with an iron bar and waking up temporally elsewhere. And while the sense of being out of step might inspire public, extravagant physical action such as blowing things up, *Connecticut Yankee,* read with its intertexts, suggests that historical unbelonging might also inspire something banal and seemingly private, such as masturbation. Conversely, this cluster of Twainian texts reminds us that directly political behavior or sentiment might be, as Castronovo (2000, 194) argues, discursively "recast . . . as nonsystemic and private, as a failing in individual hygiene." In other words, as Castronovo demonstrates, nineteenth-century American social conflicts were often displaced onto psychic or libidinal conflicts within the individual.

Castronovo's analysis of analogies between masturbation and slavery also clarifies that Hank's stint in Camelot under a slave driver is not just a Prince-and-the-Pauper-like exchange of the aristocratic body for the bondsman's intended to bring to light the injustice of US slavery, which had in any case been abolished by the time of both Twain's writing and Hank's 1879. Nor, though *Connecticut Yankee* can certainly be read as an indictment of the post-Reconstruction era as a return to slavery, does Hank's time as a slave frontally index racial injustice. Instead, the enslavement of Hank, a white man—as with the metaphor of the slave that eventually attached to Shakers—is a sign of his essential hankiness, his inability to master his desires. This is, itself, symptomatic of his own nineteenth-century moment's construction of whiteness, even as Hank projects his desires onto the denizens of Camelot. For Castronovo (2000, 196) correlates the flowering of antimasturbation literature in the American 1830s and 1840s with "agendas of self-culture that encouraged young [white] men to discard allegiances to dead institutions and live according to the rhythms of natural law," individualist agendas most clearly distilled in the Emersonian doctrine of self-reliance. Castronovo also sees the antebellum era's obsessive interest in white male self-governance as a mode of containing anxieties about the presence of chattel slavery in a supposed democracy.

Within these terms, Twain's satirical attention to masturbation in 1879, and Hank's status as a wanker in an 1889 novel, seem somewhat anachronistic. But *Connecticut Yankee* is deeply concerned with individualism, if not precisely with the doctrine of self-reliance: the novel's biggest questions are whether and how men may be trained, and whether or not there is a core to them that resists training. Hank's contempt for the knights of Camelot is in part based on the fact that even before he defeats them and makes them into literal objects, they are merely material: "They did not exist as individuals, but merely as homogeneous protoplasm, with alloys of iron and buttons" (Twain [1889] 1982, 249). *Connecticut Yankee* famously compares the men of Camelot to "white Indians" whose stoicism, Hank declares, is "not an outcome of mental training, intellectual fortitude, reasoning" but is "mere animal training" (19). Yet as Walter Benn Michaels (1987) has noted, Twain's "Indians" are also those who *resist* training and thus, paradoxically, embody a salutary, individualist antipathy to groupthink and tyranny. Despite their fey Frenchness, they also emblematize the Teutonic "essence" that Anglo-American disciplinary historians sought to establish as having been passed down to the English and their descendants in the United States (Tolliver 2015, 29).

The fact that Twain calls the schools where he retrains young Arthurians who show this kind of gumption "Man-Factories" clarifies this paradox: "men" are those whose resistance to ideology qualifies them for Hank's project of turning them into more sophisticated automata. Hank purports to want to lead his men away from the superstitions of the Catholic Church and their blind allegiance to an unelected king and toward freedom, but of course he is simply transforming them into factory workers of the sort whom he "bossed" in the nineteenth century.

The fact that the product they make is themselves, of course, links Hank's man-factories with just the sort of self-governance promoted by antimasturbation literature in the antebellum years. At the same time, Hank's factories manufacture another product, soap: in short, they are purveyors of the kind of cleanliness celebrated by antebellum reformers and the social hygienists of Twain's Progressive Era alike. And finally, Hank's factories make one more product, soap "missionaries" who wander the countryside wearing placards that read, "Persimmon's Soap: All the Prime-Donna Use It" (Twain [1889] 1982, 78). Hank's factories are purveyors, then, of consumer desire, the very thing that threatens to undermine individual autonomy even as it seems to provide a relay to a new kind of individuality founded on freedom of choice and self-expression.

And this is where Twain provides an updated, if also old-fashioned, picture of the problem of masturbation as a response to and figure for his own historical moment. It is updated because Twain wrote *Connecticut Yankee* after his coauthored novel *The Gilded Age* (1873) but still during that era in which speculation and finance capitalism indexed and inflamed all kinds of desires. It is old-fashioned because Thomas Laqueur (2004, 13) has connected the emergence of the antimasturbation panic, which sprang full-blown in medical discourse "in or around 1712," when, with no precedent in legal or religious doctrine, the pamphlet *Onania* appeared and was distributed. Laqueur connects the emergence of antimasturbation discourse in the eighteenth century with the emergence of two new forms of imaginative work: novels and credit. Like reading novels, he argues, masturbation was a solitary bedroom activity. Like credit, masturbation trafficked in imaginings of limitless satisfaction, of ever-escalating desires met by instantaneous gratification.

Twain's late nineteenth century is more like Laqueur's emerging eighteenth century than it is like Castronovo's early republic or, of course, like Camelot: Hank looks like a masturbator simply because he is a financier, and joins the long history of representation in which sexual deviance and the fluctuations endemic to the market stand in for one another. For example, Hank declares that

> knight-errantry is a most chuckle-headed trade, and it is tedious hard work, too, but I begin to see that there *is* money in it, after all, if you have luck. Not that I would ever engage in it as a business, for

I wouldn't. No sound and legitimate business can be established on a basis of speculation. A successful whirl in the knight-errantry line . . . it's just a corner in pork, that's all, and you can't make anything else of it. . . . And moreover, when you come right down to the bed-rock, knight-errantry is *worse* than pork; for whatever happens, the pork's left, and so somebody's benefited, anyway; but when the market breaks, in a knight-errantry whirl, and every knight in the pool passes in his checks, what have you got for assets? Just a rubbish-pile of battered corpses and a barrel or two of busted hardware. (Twain [1889] 1982, 98)

Hank equates financial investing in what we would now call "futures" with a form of courtship he loathes: heterosexual knight errantry. The problem, as he sees it, is that knights go lumbering quixotically around, fighting imagined demons on behalf of unattainable women, returning only with fantastic stories, the equivalent of kited paper checks.

Yet despite Hank's protests, Twain's invented history of "what might have been" also follows the logic of "gambling away your life sexually" that he seems to condemn in his speech to the Stomach Club—a logic in which investments tend toward a future not yet realized, in which high risk may yield high profits, and in which the virtual supplants the material just the way paper money supplanted the gold standard. Hank rebuilds Camelot in the image of nineteenth-century America while acknowledging that his project must remain incomplete. He averts his own execution in what he calls a "saving trump" (Twain [1889] 1982, 30) by predicting an eclipse and claiming he has the power to blot out the sun: "In a business way," he claims, "[the eclipse] would be the making of me" (31). He names the new currency of Camelot the "mill," and claims that "our new money was not only handsomely circulating, but its language was already glibly in use" (175), suggesting a collapse between linguistic and financial signs that undermines any pretense to a gold standard; indeed, part of what makes Hank an unreliable narrator is not only his own rambling, "glib" narration but also the way his actions fail to back up his words.

In all of these ways, then, Hank is an exemplary capitalist, a status that threatens to make him an exemplary masturbator. And this intersection is part of his relationship to time. Peter Coviello (2013, 33) writes that we might think of a nonreproductive, dissident, or culturally aberrant sexuality as a way of "inhabiting a unique temporality, one that renders the body at once out of step with modernity's sped-up market-time and exquisitely responsive to the call of an intuited but inarticulate future." In *Connecticut Yankee*, Hank's onanistic sexuality is in a kind of two-step with market time, emblematic of it in Laqueur's terms, but also continually getting in the way of it insofar as his reveries thrust him into a time before capitalism. What Hank hears, though, is not the call of the inarticulate future. Instead Hank's body is tuned to an inarticulate *past* of erotic possibility, a fantasy of what Carolyn Dinshaw (1999) has named "getting medieval." In fact, Laqueur (2004, 22) has also written of masturbation that "no form of sexuality is more profligate with time," and among the many physical and mental ills with which it was associated by the nineteenth century, a striking one is memory loss. Samuel Tissot's *Onanism* ([1758] 1832, 14), for example, describes masturbation causing impairment of "all the faculties of the mind, particularly the memory"; memory loss is also mentioned in Benjamin Rush's *Medical Inquiries and Observations, upon Diseases of the Mind* (1812) and Homer Bostwick's *A Treatise on the Nature and Treatment of Seminal Diseases* (1860). With this symptom, masturbation becomes a figure not only for the time of capitalism but also for history, or historiography, gone awry. Indeed, Hank suffers from memory troubles at the novel's end, when he babbles about times gone by but does not seem to remember his nineteenth-century self. More generally, both Hank and the novel suffer from a kind of cultural amnesia about the complexities of the medieval era. Hank's most damaging quality is that he is completely ahistorical: a living anachronism, he actually supposes that he can introduce new technologies and modes of production to the Middle Ages, and force a revolution against feudalism before the contradictions of this system have come to a head on their own.

Eve Sedgwick (1991, 820) has cited masturbation's "affinity with amnesia, repetition or the repetition-compulsion, and ahistorical or history-rupturing rhetorics of sublimity," which is an accurate description of *Connecticut Yankee* as well: Hank goes back in time to repeat the medieval with a modern difference. And the novel resolves its own historical contradictions—predominantly the one that Hank's interference in medieval culture would also have resulted in a very different *nineteenth* century—by blowing everything up in a last blast of the technological sublime. In other words, *Connecticut Yankee* is less a novel about time travel per se, than about doing history badly. *Connecticut Yankee* casts the somatization of history in comic terms and is skeptical that the outcome of a corporeal sense-method will be salutary in world-historical terms.

By interlacing the themes of sexual deviance and faulty historicism, *Connecticut Yankee* points to a longer history of the problem of history. This problem is that doing history badly, as the case of amateur historians shows, frequently appears as a kind of perversion. Not only a late eighteenth- and early nineteenth-century phenomenon, the specter of the sexually deviant "bad" historian runs through the Frankfurt school condemnation of pleasurable sensation as always already antithetical to proper historical consciousness, to contemporary Marxist dismissals of queer theory as ludic and ahistorical.[7] Marx and Engels's ([1845–46] 1970, 103) famous statement "Philosophy and the study of the actual world have the same relation to one another as masturbation and sexual love" puts the issue succinctly: masturbation is as much a part of the sexuality of history as it is part of the history of sexuality.[8] *Connecticut Yankee,* then, is best read as an inquiry into the erotic logic of nineteenth-century habits of historicizing, and perhaps even our own contemporary ones— and an excursus into possibilities for rethinking these habits.

Twain is not the first author to displace the threat of sexual-historical deviance onto the bad timing of the French, either. As Marx famously writes in the *Eighteenth Brumaire of Louis Bonaparte*, citing Hegel, events in world history "occur, as it were, twice. [Hegel] forgot to add: the first time as tragedy, the second time as farce" (Marx [1869] 1963, 15). Marx is speaking specifically of the younger Bonaparte's coup of December 2, 1851, that restored the French empire after the revolutions of 1848, repeating his uncle Napoleon's coup in November 1799 that overthrew the revolutionary government. This latter, original coup was called the "Eighteenth Brumaire" because it occurred on the eighteenth day of "Brumaire" in the year 8 on the French revolutionary calendar: Marx is, then, ironically applying a calendar that ended in 1805 to a mid-nineteenth-century imperial act that seemed to turn the clock back by half a century. And French history's temporal drag (see Freeman 2010)— the insistent, distorting pull of its past failed glories on its imperial present—appears, in Marx, as camp performance: he describes the Protestant revolution as "Luther don[ning] the mask of the Apostle Paul," the revolution of 1789 "drap[ing] itself alternately as the Roman republic and the Roman empire" (Marx [1869] 1963, 15), the revolution of 1848 as a parody of 1789, and the coup of 1851 as the resurrection of Napoleon I. For the Marx of the *Eighteenth Brumaire,* there is no turning back to the past that is not rearguard, and looking backward is an act of what Hank Morgan might have called "dudery," or dress-up.[9]

Connecticut Yankee has in common with *The Eighteenth Brumaire* the use of stigmatized sexual activity as a metaphor for a faulty relationship to history: just as costume drama stands in for a failure to apprehend the present in Marx, in *Connecticut Yankee* drag, masturbation, and an unseemly interest in boys stand in for the failure of particular kinds of pseudohistoricist consciousness. At first, Hank seemingly returns to the period *before* the Norman Conquest, the Anglo-Saxon era celebrated by commentators from Blackstone onward as prior to feudalism and hence possessed of an originary freedom (Horsman 1981, 14). Hank's use of parodic Germanic "abracadabras" such as "Transvaaltruppentropen- transporttrampelthiertreibertrauungsthraenentragoedie!" (Twain [1889] 1982, 125) to accompany his feats of technological violence skewers an invented political etiology in which the period of Germanic rule counted as the apex of national sovereignty (and invoking "Transvaal" also slyly alludes to the South African Republic's defeat of the British in the first Boer War, foreshadowing Hank's demise). Yet the denizens of Camelot also, like D'Un Lap of the Missouri Rangers, bear suspiciously Franco- phone names such as Le Fay, Le Desirous, and Le Poulet.

The anachronistic Frenchness of Camelot is doubtless influenced by the nineteenth-century vogue for the Arthurian romances pioneered by Chrétien de Troyes in the twelfth century, but it also allows Twain to poke fun at the aristocracy by way of an effeminacy coded as French, though it is a gendered drag less immediately weighed down by the past than that condemned by Marx. Hank Morgan's same-sex infatu- ations and dubious masculinity are signs not just of his scrambling Norman and Saxon history but also of his investment in coding me- dieval times as a restorative tonic for American dissipation, and as the prototype for British and US manhood, in a way typical of many of the writers who retooled the medieval era in the image of the nineteenth century—most egregiously, in Twain's eyes, Sir Walter Scott. Both Twain and Marx, then, suggest that to lack historical consciousness is to be addicted to costume play and/or, we might say, to be a bit of a wanker.

Yet *Connecticut Yankee* risks the poetry of the past, and this pastness is both temporal and historical: Hank himself is portrayed as sexually regressive through references to his onanistic tendencies and interest in Clarence, and historically regressive through the figure of time travel. *Connecticut Yankee*'s narrative mode is also regressive: it allegorically tells a story of nineteenth-century America's failures through a return to medieval texts such as *Le Morte d'Arthur*. But it is less what Michael Colacurcio (1984, 425) calls "an allegory within history," which stops historical time, than it is an insistence on the historicity within allegory. Critics have produced historicist interpretations of the novel almost as constantly as Hank's "Man-Factory" churns out men ready for nineteenth-century life within the novel. According to the scholarship, *Connecticut Yankee* allegorizes the modernization of China (Hsu 2015). Or it critiques US imperialism (Rowe 1995). Or it accedes to the logic of nineteenth-century industrialization, in which people are machines (Weinstein 1995). Or it transcodes Twain's experiences with the Paige typesetting machine (Collins 1986; Gelder 1989). Or it is about the crisis of realist representation during the Gilded Age (Michaels 1987). Or it condemns feudalism in Hawaii (Lorch 1958). And so on, as we move backward in time through literary criticism. In this way, *Connecticut Yankee* is as much about an excess of historical meaning making, or about historical meaning making as inherently allegorical—and thus inseparable from fiction—as it is about anything else. By making a mockery of all our attempts to historicize it, by generating a surfeit of historicist readings that all boil down to more allegoresis, *Connecticut Yankee* suggests something that the *Eighteenth Brumaire* entirely renounces: that the making of history is a process in which events and texts are invested and reinvested with meaning, prepared for future use in a process that is, as Pauline Hopkins's *Of One Blood* clarifies, ultimately libidinal.

"Over the Surface of History": *Of One Blood*

A generation after Twain, African American writer and historian Pauline Elizabeth Hopkins would also take up the project of historical reenactment through literature. Cedric Tolliver (2015, 26) describes her novel

Of One Blood, serialized in the *Colored American Magazine* in 1902–3, as the Africanist counterpart to exactly what *Connecticut Yankee* mocks: late nineteenth- and early twentieth-century academic historians' concern with the Anglo-Saxon past as the blueprint for a more perfect future. Tolliver cites George Bancroft, William Prescott, John Motley, E. A. Freeman, and Francis Parkman as the era's preeminent "Teutonic-Whig" historians, whose project was to track an unchanged spirit of liberty in those descended from the Anglo-Saxons (Tolliver 2015, 28). As with Twain, Hopkins's work suggests familiarity with these dominant historiographical texts of her period, and also with Afrocentric historiography such as the aforementioned *History of the Negro Race in America* (G. W. Williams 1883), which used the writings of Herodotus to argue that Egyptian civilization derived from Ethiopia (Bruce 1984a), with Volney's work on Egypt, and with the abolitionist writings that drew from Volney to argue for the greatness and priority of ancient African civilization (Bruce 1984a, 691). Hopkins's interest in ancient Ethiopia as a setting was not mere antiquarianism or even entirely tuned to the project of locating precedents for the black freed person's value and potential to contribute to American civilization. As Dana Luciano (2003, 150) has clarified, Hopkins was also part of a project, according to the *Colored American Magazine*'s stated aims, of "reviving black history," which involved not only, or even primarily, recovering the forgotten or repressed events and texts from the African American past but also galvanizing the African American future: "perpetuating" history, as the magazine put it, or, I would add, animating its body.

This project, in *Of One Blood,* is not just a matter of print culture but also a matter of sex. What makes the novel unique among its contemporaries in fiction and among Africanist historiographical writings of the period is the fact that it combines the heterosexual romance infused with racial questions that was common to the nineteenth-century African American domestic novel, with the fabulations of time and space developing in the emergent genre of American science fiction, but with an eye toward reconstructing the past rather than just the future.[10] In short, *Of One Blood* is a romance of alternate history.[11] Its closest analogue in fin de siècle African American fiction may be Griggs's *Imperium in Imperio* ([1899] 2003), discussed in the previous chapter, whose plot turns on the existence of a secret African American secessionist empire within the post-Reconstruction United States—except that Griggs's empire fails to integrate women or heterosexual marriage, and thus is not motored by sex in quite the way that Hopkins's revival of ancient Africa turns out to be. And rather than wrinkling national space as Griggs does, Hopkins wrinkles transatlantic space *and* time. Her love story crosses from one possible historical moment to another, for while its protagonist falls in love in the postbellum United States, that love is eventually fulfilled by his marriage to the queen of Telassar, the sole surviving city of the ancient Ethiopian kingdom of Kush, located on the present-day map by the ruins in the capital city of Meroë, now in Sudan. Telassar, which Hopkins named after the biblical home of the people of Eden, marks a challenge to European American historiography: what if African civilizations were understood as the crucible of modernity? *Of One Blood* even challenges the course of history itself: what would human society look like if Kush, among other ancient African empires, had not been conquered?

Hopkins's novel bridges the two sense-methods that the previous chapter and this one thus far have discussed, thanatomimesis (playing dead) and erotohistoriography. For in *Of One Blood*, episodes of feigned or near-death mark the blurring of boundaries between distinct eras: as Luciano (2003) demonstrates, reviving dead or seemingly dead bodies in this novel also reanimates encrypted and foreclosed histories. These revivals are also erotic, for they are galvanized by a melancholic sexual desire: the protagonist's longing to be united with a woman who appears first as a phantom, then as a dead body, and finally as a queen in ancient Telassar. Importantly, erotics is the relay to the kind of historical reconstruction and realignments that can, in Hopkins's view, potentially move African Americans out of the structural position of social death and into the dialectic of history. In Hopkins, visceral encounters with the past work in the service of creating a mode of black being that is not so much structurally alive and human in liberal terms as incipient and charged in historical-materialist ones: *Of One Blood,* among its other accomplishments, provides a response to contemporary Afropessimism that does not cede to liberal humanism.

Of One Blood also understands historicism as a sense-method, one that expands beyond the genitality of masturbation and the whiteness of *Connecticut Yankee,* to encompass voice and skin. Like Twain's novel, Hopkins's is both authored by an amateur historian—from 1900 through

1902, Hopkins published essays about famous African Americans throughout history—and about one, for the main character is an African American doctor who explores ancient African civilizations as part of a team of archaeologists. And, as with *Connecticut Yankee,* its action begins with an erotic charge between an avatar of the past and a denizen of the fin de siècle present. In the opening chapters of the novel, protagonist Reuel Briggs sees the phantom of a beautiful woman in the woods. That evening, he goes to hear the Fisk Jubilee Singers and falls instantly in love with one of their members, Dianthe Lusk, whose performance almost literally enchants him, as he recognizes the face of the singer as that of the phantom he saw earlier.

Dianthe's status as a phantom is not her only connection to pastness. As Daphne Brooks (2006) has demonstrated, her singing is already, itself, a historiographic sense-method, before the more properly historicist aspect of the novel unfolds. For the Jubilee singers were "perceived by many as the physical and aural manifestation of slavery's traumas" (Brooks 2006, 298), and the scene of Dianthe's concert suggests that the theater is a place where historical meaning and desire are "improvised and renegotiated" (Brooks 2006, 302). Dianthe's rendition of "Go Down, Moses," Brooks writes, is encrypted with historical references; these catalyze not only Briggs's sexual desire but also his desire for a collective past, for his love for Dianthe eventually leads him to join an expedition to Africa in the hopes of making himself wealthy and worthy enough for her. While in *Connecticut Yankee* the figures of white male dudery, dress-up, and drag index a promisingly faulty historical methodology, in *Of One Blood,* as Brooks demonstrates, the figure of the black female diva does a similar, more expansive kind of work.

After the concert, Briggs sees Dianthe again in the woods on Halloween, where she tells him, "You can help me, but not now.... The time is not yet" (Hopkins [1903] 1988, 461–62). Dianthe's forestalling of the present time foreshadows her entanglement with multiple temporalities, the first being, in an echo of the theme of playing dead, the time of life and the time of death—for the next morning, Briggs is summoned to the hospital, where Dianthe is seemingly lifeless after a train wreck. In this episode of reversible death, the novel's first, Briggs diagnoses Dianthe with "suspended animation," claiming that "this woman has been long and persistently subjected to mesmeric influences" and that the train accident has induced a "cataleptic sleep" (465). Mesmerism here is not yet a direct conduit to other times, as it will become later in the novel, but rather indexes the long history of the sexual violation of black women, for it was, in eighteenth- and nineteenth-century Anglophone literature, a figure for rape.[12]

Yet Briggs is not innocent of sexual intent himself. He senses a "mysterious mesmeric affinity" between himself and the catatonic singer (Hopkins [1903] 1988, 466), and revives Dianthe in front of a group of fellow physicians with a secret technique he calls "volatile magnetism" (468). Though Briggs explains volatile magnetism in technical terms, as a compound made up of salt, ammonia, and a magnetic agent found in the human body, he also tells his colleagues, "I supply this magnetism" (468), hinting that his own body, and specifically his erotic longings, precipitates both Dianthe's return from the dead and her enmeshment in what we will later learn are complex relations with dead ancestors and previous historical eras. In other words, Dianthe's state of suspension between life and death is not simply corporeal but also sexual; not simply masturbatory, as in Twain, but also other-relational; and not simply structural, as in narratives of playing dead, but, as the novel will reveal, world-historical as well.

In *Of One Blood*, thanatomimesis becomes sociopolitical because it invokes an alternate, Afrocentric global history. Once Dianthe is revived, *Of One Blood* begins to shuttle between the past and the present, both in the structure of its plot and historically. Dianthe has no memory of her past or her racial identity, and so Briggs—who has been passing for white—and his white friend Aubrey Livingston conceal her true identity, renaming her Felice Adams and bringing her into the fold of their white friends, who include a college chum named Charlie Vance and his sister Molly, Livingston's fiancée. Here, Dianthe is no longer suspended between life and death but between white and black, and then between virginity and marriage, for though Briggs marries her, they do not consummate their nuptials. Instead, seeking to be wealthy enough to support Dianthe and goaded by Livingston, who has also fallen in love with her, Briggs goes to Africa with Vance for two years to research the history of ancient Ethiopia, the two men accompanying a scholar who hopes to prove that all of mankind is descended from that first major human civilization. In Ethiopia, Briggs dreams of Dianthe calling to him for help, and then learns that she, Livingston, and Molly are all dead; Dianthe's telecommunication marks yet another moment when the boundary between living and dead seems to be violated by a romantic attachment.

Despairing, Briggs wanders alone into a pyramid at night, falls unconscious, and wakes up in a secret Ethiopian city, Telassar, where the original high civilization has continued undisturbed for six thousand years: indeed, Telassar is an entire city that has "played dead" for millennia. Briggs's African heritage, which the novel has only implied earlier, is made explicit as he learns that he is the heir to the Telassarian throne and, thinking he is a widower, marries their queen, Candace—a woman with a distinct likeness to Dianthe. The novel then flashes back to reveal that Livingston has preyed on Dianthe's suggestible mind, recapitulating the association of mesmerism and sexual assault. As Dianthe's memory returns and she realizes that she is African American, Livingston convinces her to marry him in secret so that she will not be destitute when Briggs—whom Dianthe thinks is white—finds out her black ancestry and abandons her. After Dianthe protests that Livingston is betraying Molly, he takes the two women on a boating trip, drowns Molly, and makes it look as if he and Dianthe are dead too, and then he and Dianthe marry in secret.

The Telassar section of the novel also inaugurates a more directly Twainian form of time travel, though it is anything but comedic in *Of One Blood*. Notably, Telassar is coeval with the nineteenth-century United States, but off its timeline, and appears to Briggs as if it were still an ancient civilization whose technological and artistic wonders were fully equal or superior to those of his own time but differently developed. Among their accomplishments, the people of Telassar have learned how to transcend death, and so the ancestors mingle with the living. As well, both the living and the dead can prophesy the future, which explains Briggs's psychic powers and links his mesmeric abilities to time travel. Finally, Telassar's own timeline is scrambled according to European American standards. On a huge sphinx in the middle of Telassar's central plaza is an engraving from Ecclesiastes 3:15, "That which hath been, is now; and that which is to be, has already been; and God requireth that which is past" (Hopkins [1903] 1988, 552). The last lines, "that which is to be, has already been; and God requireth that which is past," refer to the fulfilling of an ancient prophesy in the form of Briggs's return and the restoration of Ethiopia to its former world dominance. But the first line, "That which has been, is now," suggests that in Telassar, "now" is no simple presence of the present. It echoes Dianthe's first words to Briggs, "not now . . . the time is not yet," and suggests that the American nineteenth century contains the residuum of a past it does not acknowledge. Thus, though the subtitle of *Of One Blood, "Or, The Hidden Self,"* seems at first to have only psychological implications—indeed, the novel's very first scene shows Briggs pondering an essay by M. Binet that he has just read, "The Unclassified Residuum," described as a work of psychology— Telassar reveals that the "hidden self" of African Americans is, in fact, historical. As Binet's essay puts it, "All the while, however, [supernatural] phenomena are there, broadcast over the surface of history" (Hopkins [1903] 1988, 442).

The engraving on the sphinx, then, links the Binet essay to a deep collective past rather than just to the recesses of the psyche—even "The Unclassified Residuum" itself, written in a time supposedly after the construction of the sphinx, has "already been" in ancient Ethiopia, where time flows two ways. The psychological texts' words, in turn, suggest that the past has a "surface," a kind of skin or membrane that Briggs is now touching in Telassar. The epidermalization of black people, that is, their reduction to skin color as described by Frantz Fanon ([1952] 1994), here becomes an epidermalization of history, or its expansion into something permeable and elastic. The Twainian trope of faulty or bad historiography as masturbatory has also expanded to a more somatically diffuse, sensory but not genitalized encounter with the past. Likewise, the African American literary trope of play with the boundary between life and death now encompasses play with the tissue seeming to separate now and then, the nineteenth century and ancient Ethiopia. *Of One Blood* confirms history's skinlike permeability and reversibility with the figure of a lotus birthmark, which the sages of Telassar see on Briggs's breast and recognize as the sign of their royal family. The lotus, in turn, signals a crossing of temporal boundaries, for its meaning in Egyptian mythology as a sign of reincarnation and creation comes from the way that it closes its petals at night and opens back up in the morning. In sum, alternate history has and is a skin: it is a literalization of Raymond Williams's "structures of feeling" (1977), a way of sensing, on the body's surface as well as in the psyche, residual and incipient events and social formations.

This crossing of temporal boundaries also indexes a tangling of the lines of kinship, in ways similar to the works I discussed in the previous chapter, for Dianthe, Livingston, and Briggs are bound by more than a romantic triangle. In a technological demonstration of their ability to confound past and present, the Telassarians show Briggs a special reflecting glass, which inaugurates the flashback that confirms Livingston's activities during the previous several months and reveals that Dianthe is still alive, and so Briggs leaves Telassar to find Dianthe. His companions on the expedition try to find him but accidentally release a nest of snakes that attack their servant, Jim, just as Briggs returns. Before dying, Jim reveals to Briggs that Aubrey Livingston is Briggs's half-brother through their father, the elder Mr. Livingston, and that Dianthe is Briggs's full sister through the elder Mr. Livingston and their mother Mira, Livingston Sr.'s enslaved mistress who was sold away along with Briggs but without Dianthe. This blood relation again confirms the sexual content of mesmerism, now fully retroped as a mixing of past and present—for Livingston Sr. had not only literally raped Mira to produce Dianthe and Briggs but also, as Briggs and readers have already learned at a party after Dianthe's revival, ongoingly mesmerized Mira, forcing her to do parlor tricks while in a trance. One of these tricks, Aubrey Livingston reveals when he tells a story earlier in the novel, was foretelling the future: Mira predicted Livingston Sr.'s ruin in the Civil War, for which he angrily sold her off.

Before Mira is revealed as the mother of Dianthe and Briggs, she has floated through the novel unhinged from time and space, appearing to Briggs as a ghost twice on his expedition and to Dianthe during the time Briggs is away, and allowing each to divine something about what is happening to the other. Mira is "mired" in time, unable to step out of her enslaved past and into the present, yet also never present in the pantheon of ancestors and descendants who are eventually united in Telassar. Given her name, Mira (meaning "look!," and an echo of "mirror"), she also seems to be the living embodiment of the Telassarian time-bending and space-overcoming reflective glass—except that her capacity to travel across temporal boundaries is entangled with, and perhaps even a result of, sexual violation. In the figures of Dianthe and to an even greater extent Mira, mesmerism and the physical encounters between past and present that it makes possible are sense-methods that do not reduce to pure pleasure as they do in Twain's onanistic historiography. They are genital insofar as they index rape, but as rape itself cannot be reduced to genital

contact, they are not only that; insofar as mesmerism registers the violation of the psyche as well as the body, it also figures the kind of porosity
that Binet's phrase "the surface of history" suggests. And unlike playing
dead, mesmerism represents and furthers contact with not only historically specific but also sexually specific forms of violence.

Mira's time bending, like Briggs's travel to and from ancient Ethiopia,
is also figured and elaborated through the distorted kin relations of which
she is a part. Through one of Mira's visitations after Dianthe is married to
Livingston, Dianthe finds out about his deception and despairingly wanders the woods, where she meets an old woman, Hannah, reputed to be
a witch. Hannah reveals herself to be a former sexual victim of the eldest
Livingston master, Aubrey's grandfather, with whom Hannah conceived
Mira, who in turn was serially raped by Aubrey's father, Livingston Sr.
(in the novel's first incestuous twist, then, Aubrey's father is already
his mother Mira's half-brother). Mira then conceived Reuel Briggs and
Dianthe, who were raised separately. Thus Hannah is Dianthe's grandmother. Hannah also tells Dianthe that Mira is her mother and that Aubrey Livingston, as well as Reuel Briggs, are her full brothers rather than
half-brothers, because Hannah had switched Mira's newborn baby boy
(Aubrey) with Mrs. Livingston's stillborn one. The third generation of
Livingstons, then, are full siblings. They all have not only the same white
grandfather in the eldest Mr. Livingston, and the same white father in
Livingston Sr., but also the same black grandmother in Hannah and the
same black mother in Mira. Dianthe is now revealed as a bigamist with
both brothers and a committer of physical incest with one, Aubrey—
sexual "deviancies" made possible, as American literature of the South so
often reveals, by the denial that black and white are kin: Hannah's baby
swap, echoed by her palindromic name, recalls the famous switching of
white and black babies in Mark Twain's *Pudd'nhead Wilson* (1894). Both
exchanges highlight the irony that under slavery a "black" and a "white"
baby might be indistinguishable, but only one would be claimed by its
white family.

This is the tangle of American kinship, the "American grammar book"
(Spillers 1987) where white supremacy by its very logic produces endog-
amy/incest, where because white fathers did not acknowledge their enslaved children the latter could end up in sexual connections with their
black or white siblings, and where the system of chattel slavery, by making

both black-white and slave marriage illegal, promoted quasibigamy in the form of white owners legitimately marrying white wives and keeping slaves as concubines, and of slaves coupling without dissolving previous unions if spouses were sold away from one another. But as later speculative fiction would elaborate in such figures as Toni Morrison's ghosts (*Beloved*, 1987), Octavia Butler's *ooloi* (*Lilith's Brood*, 2000), and Jewelle Gomez's black lesbian vampires (*The Gilda Stories*, 1991), Dianthe's sexual aberrations are part of the production and repression of alternate *histories* rather than just bodies or kin networks. *Of One Blood* clarifies how Anglo-European repression of the Ethiopian past, which is clearly also an allegory for the American repression of its own past of slavery and of African American history in general, produces "perversions" in the social field as well as the historical record. Hopkins suggests that a white-supremacist history bent on repressing the contributions of people of African descent has ramifications for the horizons of African Americans as a people and for humankind in general: it is not that the condition of not knowing one's collective history makes one a practitioner of incest or a bigamist in the literal way that not knowing one's personal history might; rather, not knowing one's collective history threatens to limit or distort the social *tout court*, for which family is here only a figure. For the phrase "of one blood" indexes not only the African blood that links ancient Ethiopia, nineteenth-century African Americans, and the three dispersed Livingston siblings, but also the entire human species, which cannot acknowledge that all are related.

Having produced a crisis in historical knowledge as a crisis in sociosexual arrangement, *Of One Blood* resolves it through a final series of episodes of thanatomimesis and eroticized time travel. In the novel's last few chapters, Aubrey Livingston finds himself immobilized by an invisible power, a mesmeric spell that Hannah has helped Dianthe cast, and one that hints at a retaliatory sexual assault. Though paralyzed, he sees his wife glide into his room and substitute a new glass of water for his customary nightly one. But Dianthe's spell breaks too early, and he overpowers her and forces her to drink the concoction, a slow-acting lethal poison. Knowing she is dying, Dianthe feigns sleep and refuses medical help, using what is left of her energy to wait for Briggs. As the life force drains from her body, a musical outpouring swells over the town—"the welcome of ancient Ethiopia to her dying daughter of the royal line"

(Hopkins [1903] 1988, 615). This burst of music, the first since Dianthe's singing scenes, suggests that song has now transcended its association with the sexual violence of mesmerism and become, directly, an agent of the reunification of past and present. Here, the historicizing function of the diva has also become collective and diffuse. Hearing the music, Dianthe calls out the names of her Ethiopian ancestors whom we assume she will be joining. One of them is "Candace," the name of the queen whom Briggs has married in Telassar. As both ancestor and double, Candace links Telassar with the underworld of death, and further cinches the novel's binding of past and present, death and life.

By the end of *Of One Blood,* making history right again makes sex right again, in ways that are somewhat less expansive than the novel's earlier figure of history and skin as mutually receptive surfaces. Briggs arrives, and Dianthe dies in his arms. From the woods, Aubrey Livingston sees Dianthe and his fiancée, Molly, gliding along together, presumably on their way to the afterlife. He is eventually charged with their two murders but acquitted. Though freed by the earthly, American justice system, Livingston has an "interview" with an impromptu court composed of two representatives from Telassar, as well as the witch Hannah, who has been revealed as a descendent of the noble court, and Reuel Briggs. There, the prime minister of Ethiopia cases a spell on Livingston, releases his soul, and whispers the prophesy to him that those in direct line of the throne—which Livingston is by virtue of his descent from Hannah and Mira—must, if guilty of the crime of murder, die by their own hand. Accordingly, and possibly also because he now knows he is legally black in the United States, Livingston drowns himself, recapitulating the opening of the novel in which Briggs contemplates suicide and asks himself if it is wrong. Briggs returns to Telassar with Hannah, whose palindromic name now reaches back and forth through time to reunite her and her nineteenth-century family and, by the end of the novel, her present-day descendants with their ancient relatives. Briggs's union with Candace, in the secret city where past and present intermingle like the blood of black and white Americans, now not only fulfills the prophesy that Telassar will be reunited with the present but also consummates his initial magnetic and otherworldly attraction to Dianthe.

The novel's solution, though, is emphatically heterosexual. Though its historiography is radical both in method and in content, *Of One Blood* finishes on a somewhat conservative sexual note, marrying Briggs out of his feigned whiteness and back into his racially pure ancestral blackness, and also out of his incestuous relation with his sister Dianthe and back into proper exogamy. In fact, Dianthe's departure with Molly actually does not make sense in the novel's economy of ancestral copresence with the living, for she too is Telassarian royalty and should end up in the secret city—but the novel must dispose of her by substituting Candace for her, in order to correlate the restoration of history with proper dynastic succession. Despite this ending, though, through its discussions of the "surface" of history and its motif of the lotus birthmark, the novel has hinted that history can be felt and made otherwise than through romantic, intraracial heterosexual love. It has suggested that the sense-method of alternate, amateur historiographies, derided and ignored by the emerging nineteenth-century profession of scientific history, is both productive of and emerges out of less sanctioned libidinal and corporeal encounters: the trauma of rape, the corporeal transfer of energy in animal magnetism, and the shape-shifting and doubling of ancestors. In short, the novel has offered up speculative history as a sense-method, and the body's sensorium as a way of transmitting and receiving history.

On Libidinal Historiography in Twain and Hopkins

But to cast things this way—to say that the body is a transmitter of history and that history has a sensible, permeable surface—is to leave out the psychic question of desire on which speculative fiction, and speculative history in particular, are based. These are genres whose plots are motored not only by corporeal contact but also by longings for and imaginations of the better presents and/or futures that could be animated by a changed past. As if to fend off this possibility, Twain's Hank Morgan seems to dismiss speculation precisely because it is based on desire, opining, "No sound and legitimate business can be established on a basis of speculation" (Twain [1889] 1982, 98) and, as discussed earlier, linking the romantic pursuits of knight-errantry to gambling. Hank's economic metaphor also gestures toward the question of what made history sound and legitimate in the late nineteenth and early twentieth centuries. Initially, then, we might read historiography in Twain and Hopkins as a cure for what ails the libidinalized marketplace that Hank condemns. After all, historiography, as nonfiction, purports to settle the meaning of the past (something that Twain satirizes and Hopkins seems earnestly invested in), offering a hermeneutic gold standard. And time travel would seem on the face of it to offer the *least* speculative, most accurate account of the past in that it ensures perfect correspondence between witness and event. This is, in a sense, the conceit of *Of One Blood,* in which African American competency for citizenship and future making is certified through Reuel Briggs's direct witness of Ethiopian technological accomplishment and the narrator assures readers that they may ascertain "the correctness of the historical records" (Hopkins [1903] 1988, 538) about Ethiopia from Briggs's descriptions of the ruins of the actual Meroë and, by extension, of the fictional Telassar.

Yet despite Hank's contempt for speculation, Twain himself establishes *Connecticut Yankee* as conjectural from the very beginning, writing in the preface, "It is not pretended that these laws and customs existed in England in the sixth century; no, it is only pretended that inasmuch as they existed in the English and other civilizations of far later times, it is safe to consider that it is no libel upon the sixth century to suppose them to have been in practice in that day also. One is quite justified in inferring that whatever one of these laws or customs was lacking in that remote time, its place was competently filled by a worse one" (Twain [1889] 1982, 4). The language of "pretending," "considering," "supposing," and "inferring" immediately establishes the novel as a self-consciously imaginary—a speculative—account of the past. Twain's historiography, then, has more in common with contemporary speculative fiction than with the disciplinary history proper to his time, or even with nineteenth-century popular histories aimed at mass audiences in which a gripping plot without any metacommentary took precedence over factual accuracy (see Pfitzer 2008). In short, Twain gleefully *admits* to speculation, showing up Hank's spurious investments in hard money and hard facts.[13] Similarly, despite its gesture toward the historical records, *Of One Blood* encodes the idea of speculation in Mira's looking-glass name, for "speculate" originates in the Latin *speculare,* "to observe."

As Hank implies when he dismisses Camelot's knights-errant as a pool of gamblers, speculation has a nonheteronormative erotic charge, for it eschews the "bed-rock" of reproduction for imaginative flights of fancy about unattainable women. It also has this charge in *Of One Blood,*

in which Reuel Briggs connects speculation with dissipation in his remark to the leader of his expedition, "Don't touch upon the origin of
the Negro; you will find yourself in a labyrinth, Professor. . . . Speculation
has exhausted itself, yet the mystery appears to remain unsolved" (Hopkins [1903] 1988, 521). Here, notably, speculation is so self-referential as
to exhaust not only its practitioners but also itself. As Briggs's metaphor
of self-exhaustion implies, the idea of imaginative risk cleaves tightly to
masturbation, the more so when the risk is financial—as, indeed, we
must remember that it is, not only for Hank but for Briggs, who "never
before built [*sic*] golden castles, but now . . . speculated upon the possibility of unearthing gems and gold from the mines of ancient Meroe
and the pyramids of Ethiopia" (496). The problem with investment, it
seems, is precisely its capacity to inflame the imagination, as, indeed, antimasturbation literature recognized in its correlation of onanism with
not only checks and credit but also reading too much of another kind of
paper, fiction. The idea that speculative writing, whether of IOUs or of
novels, is inherently libidinal, had been around for almost two centuries
prior to the nineteenth.

The literary mode that would correspond to history's hermeneutic
gold standard would, on the face of it, seem to be allegory. Just as history
purports to fix the meaning of the past, allegory purports to fix literary
meaning by anchoring one text firmly to another. And both Twain's and
Hopkins's novels can be read as allegory—*Connecticut Yankee* in all the
ways critics have read it as a retelling of American imperialism, industrialization, economics, et cetera, and *Of One Blood* as an allegory for
the repression of slavery in dominant American historiography and as a
series of scriptural allusions and rewritings that culminate in Acts 17:26,
"[God] hath made of one blood all nations of men for to dwell on all
the face of the earth, and hath determined the times before appointed,
and the bounds of their habitation." Yet as Fredric Jameson (1982, 30)
reminds us, allegory can also unfix meaning, serving to prepare a text
"for further ideological investment," that is, for new ways of figuring the
relationship between an individual and "transpersonal realities such as
the social structure or the collective logic of History." In other words,
allegory is a way of critiquing the present, perhaps even of dreaming the
future, of making history in the sense of assuming historical agency by
setting up the past as a transactional site—one that primes the desire to

understand one's position within larger coordinates in the present and presumably, through such understandings, to change those coordinates.

On this model, Hank Morgan's faulty historicism, represented variously as masturbatory vicariousness and prurience, as the failed narrative drive of his tale, as his attempt to short-circuit the stadial movement of History-with-a-capital-H from feudalism to capitalism, and even signaled by Twain's incitement of the critical desire to anchor his tale in events of the nineteenth century, looks like something queer historians might want to claim. While Twain's contemporaries prepared the Middle Ages for a rearguard ideological investment in Anglo-Saxonism, he himself seems to have prepared them for something else. We might also claim several aspects of *Of One Blood:* Reuel Brigg's amateur historical inquiry, represented as both a suspect sexual violation of Dianthe and a more promising open and porous body; the black female characters' use of haunting, voice, and prophesy as historical methods; and the amateur historiography signaled by Hopkins's own traffic in speculation, reworkings of secondary histories by her contemporaries, and the biblical model of prophesy and recapitulation. While Hopkins's Afrocentrist contemporaries prepared ancient Africa for ideological investments that, as Saidiya Hartman clarifies in *Lose Your Mother* (2008), can produce an African continent innocent of participation in the slave trade, Hopkins, like Twain, prepares her readers for something else. In other words, these "bad," literary, corporeal, allegorical histories may prime their readers to make history otherwise.

The world-historical investments made possible by allegory, in turn, are matters of race, gender, and sexuality. Allegory can be understood not only as a form of historiography, a narrative mode that, by pointing to an anterior time, can suggest violence, ruination, and change, and thus future making, but also, since Walter Benjamin ([1963] 2009), as a form of drag: a way of dressing up the future in the garb of the past. But what is Twain "getting up" in the persona of Hank, or of medieval culture in general? Countering his historicist critics, I would suggest that Twain is less interested in retelling a particular aspect of nineteenth-century culture through the medieval conceit than he is in revealing and exploiting the libidinal logic of historiography itself. *Connecticut Yankee* suggests that our habit of historicizing—our hank for it—is fundamentally erotic, perhaps even autoerotic, and that this might not be such a bad thing. Twain's looking backward is neither triumphantly nostalgic nor properly political in the Marxist sense of what it means to do history: it simply marks a refusal, like Hank's final one, to accede to contemporary norms of gendered and sexualized identity, even as it fully accedes to the norms of whiteness.

Likewise, the erotics of *Of One Blood* become both clearer and queerer when read through this lens. By going back to and rewriting Western history in terms of a forgotten biblical city and the Bible as a whole—a text that the ghostly Mira literally writes her name in, as well as underlining a prophetic passage, when she appears to Dianthe—Hopkins participates in the logic of allegorical recapitulation that animates that very Bible, a logic that supersedes the heteronormative alliances that *Of One Blood* seems to champion at its end. For in Hopkins's novel, mesmerism, reanimation, reincarnation, and the transmission of both melancholic affect and historical understanding across generations take the place of pregnancy and childbirth; parent-child relations are so distorted by slavery as to make biological reproduction an untenable blueprint for the future. Sexual longings, in this novel, do get resolved into the privatized and personal figure of exogamous marriage, but they do not get resolved into pregnancy and parenthood. Instead, they retain a historical and collective charge insofar as they revive and reinvest a dormant past for future use. *Of One Blood* looks backward to an invented history on another continent, furnishing ancient Ethiopia with technologies reminiscent of the nineteenth century to repudiate the racist present of a nineteenth-century United States in which black people counted as primitive and uncivilized, imbuing that refusal with a libidinal logic in which people connect through time via bodily affinities rather than descent. *Of One Blood* thus might be called, with a nod to Claudia Tate (1992), an *anti*domestic allegory of political desire.

All of this brings me, at long last, to the epigraph with which this chapter begins, Nietzsche's remark about his *Untimely Meditations* ([1873–76] 1997): "The four *untimely essays* are altogether warlike. They demonstrate that I was no 'Jack o' Dreams,' that I derive pleasure from drawing the sword—also, perhaps, that I have a dangerously supple wrist" (Nietzsche [1908] 1992, 54). Here, Nietzsche paradoxically suggests that his articles, which include "On the Use and Disadvantage of History for Life," are military in their temporal *im*precision, foiling the idea that collective political action requires the temporal simultaneity of the drill or the progressive directionalities of nation and empire. Counterposing fantasy, or "dreaming," with historiography's "drawing [of] the sword," Nietzsche stakes a claim for the "unhistorical" in the battle against the status quo, echoing his assertion in "On the Use and Disadvantage of History for Life" that forgetting is necessary to action. But this insistent ahistoricism brings with it a dangerous supplement (see Derrida 1998). Drawing the analytic blade of the untimely is not so distinct from the other manual exercises associated with dreaming: indeed, the creative abuse of history that Nietzsche champions implies, with that supple wrist, a bit of self-abuse.

By the early twentieth century, the (a)historical allegory—in which the past will neither retreat altogether, as in biblical allegory's fusion of past and present into recurrence and eternity, nor provide a triumphant origin story for the present, as in Anglo-American nationalist allegory, but hovers as a site of potential critical investment, as in *Connecticut Yankee* and *Of One Blood*—would become the refuge of those inheritors of the masturbator and the nonprocreator, the newly specified "homosexuals" whose erotic interests were "wrongly" invested. Fixating on a past in which they could not have lived, even fixing their own protagonists within an invented but historically specific past, inverts and others whose sexual practices did not fit into the heterosexual-reproductive matrix could practice a kind of dialectical nostalgia: the past might be embarrassing, but it could also signal the validity of a different lifeworld, including its norms of gender and eroticism (Nealon 2001). And, crucially, by featuring an archaic historical period that could not be dissolved into a moment on a personal timeline, or even be situated in a coherent, quasinationalist political progress narrative, sexual dissidents could signal the absolute inaccessibility of these alternate lifeworlds, these temporal and sexual *imperiums in imperio,* to so-called normals.[14]

This logic might explain the peculiarly regressive moves of explicitly lesbian and gay literature later on, such as the ending of Radclyffe Hall's "Miss Ogilvy Finds Herself" (1934), in which the main character, a classic version of what Esther Newton has called the mythic mannish lesbian, slips into a dream sequence and finds herself a caveman courting a cavewoman, never returning to consciousness or the present moment (see Newton 1984). And it may help explain the queer, pseudohistoricist oddities, often classed as decadent works, that were contemporaneous with *A*

Connecticut Yankee and spanned the decades in which sexology rose and fell, from Flaubert's *Salammbô* (1862, another African historical fantasia) through Virginia Woolf's *Orlando* (1928, in which the main character changes from male to female while in Turkey). For these texts, each in their own way, embrace bad historicism as an erotics. They toy with allegory's shuttling movement to prior texts, but no overarching interpretive point guides their time travels. They delight in the sheer alterity of other sex/gender systems, but use these as material for fantasy, courtship, and erotic worldmaking rather than for analytic distance.

These other literary works are also doggedly and determinedly colonialist, in a way that Twain mocks in the figure of the blustering Hank Morgan, and that Hopkins reflects on in the final chapter of *Of One Blood*—which may be explained by the fact that they are white-authored. In *Of One Blood,* Briggs "views . . . with serious apprehension, the advance of mighty nations penetrating the dark, mysterious forces of his native land" (Hopkins [1903] 1988, 621). Having assumed the role of "native" despite his status as a (re)settler, Briggs seems faintly to recognize that his own incursions into Telassar have not only reunited the royal family but also represent an early form of what we might now recognize as heritage tourism, the very activity of which Saidiya Hartman (2008) is so skeptical in *Lose Your Mother*. Works such as "Miss Ogilvy Finds Herself," *Salammbô,* and *Orlando*, similarly, engage in what Joseph Allen Boone (2014) calls "the homoerotics of Orientalism," in which spatial alterity offers sexual adventure; these texts temporalize that alterity. Through them we can see, on the one hand, that the fantasy of feeling history with, on, and even as the body is a powerful alternative to disciplinary histories that, in denying the libidinal investments of historiography, understand themselves as innocent of imperialist violence. Libidinal historiography offers constituencies whose bodies are understood as the basis of their inferiority a way to mobilize that stigma into a world-historical imagination. But on the other hand, it also risks preparing the past for a future that, as Briggs recognizes, might further rather than reduce "caste prejudice, race pride, [and] boundless wealth" (Hopkins [1903] 1988, 621).

Finally, the limits of libidinal historiography are, ironically, corporeal. For they depend on the fiction of able-bodiedness that attends all travel literature: the conceit that feeling historical, as a sense-method, is a matter of action, of making the body literally go places. I have thus far treated populations whose physical movements could be understood as political ones: Shaker rhythms as a critique of heteronormative gender roles and of whiteness; playing dead as a confrontation with social death; amateur historiography, literalized in time travel, as a form of queer and queer-of-color worldmaking. But during the early nineteenth century, which celebrated a masculine-capitalist body in control of its energetic capacities, and the Progressive era, which celebrated a masculine-imperial body moving through a temporalized space and eventually a spatialized time, the sense-methods of those who could not "go" so completely were very different. As the following chapter will show, the inability or unwillingness to move, or to be moved, is a sense of another kind, with a politics of its own.

4   THE SENSE OF UNENDING

Defective Chronicity in "Bartleby, the Scrivener"
and "Melanctha"

> How much wood would a woodchuck chuck if a woodchuck
> would chuck wood? And how much wood would a woodchuck
> chuck if a woodchuck only could? Now a woodchuck could
> make good and would, but there ain't no reason why he should.
> But how much wood would a woodchuck chuck if a woodchuck
> would chuck wood?
>
> THEODORE F. MORSE AND ROBERT HOBART DAVIS,
> "The Woodchuck Song"

At the end of *Of One Blood,* Reuel Briggs wonders in relation to the imperialism threatening Telassar, "When will it stop? What will the end be?" (Hopkins [1903] 1988, 621). This question emphasizes duration, and turns us toward the idea of ongoingness, rather than inquiry into the past, as a sense-method. Not to stop, at least periodically, not to have an end or even a picture of what the end could be, is a condition of being uninflected by tense. This lack of inflection was particularly threatening at a historical moment concerned, as *Of One Blood* is, with anchoring the present in the correct past, and also—as we can see from that novel's program of realigning Briggs with a technologically advanced African dynasty unadulterated by whiteness—with the eugenic movement toward a perfected future. If the erotohistoriographical project of using the body to recalibrate the past and the eugenic project of using it to procreate the future both conjure up states of somatic capacity, the state of tenselessness invokes a less capacitated body, whose directionality and endpoints cannot be guaranteed. In a century marked by the machinic rhythms of industrial capitalism, the increase of work time due to electric lighting, and other methods by which the body's actions were extended and prolonged, a tenseless and perpetual mode of being, unhampered by memories, energy fluctuations, or pessimism about the future, might seem ideal. But the lure of the perpetual brings with it another mode of tenselessness: the threat of inertia, of not starting in the first place, of being persistently out of commission—a possibility made starkly evident by the Great Railroad Strike of 1877.

Perhaps inflected by technology's ability to produce bodies marked by both perpetuity and inertia, in the late nineteenth century a key temporal term, "chronic," took on pejorative connotations: it came to mean, simply, ongoingly bad, as in chronic weather or a chronic flavor. At its simplest, "chronic" simply means "of time," though that meaning does not seem to have survived the early modern period. To say that something was *chronic,* before about 1600, was to say that it was timeish, about time, that it took time as its primary subject or material, as in the modern "chronological."[1] But by the eighteenth century, "chronic" had narrowed to designate only lingering medical conditions. Chronic sufferers were (and are) marked by unspecified or unknown etiology and uncertain outcome: they are, as the anthropologist Jean E. Jackson (2005, 344) puts it, "out of place temporally, if no one knows whether the painful state will improve, deteriorate, or remain the same." The time of the chronic is different from what anthropologist S. Lochlann Jain (2013, 27) has described as "living in prognosis," which involves reimagining the past in light of one's disease (in Jain's words, "what alternatives and what necessities [the past] contained" [Jain 2013, 44], unbeknownst to us), or knowing the end from what becomes a new beginning point, the time of diagnosis. With a chronic disease, prognosis is really more of an agnosis: as long as a condition remains chronic, one simply has it; one can go into remission or experience relapse or return, but one is never fully cured. Nor are chronic diseases necessarily terminal. By definition they do not terminate in a cure, but they also do not automatically terminate in death; one can have a chronic disease such as lupus and not die of it. Indeed, "chronicity" correlates with a certain shapelessness in time, and chronic conditions seem to belie narrative altogether. The chronic foils differences between not only beginnings and ends but also transgression and the reproduction of the status quo, ability and disability, action and passivity. Chronic conditions, like the original meaning of "chronic," are simply time-ish.[2]

Perhaps the nineteenth century's most famous avatar for this lack of tense—its ability to indicate either machinic perpetuation or complete inertia, along with its connotations of pathology—is the protagonist of Melville's short story "Bartleby, the Scrivener" (Melville [1853] 1979). Bartleby seeks employment as a copyist at a law office and, once hired, simply refuses to do his job. As a scrivener, he figures the industrial nineteenth century's fantasy of unceasing labor, for he is the human precursor to the photocopy machine. And he is tenseless, without past, present, or future. First, as the lawyer who employs him and narrates the story declares, "Bartleby was one of those beings of whom nothing is ascertainable except from the original sources, and, in his case, those are very small" (103). Second, Bartleby's present consists of standing in reveries before walls. Finally, without a futural orientation, he ends up dead, curled in the fetal position against a prison wall. In short, the scrivener is, according to the lawyer, altogether "deficient in what landscape painters call 'life'" (105). His lack of vitality is captured in the story's most famous phrase, Bartleby's continual declaration that "I would prefer not to." He is also, the lawyer finally decides, a chronic: "What I saw that morning persuaded me that the scrivener was the victim of innate and incurable disorder" (122).

Bartleby's fin de siècle sister is Gertrude Stein's Melanctha, from the triptych *Three Lives* (1909). A mixed-race African American woman, Melanctha wanders through life recurringly doing things that do not add up to a purpose. She has a somewhat foreshortened past, told in a set of digressions by the narrator, but her main problem seems to be her lack of movement toward the futures dictated by her subject-position: marriage and reproduction, and/or the kind of public service dictated by Progressive-era ideals of racial uplift. Instead, Melanctha drifts in an eternal present, a series of moments that do not accumulate into a life story. Stein does not use the language of disease to describe Melanctha; rather, her story is mostly a series of dialogues with a doctor, her lover Jeff Campbell, narrated in a patterned syntax that features repetition, a kind of stuttering copying of previous phrases that echoes both the work of

Melville's scriveners and the repetition of Bartleby's "I would prefer not to." Melanctha's lack of forward motion, of the characterological development that readers of Stein's era might expect from a novel, is encoded into Stein's very grammar, in sets of sentences such as "Melanctha Herbert had always had a break neck courage. Melanctha always loved to be with horses; she loved to do wild things, to ride the horses and to break and tame them" (Stein [1909] 2000, 92). Typical of the writing in "Melanctha," the anaphora of Melanctha's name, the repetition of the infinitive "to," and the doubling of the words "break," "loved," and "horses" give these sentences a static quality, even as they describe intense emotions and physical action. Mirroring this syntax, Melanctha's life consists of what we might now call repetitive behavior patterns, alternately narrated in the third person and recounted in habitually complaining conversations with her lover and a couple of other friends.

"Bartleby" and "Melanctha," as I will go on to demonstrate, offer up the chronic as a method of knowing and inhabiting the latter part of a "long nineteenth-century" world that demanded temporal obeisance in the form of punctuated periods of activity and rest for the purposes of maximum productivity, and forward motion connected to national progress.[3] While these two stories are not precisely disability narratives, I want to claim them, following Jasbir Puar (2017), as debility narratives, or stories of attrition, erosion, exhaustion, and decline that are also stories of endurance, protraction, persistence, and dilation in spite of it all. "Bartleby" and "Melanctha" stake a claim for the chronic, or for a tenseless modality of being that is understood, though not necessarily lived, as a pathology. And they do so in the form of the case, perhaps the preeminent genre in which what counts as a life is negotiated. Melville suggests this way of apprehending Bartleby with the invocation of documentary sources that could explain the scrivener and "his case" (Melville [1853] 1979, 103); Bartleby becomes a legal case as the lawyer tries to figure out how to evict him; he finally becomes a clinical case when the lawyer diagnoses him as having some innate and incurable disease. Similarly, Stein positions Melanctha as a case by giving her protagonist a doctor for an interlocutor. Furthermore, Stein's simple title for the triptych containing "Melanctha," *Three Lives,* is not only a claim to the form of "a life" on the part of Melanctha and the other subjects in the triptych but also an indicator that what is to follow will exemplify something, as cases do. But these two literary figures' positions in and as chronic cases (or cases of the chronic), I will argue, are more than just studies of dysfunction. They engage with the question of human energy and its conservation, eventually offering up a sense-method that I call chronocatachresis: opposed to producing and channeling human vitality toward industrial-capitalist projects tuned to the reproduction of profits and populations, chronocatachresis involves the stretching out of time beyond its instrumental uses.

Bartleby: A Story of Wouldn't

Melville's Bartleby, though his name echoes two verbs ("barter" and "be"), is a man of stunning inaction. When first tasked with cross-checking his copy with that of the other scriveners, he famously replies, "I would prefer not to" (Melville [1853] 1979, 112). He eventually prefers not to copy, eat, leave his place of employment, or live at all. Critics have generally focused on Bartleby's famous verb "prefer" (see Deleuze 1997), but that verb is a feint, a way for Bartleby to signal a potential for an action, even an emotional one, that he never realizes. For "prefer" is actually optional to his meaning. Bartleby, that is, could have eliminated "prefer" and said, albeit somewhat archaically, "I would not [do that]." In fact, the word "would" appears in Melville's story of 14,463 words exactly ninety-eight times, most pointedly in Bartleby's fifteen statements that he "would prefer not" to do what he is asked to, and his two that he "would prefer" to be left alone or do something else. As with my epigraph above, "The Woodchuck Song," Melville's repetition of the word "would" echoes the word "wood," suggesting that Bartleby's ligneous opacities and vexed relation to paper reduce him to the status of a thing, what we might now call a blockhead. The story's conundrum is precisely whether and how not doing something can count as an act of human will; indeed, the lawyer asks, incredulously, "You *will* not?" (Melville [1853] 1979, 116; emphasis in source) and receives in answer, "I *prefer* not" (117; emphasis in source), an answer that equivocates the question of will.

At the center of the story, then, are not so much Bartleby's preferences, as the verb "would," whose function exemplifies the tenselessness I have been discussing. Grammatically, "would" is a modal verb. In linguistics, modal verbs are called "defective" (see, e.g., Baerman and Corbett

2010) because they are not inflected for tense (there is no "will would," or "woulded"). They are, simply, incompletely conjugated, as yet undone. "Would" is also distinguished by what linguists call the "dynamic modality," in which the condition of possibility for the verb is internal, concerned with the subject of the sentence's ability or willingness to act (Palmer 2001, 9–10). As the past tense of "will," "would" is connected with questions of agency, drive, inclination, disposition, appetite, desire, pleasure, vitality: all aspects of what it means to live and have a life.[4]

What does it mean to be able to do something, at least theoretically, but not to do it?[5] The lawyer actually knows the answer to this question, for he himself has preferred not to do much of his job, especially not the part that involves going to court: "I am a man who, from his youth upwards, has been filled with a profound conviction that the easiest way of life is the best. Hence, though I belong to a profession proverbially energetic and nervous, even to turbulence, at times, yet nothing of that sort have I ever suffered to invade my peace. I am one of those unambitious lawyers who never addresses a jury, or in any way draws down public applause; but in the cool tranquility of a snug retreat, do a snug business among rich men's bonds and mortgages and title-deeds" (Melville [1853] 1979, 104). In fact, the "unambitious" lawyer has exempted himself from the "energetic and nervous" pace of mid-nineteenth-century American business life, and retreated, just like Bartleby, behind a series of walls and screens.

Importantly, one of the ways that the lawyer has achieved equanimity amid the hustle-bustle of Wall Street pertains to the only temporal function that "would" actually has: to indicate habit or repetition in the past. The lawyer employs two other clerks, Nippers and Turkey, each of whom is dysfunctional for half the day. During the morning, Nippers has indigestion, and spends most of his time banging at his table and adjusting its height until the lunch hour, after which he is "comparatively mild" (Melville [1853] 1979, 109). In the afternoons, though, Turkey arrives back from his lunch drunk, and there is "a strange, inflamed, flurried, flighty recklessness of activity about him" (105–6) as he blots documents, bumps his chair, throws his pen, and stirs up his papers. The lawyer's solution is to make the most of his employees' habits, relying on Turkey in the morning and Nippers in the afternoon. "Their fits relieved each other like guards," he reports: "When Nippers' was on, Turkey's was off; and *vice versa*. This was a good natural arrangement under the circumstances" (109). This is, effectively, a rhythmic arrangement, but one attributed to nature rather than to the lawyer's power as an employer. Indeed, the lawyer further naturalizes this oscillation insofar as he keeps time more or less by his copyists' skin tones, relying for a clock on Turkey's flushed face, "which gaining its meridian with the sun, seemed to set with it, to rise, culminate, and decline the following day, with the like regularity and undiminished glory" (105). The third clerk, a copyboy named Ginger-Nut, is notable only for the fact that he goes out and gets cake and apples for the other two on a daily basis. By naming his employees after purely physical characteristics and counting on their habits—naturalized, perhaps even racialized, as complexion—to mark the days, mornings, meridians, afternoons, and evenings, the lawyer arrogates clock time back to natural time, beating the mechanical time of wage capitalism, and exempting himself from the anxiety-making tempo of Wall Street. The lawyer's use of his employees as chronometers is reflected in the other predominant use of "would" in the story: it is generally used to indicate a repetition in the past, as in "[Turkey] would be incautious in dipping his pen into his inkstand" (106). For the lawyer, then, habit organizes time so that it is bearable.

The lawyer's use of "would" emphasizes predictability, making the verb itself akin to copying, the repetitious activity to which much of the lawyer's office is dedicated: in the locution "[Turkey] would be incautious," Turkey repeats his own actions often enough that they can be anticipated—they also form a rhythm of sorts. But Bartleby's "would" interrupts the "would" of habitual repetition, the accretions from the past that give "would" a claim on the future and that get things done in a safe and "snug" way. Thus it is important that Bartleby utters his first "I would prefer not to" in response to the lawyer's request that he read a copy of a document out loud while the lawyer cross-checks it with the original. Bartleby's first "would" interrupts the routine of the office (so tacit that the lawyer has called Bartleby to him without raising his head, merely extending the copy in his hand), the repetition of legal documents in the process of copying, and the tense of habitualness that makes both the past and the future possible. Bartleby's habits are not like Turkey's, Nippers's, or Ginger-Nut's—punctual episodes that make time livable because their intervals are clearly patterned. Rather, Bartleby's habits are an incalculable mass of resistance, the doings of an "unaccountable scriv-ener" (Melville [1853] 1979, 119) whose actions cannot be broken down into predictable parts. As the lawyer remarks, "Nothing so aggravates an earnest person as a passive resistance" (115).

But though this comment would seem to indicate that the lawyer understands Bartleby's actions as a form of social protest against the mo-notony and hierarchy of his work environs, he moves quickly to diagnose his clerk in the individualizing, privatizing terms of medical pathology. Describing his turn from sympathy toward Bartleby to repulsion, the lawyer rationalizes that the heart cannot bear a misery it cannot alleviate, and that his recoil from Bartleby stems from "a certain hopelessness of remedying excessive and organic ill" (Melville [1853] 1979, 121). Incur-able, hopeless, excessive, organic, ill: this is the language of chronic dis-ease, of the static bodies it indexes and the defective temporalities it en-genders. The modality of the chronic, then, is less the safely habitual than the compromised, the unconjugated, the "would" in the sense of being able or unable to realize one's will. Or, in its more recalcitrant modes, the modality of the chronic might run something more like this: rather than succumbing to incapacity ("I would if I could but I can't"), actually *liv-ing* with chronic illness might involve expressing not doing as a matter of preference ("I could, but I would prefer not to," or "I could, but I would not"), so as to conserve oneself for more important things.[6]

"Bartleby" was published in 1853, before chronic disease became a matter of public, national-level discussion in the United States in the early 1900s. But it anticipates some things about that discussion. First, Bartleby, who eats as little as possible and does as little as possible, seems intent on safeguarding himself and his energy. And in fact, during Theo-dore Roosevelt's administration the US government became interested in public health, including chronic disease, as part of what we now know as the nature conservation movement—a movement originally imagined to involve the preservation of both people and the environment. In 1908, responding to the exploitation of natural resources that had marked the rise of industrial capitalism and the wealthiest classes, Roosevelt appointed the Federal Commission on the Conservation of Natural Resources. Two Yale economists, J. Pease Norton and Irving Fisher, had already seized on the question of health as part of the national wealth. Accordingly, the American Association for the Advancement of Science set up a Committee of One Hundred on National Health to advocate for a federal department of public health (Rosen 1972). Fisher submitted his *Report on National Vitality, Its Wastes and Conservation* (I. Fisher 1908) to Roosevelt's Commission, though it took until the Taft administration for a cabinet to be established. With the Fisher report, the idea of human resources was born, inaugurating an American-style biopolitics that, in a capitalist rather than a state vernacular, took as its object the optimization—the capacitation—of dominant populations (see Foucault 1990 and [1978–79] 2008).[7] This capacitation included not only work but also rest, leisure, and preventative health programs that would preserve and restore the worker.

Second, "Bartleby" anticipates the conservation movement, and the *Report on National Vitality* in particular, because Melville's story is shot through with the language of liveliness and the lack thereof, from "the life of Bartleby . . . the complete life of Bartleby" (Melville [1853] 1979, 103), to the "life-lease of . . . profits" (104) that the lawyer counts on as Master of Chancery, to the lawyer's "predestinated purpose of . . . life," (131) to the "errands of life" (140) on which the letters at Bartleby's former place of employment, the Dead Letter Office, famously speed "to death" (140). Likewise, the most important aspect of Fisher's report, besides its generally eugenic thrust, is its insistence that the American population lacks "vitality," that the country's "vital assets" are "three to five times the physical" ones that comprise its property (I. Fisher 1908, 1). In Fisher's view, the promotion and preservation of "human vitality" (2) means preventing rather than just curing diseases, and it means reducing the "incapacitation" of the workforce in order to conserve "national efficiency" (3). In other words, Fisher characterizes the United States as a particular kind of body: lively, propertied in itself, capable, waste-free, and time-conscious. Conservation of the individual body is here recycled, as it is emphatically not with Bartleby, into the conservation of national time. Indeed, Fisher went on to influence the insurance industry, through his founding of the Life Extension Institute in 1913, promoting the quest for more and better quality lifetime. And the insurance industry eventually began to require periodic physical examinations for the insured (Rosen 1972, 19), the most important means of identifying the chronic illnesses that were asymptomatic in everyday life.

What makes Bartleby chronic, then, is less his physical pain or ill-ness, than his refusal of vitality and especially of its temporal regimes of prevention, conservation, and efficiency in the name of a greater good. He spurns the system of discipline that manages the story's other chron-ics, the alcoholics Turkey and Nippers, whose episodes of dysfunction can be timed and worked around so that the law offices remain efficient, and who relegate their incapacity to specific parts of the day so that the lawyer's work can get done. Bartleby, by contrast, conserves, but con-serves himself, only for himself, or perhaps for nothing at all: part of the reason that the lawyer repudiates him so thoroughly is that when he goes back into the office on a Sunday, snoops in Bartleby's desk, and finds the scrivener's savings knotted in a handkerchief, he realizes that Bartleby spends no money, and recalls that Bartleby neither reads, nor drinks beer, tea, or coffee, nor goes for walks, but remains mostly motionless behind his screen. In other words, Bartleby refuses the rhythms of work and leisure, the measures that would restore him to decent health and concomitant productivity, preferring not to waste the energy that it takes him, first to compare copies, then to copy at all, then to do any work for the lawyer, and finally even to eat in the prison, or live at all. If by the early twentieth century Fisher was advocating temperance, nonsmoking, exercise, a low-protein diet, and a shorter workday to preserve "national efficiency," even in the mid-nineteenth we find Bartleby both invoking and refusing at least some of the habits that would presumably make his body a fitter part of the workforce.

Bartleby's one-man conservation efforts exemplify what Michael Sne-diker (2015, 19), in an essay on "Bartleby," Stein, and chronic pain, calls "degeneratively tak[ing] up space as though in a parody of functioning." But importantly, Snediker refers here to words, specifically to the lawyer's attempt to steer Bartleby from preferring not to do things to "liking" a career as a clerk, a bartender, a bill collector, or a traveling companion. Snediker writes, "The lawyer's unsuccessful attempt to force Bartleby's preferences into the deeper (less *neutral*) shade of liking has everything to do with the lawyer's wish to calibrate language (Bartleby's and his own) along an axis of utility. Which words *do* something, versus which ones degeneratively take up space as though in a parody of functioning?" (Sne-diker 2015, 19, emphases in source).

Snediker sees "preference," or "liking," as this sort of parodically functioning word, but the defective modal verb "would" is even more exemplary of this condition, and of Bartleby. Scattered throughout McIville's story, and appearing in almost every one of his protagonist's refusals, "would" blocks function, and specifically the function of tense, while also blocking the fantasy of machinic perpetuation that tenselessness seems to promise. If machines and preferences can be calibrated, "would," and the dumbly opaque natural substance it conjures up, wood, cannot.

As Snediker shows through his pairing of Melville and Stein, there is no better parody of function than Gertrude Stein's syntax. Famously exemplified by her phrase "Rose is a rose is a rose" (Stein [1913] 1922, 187), Stein's words and sentences refuse utility and functionality and, in early works such as *Three Lives* and *The Making of Americans*, expand to fill up paragraphs' worth of space without advancing anything like an ordinary novelistic plot. Bartleby's status as an arrested copyist, the attenuated etiology and nonfuturity of his actions, his lack of vitality, and his "defective" tenselessness are aspects not only of Stein's portrayal of the most Bartlebian heroine in American literature—Melanctha Herbert, of *Three Lives*—but also, as I'll go on to argue, of Stein's method of writing, and of the sense-method of chronocatachresis that she eventually develops in contradistinction to the progressivism of Irving Fisher and his compatriots in public health.

Melanctha, or, Each One as She Would (Not)

The middle narrative in Gertrude Stein's novella *Three Lives* (1909), "Melanctha" is the only one of the three stories whose protagonist is unmodified by an adjective. The other narratives are "The Good Anna" and "The Gentle Lena," their adjectives implying that there are other Annas and Lenas (and that these particular ones, through their goodness and gentleness respectively, have achieved normative femininity), whereas Melanctha remains singular. "Melanctha" is also the only heroine in the triptych to be qualified by a modal auxiliary verb—for while the other titles stand alone, the subtitle of "Melanctha" is "Each One as She May." With the singular quality of Melanctha and the subtitle, our attention is immediately called, as with "Bartleby," to questions of agency, permission, and possibility: "Each One as She *Will*" would characterize Melanctha as a creature of intent, but "Each One as She *May*" suggests a certain suspension of will or action for possibility and inclination (indeed, "may" is in this phrase yet another dynamic modal auxiliary). Finally, "Melanctha" is the only section of the triptych whose protagonist is black, tying issues of the case study, of will and agency, and of tense to issues of racialization in the United States in the early twentieth century and beyond. Whereas "Bartleby, the Scrivener" attaches chronicity to white fragility, repeatedly calling the clerk "pale," "Melanctha" attaches it to the condition of being black and poor in America. In Stein's story, that is, we can see debility more clearly as an effect and a motor of racialization.

Of the stories in *Three Lives*, "Melanctha" is the most obviously situated within the medical discourse of its own historical moment, for it is a psychological portrait, a map of desires and frustrations. Furthermore, opening with the birth of an African American baby who does not survive beyond a few days, "Melanctha" hints at its own eugenic context, the same one in which Irving Fisher (1908, 101) could advocate that "'sterilization' laws will reduce the number of marriages of degenerates." Finally, the bulk of the story reads like the transcript of a psychoanalytic session, for it consists of dialogues between Melanctha and Dr. Jeff Campbell about the proper way to live a life.

Melanctha's very name is charged with racialized questions of agency and pathology as well as sexuality: possibly a compound of the ancient Greek *melano* (black) and *anthos* (flower), the name also chimes with the timid and often ill Reformation theologian Philip Melanchthon, and with the words "melancholy" and "malinger," at once granting Melanctha some psychological complexity and recalling the myth that black people do not feel pain.[8] The moniker, then, is a tangle of stereotype, historical precedent, and diagnosis, all of which inflect the genre of the case study. But Melanctha the character is not so easy to assay. While she could be described as a nymphomaniac, a repressed lesbian, or a person suffering from repetition-compulsion, the story avoids attaching nouns to her or her condition. Instead of naming her psychological complex, the narrator calls Melanctha "complex with desire" (Stein [1909] 2000, 89). Within the terms of literary analysis, too, Melanctha cannot be described as a heroine whose choices help her triumph over circumstance as in the bildungsroman. She also refuses the part of the tragic mulatta, a victim whose death from consumption, which Stein portrays as incidental and tacks onto the end of the story, would culminate a plot of decline. Melanctha's many long dialogues with Jeff are an endless duet of mutual dissatisfaction, though unlike Jeff, who prizes middle-class respectability, Melanctha knows a lot more about what she doesn't want than what she does want. Directionless, she seems determined only to wander, a term that appears fifty-six times in the story. Her connection with psychopathology and sickness, her long complaining arias, and her plotless life story all point to a state of tenselessness that counters the dominant temporal patterning of the American (and even African American) turn of the century, about which more below.

Like "Bartleby," "Melanctha" initially seems to foreground space more explicitly than time. If Bartleby is hemmed in by walls, Melanctha is cramped by her story's small number of characters (Melanctha's parents; her friends Rose and Sam; her lovers Jane, Jeff, and Jem); its segregated setting (the fictional Bridgepoint, a middle-class black town); and its poverty of physical spaces (the town, people's houses, and architectural features such as stairs and rooms are named but never presented pictorially). But even more than with "Bartleby," whose narrator has a huge lexicon to balance the spareness of its main character's, what feels most impoverished and shrunken about "Melanctha" is the story's language, in both its narration and its dialogue. Stein's sentences, paragraphs, and even plot structure are so repetitive, with such a limited vocabulary, that they annoy most readers: as an anonymous reviewer on Goodreads has written online, "I never want to read the story of Melanctha again in my life. No never no more do I want to read Melanctha. Never no more in my life do I want to read Melanctha. No never no more again" ("Andy's review" 2010). That's actually pretty fair parody of what "Melanctha" sounds like. Stein's monochromatic prose, her long sentences made up of basic, mostly one- or two-syllable words, echo Bartleby's flat repetitions of "I would prefer not to."

Though Stein is a canonical modernist by now, the surprise of "Melanctha," and its unbearability, do not lie in modernism's usual set of juxtapositions, neologisms, or fragments, textual imitations of the collage aesthetic or the "shock" of synthetic cubism. Rather, "Melanctha" is the linguistic version of analytic cubism, whereby a single motion is broken down into linked, only slightly differing increments, as in Marcel Duchamp's famous painting *Nude Descending a Staircase (No. 2)* (figure 4.1).[9]

4.1 Marcel Duchamp, *Nude Descending a Staircase (No. 2)*, 1912. © Association Marcel Duchamp/ADAGP, Paris/Artists Rights Society (ARS), New York 2018.

However, in "Melanctha," what is broken down and made incremental is not physical motion but thought itself. For example, Jeff describes himself as a "very quiet kind of fellow" (Stein [1909] 2000, 113) and then, a few pages later, as a "very slow-minded quiet kind of fellow" (116); the narrator refers even later to his "slow fighting resolution" (132) and "slow way" of doing things (157); and eventually, Melanctha comes to hate what Jeff already recognizes as "the cold slow way he always had to feel things in him" (146). This portrait of Jeff is built up bit by bit, with a single word placed at different syntactic angles to other words, which allows for slight semantic changes not so much in the word "slow" as in Jeff's personality as a whole: in the first phrase, his slow-mindedness dominates his quietude; in the third it has receded; in the next it has become a kind of strength; by the final one it has become a sign of his lack of humanity. This is something like the movement of, for instance, the hip in *Nude Descending a Staircase*, which is seen at various angles in succession, all on the same plane.

Just as analytic cubism features repetition across space, "Melanctha's" prose style performs at the level of the sentence a possible way of living that features repetition over time—habit, or constancy. Jeff Campbell, like "Bartleby's" lawyer and even his other employees, is an impresario of this quality: "Dr. Campbell said he wanted to work so that he could understand what troubled people, and not to just have excitements, and he believed you ought to love your father and your mother and to be regular in all your life, and not to be always wanting new things and excitements, and to always know where you were and what you wanted, and to always tell everything just as you meant it" (Stein [1909] 2000, 109).

Here is the middle-class doctor's version of the Melvillian lawyer's proclamation that he suffers nothing of the turbulent lawyerly profession to invade his peace. Jeff Campbell wants, above all, to be oriented—to know where he is in space ("where you were") and what is the point of his directionality ("what you wanted"), and to speak intentionally. However slow and fixed he seems, then, he is cumulative, like the nude on the staircase: on the map, moving toward something, in control of his language. Melanctha's other heteronormative friend, Rose Johnson, captures this way of being succinctly, as "proper conduct" (Stein [1909] 2000, 90).

Melanctha's actions and thoughts, on the other hand, do not accrue into any kind of consistent direction for her life. Jeff accuses Melanctha of transgression, of wanting "new things" and "excitements" (Stein [1909] 2000, 134), and suggests over and over again that being habitual and punctual will grant her happiness. But Melanctha's plot and the sentences that describe it are as repetitive and incremental as Jeff's; it's just that unlike his, they don't add up to anything. Ironically, Melanctha's movements toward events, novelty, and difference become a sign not of her brilliance at rupturing the status quo but of her stasis and incompleteness. She can achieve neither departure from nor completion of the dominant form of a life. Instead, Melanctha occupies what Lauren Berlant (2011, 4) has called the "impasse": a stretched-out scene demanding of its denizens a "wandering absorptive awareness" and an alert scavenging for whatever looks like a possible form to inhabit momentarily, if only to take a rest.

As the repetition of the word "slow" in the depiction of Jeff, and the tooth-grinding difficulty of remaining attentive to such a reiterative story suggest, though, what look like problems of space—Melanctha's inability to fit into a narrative genre that would give her life meaning; the historical situation of Jim Crow; the counterpoint between proper houses and dangerous streets and alleys; the attempts of various men in Melanctha's life to limit her movement—are also, and perhaps predominantly, problems of time. "Melanctha" highlights the role of what I have elsewhere (Freeman 2010, xxii) called *chrononormativity* in the assessment of lives as meaningful and worthy of enhancement. Rather than following a culturally sanctioned sequence or even just inclining herself toward recovery, Melanctha represents those who fill time, wait till it's time, do time, or kill time. The story's style suggests that Melanctha's relationship to time is simply that she is in it—*for* life, but not *as* a (sanctioned) life.

In light of Kyla Schuller's (2017) discussion of sentimentality, sensation, and whiteness, referenced in the introduction, let us recall that these questions of how bodies are timed and how they adjust or maladjust to normative temporal schemata are inseparable from the question of race. At base, the optimization of some lives and the debilitation of others, described by Foucault ([1978–79] 2008), Puar (2017), Schuller (2017), and others as biopower, is a racializing technique. For not only are the bodies that biopower marks as disposable or unworthy of improvement often those of people of color, but that very process of degradation is used to buttress arguments about the relative strength and weakness of racial groups (in this sense, biopolitics is merely a seemingly kinder, gentler eugenics). Likewise, no discussion of "Melanctha" could be complete without acknowledging its focus on African American life and the period of eugenic thinking in which it was written. Despite its representation of a psychologically complex African American female character, "Melanctha" also contains all kinds of racist imagery: Rose is described as "a simple beast" (Stein [1909] 2000, 87) and "sullen, childish cowardly, black" (87), and, most (in)famously, the narrator speaks approvingly of "the warm broad glow of negro sunshine" (87). Yet it is a mistake to assume that the story's racial dynamics can be contained by a description of the stereotypes in which it traffics. Rather, these dynamics seem to be nonrepresentational, not dependent on the "visible" in the way that stereotypes are.

Stein's portrait of Melanctha as a mixed-race woman with a chronic desiring condition—one that inflects both her speech and her actions or lack thereof—inflects the question of race temporally. On the one hand,

Melanctha exemplifies both the turgid, unresponsive racial other and the impulsive, enthusiastic one that Schuller describes. The slowness and stasis of her story, and the character's floundering among a limited set of stereotyped narrative possibilities, or genres, also perform on a syntactic and structural level the continual deferral of African American mobility and autonomy, perhaps even that population's "slow death" (see Berlant 2011), and certainly its status as the target of debilitating laws and policies. Yet the very terms offered for mobility and autonomy, in the character of Jeff, are a form of further discipline in and through time: ways of capacitating the black body for sanctioned modes of production and social reproduction. In short, where racism appears most consistently in "Melanctha" is not just in Melanctha's characterization as too slow or too quick but in the two poles of chrononormative possibility for late-nineteenth-century African Americans: endless waiting and debilitation, or mandatory capacitation according to the march of progress.

By tying Melanctha's way of being in time to her race, Stein reminds us that the model of chronicity is shot through with progressive, developmental, industrial-capitalist, and/or teleological uses of time that have moral valence: chronic conditions require management, which in turn implies self-discipline, adherence to protocols that are often very much tied to Western clock and calendar time, and most importantly, a future-directed outlook on the parts of doctors, patients, and populations. What we can see in the Fisher report published contemporaneously with "Melanctha," and what continues in contemporary biomedical discourse, is that chronicity itself has been arrogated for a biopolitical narrative of futurity. At the turn of the century, Fisher wrote, "As it is usually the normal healthy man who provides life insurance for his family, so it will be the normal healthy nation which will take due care of its resources for the benefit of generations yet unborn" (I. Fisher 1908, 13). In his view, just as citizens' bodily self-regulation guaranteed a future in which family members would not depend on the state, conservation of national resources guaranteed a healthy future population. In contemporary biomedical discourse, the chronic has been paradoxically associated with the "modern," according to a paradigm in which nations industrialize, eliminate, or contain acute infectious diseases (polio, smallpox, and malaria), only to find their populations beset with the chronic conditions that are associated with toxic chemicals, overconsumption, sedentary occupations, and disrupted kinship and community ties (cancer, asthma, diabetes, obesity, and depression) (Manderson and Smith-Morris 2010, 5). Puar (2017) and Berlant (2011) have described this as a shift from the epidemic to the endemic. The "chronic," then, does not just demand a future-oriented outlook but now also proclaims the arrival of a population *to* its own future, as suggested by Fisher's description of neurasthenia as "on the increase" and prevalent among "persons who take no reasonable recreation—businessmen among others" (I. Fisher 1908, 39). We can glimpse in Fisher's diatribes against smoking, overly protein-rich diets, and fatigue the way that the medical crises arising via modernity, in turn, are referred to a moralizing, individualizing narrative of "lifestyle excess and cost," in a model of what another anthropologist, Dennis Wiedman (2010), calls "the chronicities of modernity."[10] And in the end, Fisher ascribes these conditions more to people of color and the poor, his "degenerates," than to the white and wealthy. In the moralizing narrative of chronicity, then, peripheral countries and the marginalized populations of dominant countries have become the "decadents" of global capitalism, whose overcivilization is leading to their decline.

This recalibration of a historically specific aspect of capitalism into a narrative of individual or demographic degeneration in the face of modernity—of those whose supposedly excessive desire and consumption, no matter how deprived their conditions actually are, mark them as modernity's inevitable waste product—is constitutive of biopolitics. In both current biomedical discourse and late nineteenth-century discourses on race, sex, and public health, the solutions to overinvestment in the pleasures of consumption, laziness, and anti- or nonfamilial affinities have been "parsimony and manual labor" (Manderson and Smith-Morris 2010, 6–7) along with marriage. In contemporary global developmental discourses of epidemiology, this means that overly modernized subjects of "developing" countries are encouraged to return to traditions of minimal subsistence and hard work for their own health, and to small nuclear families. During the post-Reconstruction and Progressive eras and beyond in the United States, this has meant that women, people of color, and sexual "perverts" have received the benefits of citizenship and inclusion insofar as they adhered to the "traditional" family, with its rhythms of production and reproduction, and to thrift and mostly manual or service labor (Gaines 1996). This sense that newly modernized subjects are prone to chronic mental and physical health problems to which the solutions are work and traditional family structures is central to "Melanctha": Dr. Jeff Campbell is a figure for the African American population's official entrance into US modernity, supposedly achieved through heterofamilial life events, the tempo of capitalist productivity, and a future-directed outlook. Melanctha, on the other hand, marches to another drummer.

The Grammar of Chronicity

Melanctha's relationship to time—her chronicity—is nowhere more apparent than in her story's grammatical *aspect*, which is somewhat different than the grammatical elements I have discussed thus far, tense and modality. Whereas tense refers to the time of an event in the past, present, or future (as in "did," "does," or "will do"), and modality refers to the question of whether an event is actualized or remains only a possibility (as in "would do"), aspect refers to an event's extension over time—its completion, duration, or frequency (Comrie 1976). Tense is the "when" of an action; modality is the "if"; aspect is the "how": the texture, feeling, or sense of time and timing. The main grammatical aspects are the perfective, or completed, and the imperfective, or uncompleted. The imperfective aspect denotes a state of sustained doing or being, rather than of moving forward or developing toward an endpoint. "Melanctha," then, is written in the past tense. But along with the familiar perfective aspect (the simple past of a completed action, as in "she slept"), the bulk of "Melanctha" uses one form of the imperfective aspect, the continuous imperfect ("was" plus a gerund, or—ing construction, as in "she was sleeping"). In her 1926 lecture "Composition as Explanation" (Stein [1935] 1993, 498), Stein calls the imperfective the "prolonged present." In this contradictory piece, she does talk about "beginning again," that is, the recursive mode so celebrated in poststructuralist theories of citationality.[11] The mode of beginning again looks more like the second form of the imperfective, the habitual imperfective, marked by the phrase "would," as in "she would go to sleep every night." But Stein is more concerned with how to use repetition to produce continuity, protraction, dilation, and extension than with repetition as return.

In attempting not just to gesture at but to calibrate alternatives to chrononormativity—to track other chronicities—Gertrude Stein was, like the Shakers I discuss in chapter 1, a practitioner of *rhythmanalysis* (Lefebvre 2004), or the use of rhythm as a methodological tool for meaning making. Stein wondered and wrote about people's modes of existing with and through time. She understood people as fundamentally rhythmic, and sought all her life to find the measure of those she encountered, as if individuals had particular frequencies that she could tune into and replicate in language. She defined personality itself in terms of "repeating being" (Stein [1903] 1993, 62), as a temporal phenomenon in which the sameness of self or identity was modified by differences of emphasis, or bodily maneuver, not always in ways the person had control over, and not always in ways that the person simply surrendered to. To Stein, personality was a kind of attenuated agency, a way of adjusting toward or aslant from the social. It did not change things dramatically, nor did it lead a person inevitably one way or another. But in meeting up with other frequencies, Stein understood, a personality could shift in small ways, could become other to itself. As the literary critic Omri Moses (2014, 135) puts it, "Stein would have us witness the way people go about extending themselves in their situation, how they feel themselves modified by the occasion. To announce an attitude over and over again is to feel it change and accumulate duration."

Moses claims that Stein refused to equate a lack of transgressive agency, a lack of dominance over time, with demise: "Stein for her part simply does not accept the charge that the habits, the temperaments, the forms of decency that incline people toward their particular brand of unthinking sociability are dead" (Moses 2014, 117). This is why both Melanctha and Jeff are very much alive, however their rhythms clash and whatever greater cultural value Jeff's life might be accorded. Yet the "unthinking sociability" to which one might attribute both Jeff's accretive regularity and Melanctha's wanderings is counter to the doctrines of will and choice that organize the lawyer's thinking about Bartleby, and to the premium on transgression and rupture that contemporary critical theory has put on its objects of analysis. "Melanctha" proffers a way of thinking about the chronic, of imagining its protagonist and its own syntax's protracted and repetitive qualities as a mode of self-stylization and other-relationality: a method of knowing and doing, and of connecting with others, through a sense of dilated and time-ish being.

Importantly, if it is not agential this mode of being is not passive either; indeed, it belies the passive/active dichotomy. It is captured in "Melanctha" by a technique that Stein calls "insistence" (Stein [1934] 1985 171), a word that she uses to describe time in terms of "distribution and equilibration" (Stein [1935] 1993, 502). The idea of distribution and equilibration emphasizes a certain constancy, marked by changes in apportionment, circulation, and balance, rather than by movement forward or backward or by the incremental progress of repetition. And indeed, Stein claims that "insistence" is actually distinct from repetition—it bears on the continuous imperfective aspect rather than the habitual one. As Stein declared later in her lecture "Portraits and Repetition," "If a thing is really existing there can be no repetition. . . . Then we have insistence insistence that in its emphasis *can never be repeating*" (Stein [1934] 1985, 171; emphasis mine). This is repetition as intensification, rather than as "working through," in the Freudian model, or as the preamble to the event of "difference," in the Butlerian model that has dominated queer theory for the last twenty-five years (see Freud [1914] 1950 and Butler [1990] 2006). As the Stein critic Ulla Dydo claims, Stein's "insistence" is not only about duration or persistence but also about rethinking energy and movement: "'Insistence,'" Dydo writes, "refers to forms of repetition that create concentrated, mounting *intensity* rather than extended, diluted repetitiousness" (Dydo 2008, 16; emphasis mine). Insistence seems to be a mode of what Berlant (2011, 95) calls "lateral agency," and Kathryn Bond Stockton (2009, 27) calls "fattening"—a thickening or extensive movement in directions other than forward or backward, whether centripetal or centrifugal. It is a kind of being the same, but more so, and not for or toward anything in particular.

On the face of it, it may seem that Stein's prolonged present just looks like stasis or eternal time. But it is actually not temporally homogeneous in the way that eternal time is: it differs from itself. A look at "Melanctha's" adverbs of time demonstrates how inadequate the term "present" is for what Stein is up to here. For instance, there are 633 instances of the adverb "now" in "Melanctha," but they most often signal a shift in status rather than the immediate present per se; that is, they appear interchangeably with but also replace the word "then" (which appears only

275 times), in clauses such as "Now Melanctha would go out" rather than "Melanctha wanted the book now." In other words, oddly enough, in "Melanctha" "now" signals a point in *past* time rather than in the present. There are also 693 instances of the word "always," most often attached to a past-tense verb, as in "Melanctha always went out," which signals the imperfective by blurring present and past. In "Melanctha," what is "continuous" and "prolonged" is as likely to be the past as the present, and the two cannot be fully distinguished. Here is where we can see the temporal heterogeneity *within* the continuities Stein seemed to privilege. Whatever "insistence" is, it is neither a return of the same nor a ruptural difference from the historically or temporally prior.

Moses (2014, 134) traces Stein's interest in theorizing the continuous, the prolonged, and the insistent to her understanding, following William James, of habit itself as a temporal mixture: "[Habit] allows one to digest and absorb the overwhelming data of experience by matching the images one takes in with memories of images from the past. . . . To the degree that one's perceptions are overwhelmed by habit, new experiences are assimilated into ready-made responses. . . . [But i]f one subtracts from the perception of an object the habit that allows the object to be recognized and therefore positioned in a context, one is left only with fugitive sensations and potentialities that overwhelm the body's capacity to act." In other words, habit is what inclines us toward a self-preserving automaticity, insofar as it calibrates new experiences in relation to a past without subsuming them to that past. It is neither absolute sameness nor complete difference. "Insistence," though, is something like the pressure or intensification *of* habit, as if habit lost its periodicity. It is about the refusal of something regular to go away, as with Bartleby, who was *"always there"* in the law office.

And this, more than anything, is what chronic conditions do. The anthropologist Angela Garcia (2010) saw a version of this intensification of ongoingness in her mid-1990s fieldwork with heroin addicts along the Rio Grande, detailed in her beautiful book *The Pastoral Clinic*: her subjects' repetitive behaviors, frequent references to long-gone events, and stories that went nowhere worked on a principle of what she calls "intensification" rather than resolution or letting go. The people with whom she worked told stories to reexperience personal pain and to connect it to larger sociopolitical events, but not to achieve closure or release themselves from torment. "Chronics," then—addicts, wanderers, recalcitrants, malingerers—are people whose queerness inheres in their relation to time, not as forward- or backward-moving but as ebbing and flowing in varying degrees of intensity and insistence, compression and dilation, irreducible to the habits that consolidate identity.

What distinguishes insistence from repetition, Stein argues, is that in insistence every linguistic recurrence contains not necessarily different words or even different syntactical positions, but a different *emphasis*. Here we can return to her distinction between repetition and insistence in "Portraits and Repetition": "If a thing is really existing there can be no repetition. . . . Then we have insistence insistence *that in its emphasis* can never be repeating because insistence is alive and if it is alive it is never saying anything in the same way because *emphasis can never be the same* not even when it is most the same that is when it has been taught" (Stein [1934] 1985, 171; emphasis mine).

To Stein, emphasis is the sign of an "aliveness" that makes pure repetition impossible, but then again does not require discontinuity to be meaningful. It also indexes a certain commitment to life, even to vitality or animacy, but not the sort associated with optimizing or maximizing that life. "Bartleby" too actually has a moment of emphasizing emphasis: "'I would prefer *not* to quit you,' [Bartleby] replied, gently emphasizing the *not*" (Melville [1853] 1979, 129). Here, insistence is doing the work that rearrangement, addition, subtraction, or accretion would otherwise do, binding Bartleby to what prevents his thriving, to his negativity, but in a paradoxical assertion of liveliness, to being still there, still, there.[12]

What exactly is emphasis, then, and how does it relate to the kind of chronicity, the "timeishness" that I am suggesting may be a product of biopower but also offers some leverage in relation to it? At a basic level, as Melville's italicized *not* expresses, emphasis is stress. When speaking we emphasize through gestures (think of pounding the table), stances or facial expressions (think of standing up to make a point or scowling while speaking a particular word), or changes in tone, volume, or tempo (think of shifting to a stern tone, speaking more loudly, or slowing down). Thus emphasis is at base a bodily matter—it involves lips, tongue, teeth, lungs, glottis, larynx, hands, face, bodily stance, and so on. One way of understanding emphasis might be to think of it as a broadened version of "accent." In *Time Binds* (Freeman 2010, 29), I argue that a certain queer corporeal accent, an out-of-kilter bodily tempo and set of daily rhythms marked by both socioeconomic and sexual alterity, troubles the chrononormativity of domestic life. This is accent as rhythmic bodily hexis, irreducible to "tone," "attitude," or even some generic "difference." In the passage above from "Portraits and Repetition," Stein also says that emphasis seems most the same when it is taught. This formulation sounds very much like Bourdieu's (1977, 78) concept of habitus: "the durably installed generative principle of regulated improvisations" that shape legible personhood in a given culture. And it sounds like Lefebvre's (2004, 41–45) understanding of rhythm as the modality in which bodies concretely live out social time (his shorthand for this process by which bodies are trained into and by time is "dressage"). Emphasis, then, is a corporeal way of playing on or with regularity, a mode of literally *making* "do" with what one already is. And as I shall argue below, it can be a way of living aslant to the chrononormativity of clinical life, as well as to the larger global discourse of the chronic, and to biopower itself.

With the Emphasis on Race

Emphasis has a relationship to contemporary African American culture and to the working-class Baltimore communities in which Stein lived and worked while at the Johns Hopkins School of Medicine in the late 1890s. By the time Stein was writing "Melanctha," "chronic" had become a noun, denoting someone whose suffering was without end, with the negative implication of malingering (the *Oxford English Dictionary* cites a magazine article from 1886 with the sentence, "We question whether the late donor intended his sanatorium to be filled with chronics"). But as I remarked earlier in this chapter, by the 1860s the term had taken on a slangy quality and began to describe the continuation of anything objectionable—the *Oxford English Dictionary*'s examples include chronic revolution, horror, and doubt—and then the state of simply being objectionable, as in, again from the OED, "The weather is chronic" and "He puts a dash of whisky into the paraldehyde to disguise the taste, which is a chronic one, I can tell you."[13] By 1992, when the rap artist Dr. Dre issued his solo album *The Chronic*, this adjectival meaning of severity and the noun form of "chronic" had come together to name a particularly potent breed of marijuana whose effects are stronger and last longer than ordinary weed.[14] In the Urban Dictionary Online, definitions of "the chronic" tie high-grade marijuana to intensity, severity, or shock: one writer offers the definition "in a very acute or intense state of being"; another describes it as "anything sick, excellent, extreme, severe or funny"; still another defines it as "something shocking but in a good way."[15] "The chronic," then, is not only about grim endurance: paradoxically, here the chronic is also the pleasurably acute. It resonates with the difference that Stein saw between "repetition" and "insistence" and that she captured with the term "emphasis": it names a connection to the visceral and the sensory, shifts in magnitude or stress rather than in subjectivity or action. And this has everything to do with Melanctha's ability to seize time beyond biopolitics.

The chronic, in the terms of contemporary African American culture and nineteenth-century medical discourse alike, is about a continued bodily state—but in the former, not one marked solely by exhaustion or desiccation. Rather, the chronic body signaled by Dr. Dre is open to the severe, and in slowing down the present, can find physical pleasure or new capacity without acceding to the demand for transformative agency. The chronic, with a black accent, is what Berlant (2011, 137) calls "a countertemporality." "Inhabiting such dense moments of sensuality" as eating, fucking dangerously, or toking up, she writes, "stops time, makes time, and saturates the lived, imagined, and not-yet-imagined world." One might add to this list of activities and their effects Bartleby the scrivener's "dead-wall reveries" (Melville [1853] 1979, 121), which Branka Arsić (2007, 74) suggests may be a result of opiate use. Another way of thinking about countertemporality might be this: the form of time marked by the chronic deregulates chrononormativity to introduce a gap that is not necessarily a life-changing event—but is not entirely meaningless either. As Puar (2017, 19) describes affect in general, the chronic is "the body's hopeful opening, a speculative opening not wedded to the dialectic of hope and hopelessness but rather a porous affirmation of what could or might be." Perhaps the chronic isn't even as tuned to the future as Berlant and Puar might have it. Perhaps, in its defective chronicity, the chronic is as much a "would not" as a "would."

This sense of the chronic as a commitment to ongoing intensity, to the emphasis that keeps one alive if not precisely going anywhere amid constraining conditions, brings us to the crux of "Melanctha." The story offers up a model of chronicity as a time-ish, body-based extension of relations to others, an "ethics" that is not so much a political movement as a stylized mode of participation with and in the existing world, a sense-method of being with it and with others. Melanctha herself is consistently described as a "feeling" person, and "feeling" is one of the story's recurrent words ("feel" or "feeling" appears 216 times, crescendoing in the story's third quintile and diminishing to almost nothing in the final quintile). The good doctor wants Melanctha to "feel right" by acquiescing to normative schedules for marrying, reproducing, and living daily domestic life. Melanctha wants to "feel" even if it's not right, even if it eschews these things and keeps her in a constant state of what the novel calls "excitement" and I am calling the chronic. If Melanctha is not precisely a drug user, she is an intensity junkie, but that's an importantly temporal state. She needs and demands the "excitement" that *is* emphasis, that is, the carnal experiences that refuse to guarantee the future through perfect rhythmic regulation and absolute temporal sameness on the one hand, or action-oriented transgression on the other. In her pursuit of sexual and other pleasures, Melanctha might be the sensory antipode of the anhedonic Bartleby, but in her refusal either to accede to the discipline of habit or to start a revolution, she is his temporal twin.

If Bartleby refuses to extend the lawyers' briefs into the future by copying them, Melanctha refuses to extend the present into the past by "remembering." Dr. Campbell constantly accuses her of not "remembering right" what he has done for her and how much he loves her, as if her waywardness were subject to a Freudian narrative cure of excavating the past. She, in turn, accuses him of "remembering" rather than experiencing things. In other words, Jeff's "feeling right" is a matter of "remembering right," of retroactively sequencing events in relation to a preexisting narrative, in the way that the lawyer also wishes he could do for Bartleby. Melanctha says to Jeff, "You remember right, because you don't remember nothing till you get home with your thinking everything all over, but I certainly don't think much ever of that kind of way of remembering right, Jeff Campbell. I certainly do call it remembering right Jeff Campbell, to remember right just when it happens to you, so you have a right kind of feeling" (Stein [1909] 2000, 151).

While Dr. Campbell strives to remember events "right," as in correctly—insofar as they reflect an ordering scheme that he understands as universal—Melanctha emphasizes "right just when it happens to you."

The word "right" turns from adjective to adverb, from moral to temporal valence, from conformity with proper conduct to a measure of immediacy. The phrase "to remember right just when it happens to you" suggests something other than forgetting or living in a fictively selfsame present. It is a way of not occupying the temporalities of recollection, memorial, anticipation, or hope. It is a way of encountering the event in time, otherwise.

Stein correlated this sense of acuteness and immediacy, interestingly, to forgetting, just as a toke of the right weed or a shot of heroin will provide both a change in the present and an escape from the past. Stein held out that *not* remembering, or emptying out the historical, had a tonic effect, declaring in "Portraits and Repetition" (Stein [1934] 1985, 179–80) that "that is the trouble with a great many so called intelligent people they mix up remembering with talking and listening, and as a result they have theories about anything, but as remembering is repetition and confusion, and being existing that is listening and talking is action and not repetition intelligent people although they talk as if they knew something are really confusing, because they are so to speak keeping two times going at once."

Dr. Campbell's problem is that he doesn't really listen, because he is too busy gauging his own behavior in terms of the regulative norms he "remembers" or has been taught. Because he is constantly trying to remember an idealized past, to get back to normal, he lives in a damaging double-time, always trying to wrench the present into the beat of the past. Melanctha's temporality, by contrast, doesn't erase the past—her actions occur, remember, in the past imperfective—but isn't dictated by it either. Indeed, the talking and (not always) listening, the dialogics that structure the story itself, are a way of making and experiencing shifts in emphasis that crack open the present.

Melanctha's emptying out of memory might fruitfully be compared to the experiments in automatic writing that Stein undertook with fellow student Leon Solomons at the Harvard Psychological Laboratory while she was an undergraduate at Radcliffe. In her single-authored piece "Cultivated Motor Automatism" (Stein 1898), Stein aimed to correlate character types with the propensity for automatic action. She instigated this automatic action in her subjects by propping their dominant arm onto a board hung from the ceiling, and putting a pencil into their hand, which hung over the edge of the board and could doodle on a piece of paper below. The experimenter could surreptitiously control the swinging of the board and thus introduce a particular motion of the arm and a corresponding doodle. Stein's interest lay in whether or not the subject resisted being guided into new motions by manipulations of the board. Though her description of the human types and their lesser or greater resistance to automaticity strike contemporary readers as comical, she correlated their resistance with the fixity of their attention on the situation of the experiment itself: those who could not forget that they were in a scientific experiment tended to return to old movements rather than adapting new ones, whereas "hysterics," as she called them, adapted beautifully to new movements because they could not attend to the experimental situation at all: "It is [the hysteric's] anaesthesia which makes automatism possible" (305). Here, resonant with Jeff Campbell's situation, a lack of feeling (anaesthesia) correlates to being automated.

But in the experiments Stein wrote up with Solomons, the two researchers honed in on "consciousness without memory" (Solomons and Stein 1896, 501), the phenomenon the authors correlated to "men completely undressing without knowing it" (492), in which the subjects were aware of having accomplished something like reading or writing but had no memory of actually doing it. The investigators were particularly invested in this distracted, rhythmic state of being because it allowed for the cultivation of new motor habits. Solomons and Stein actually suggested that a chronic condition could provide just such new possibilities: "Imagine an arm in the condition of 'chronic rest' of an hysterical paralysis. Is it not altogether likely that it often acquires great sensitiveness from this, so that stimuli reaching it along the automatic path, not strong enough to produce a reaction in a normally exercised arm, may yet produce a reaction in a hyperaesthetic arm?" (Solomons and Stein 1896, 503). Here, hysteria correlates with an excess of feeling, a hyperaesthesia. Lacking the muscle memory of the "normally exercised" arm, the chronic arm can adapt to new movements because it feels sensations otherwise imperceptible, *right when they happen to it*, just as Melanctha the chronic, lacking the proper form of habituated memory that Jeff exemplifies, feels things right when they happen to her.

This remembering right when things happen also gives us another way into the temporal politics of race in the story. The Stein critic Claudia

Franken (2000, 122) writes that "[a]s a literary form, insistence aims for a certain independence in the mental relation to an object of attention. Repetends and extensive parallelisms [have] been used in religious language. Suggestive of a time that goes on and on forever, religious 'insistence' may satisfy a desire to forget and provide a rise or standstill of feelings." This simultaneous forgetting and rise of "feeling" also seems to me to be a way to conceptualize racial belonging in general. For example, performance theorist José Esteban Muñoz (2000) describes racial belonging as "feeling brown" a phrase that disrupts the legalistic and lexical sense of race as an identity and redescribes it as a sensory apparatus, something durable and installed but not fully biological, something of the body but not reducible to it, something ongoing that one nevertheless feels at varying states of intensity, something that indexes not just the misery of oppression but also the joy of connection with others.

While I can't credit Stein with a coherent critical theory of race and racialization, I do think that her using black characters to explore the relationship between repetition and memory is important. Clearly, her sense of what black cultural continuity might mean was not reproductive: nobody in "Melanctha" has a child that lives, and in this the story flirts dangerously with a eugenic mindset. Yet I think it also goes beyond the "repetition with a difference" or "beginning again" that James Snead (2003), Fred Moten (2003), and other African American critics have recognized in cultural forms such as jazz and rap. It has something to do with the kind of accrual or persistence that can counteract false memories of a time "before" a supposed social or physiological breakdown, or can contest demands that black people give up particular activities in the name of personal uplift, racial solidarity, or national vitality. In other words, insistence and emphasis, or what I am calling the chronic, are forms of duration in which past and present admix, but not in which the past or the future block access to pleasure: rather, the chronic is a mode of continuity without sacrifice. And as with Muñoz's formulation, Melanctha's insistence on "feeling" is not just the presentism that is often described as the fatal flaw of racialized and class-marked cultures (as in the idea that black and/or poor people buy things for immediate gratification, such as cars). Rather, Steinian insistence, and Melanctha's insistence in particular—what I am calling their *chronic* characteristics—have an important relationship to the politics of memory, as Franken's words suggest: "forgetting" the past in order to allow the "rise of feelings" or new intensities may be key to inhabiting the now otherwise.

Stein herself correlated automatic writing and its evacuation of the past with religious ecstasy, writing in her scientific work that "I have found a number of instances of [automatic writing] which reminded me of the rapid and incessant movement seen in revival meetings, where people under the domination of religious frenzy swing their arms and beat their breasts in rhythmic time" (Stein 1898, 300–301). And indeed, Franken (2000, 122) isolates a key moment of insistence in Gertrude Stein's play *Saints and Singing*, a moment saturated with religious imagery that captures the work of insistence, emphasis, and chronicity that I have been tracking:

> Saints and singing do not come to this as an ending. Saints and sing-
> ing. Read me by repetition. Saints and singing and a mission and
> an addition.
> Saints and singing and the petition. The petition for a repetition.
> Saints and singing and their singing.
> Saints and singing and winning and.
> Do not repeat yourself. (Stein [c. 1922] 1993, 399)

First, in this passage we can see Stein enjoining us against the terminal: though saints and singing may conjure up images of the pearly gates and the end of time, Stein asks us not to stop there. Then, too, there is something more here than repetition with a difference, even "repetition" "and an addition." There is song, reminding us that the emphatic part of insistence lies in what the body can do, what it must do, to carry on. There is a mission, but not the kind of missionary work that attends to saving souls or curing bodies, because there is also the sound of "omission," or what that model cannot see or hear. There is a petition within repetition, a kind of recurring demand or the demand that lies *in* recurrence, even recurrence without any transformative difference. This "petition" is a way of asking that equivocates between mission and omission, between doing and not doing, whose most salient characteristic is its constancy. As Franken (2000, 122) writes, "Yet another formulation of the concept of 'insistence' contrasts with 'repeating' . . . insistence now appears as an addition, an act of *asking or demanding something from life*." Yet in Stein, that dem/and is just an "and," not an end.

Finally, Stein enjoins us, "Do not repeat yourself," which of course points to the deadening possibility that what we will pass on down is our habituated "selves," our identities. But her call to us not to "repeat" but to read *her* by repetition suggests that she wishes for a constant reader, a way of being ongoing with us, of talking and listening without remembering but without abandoning continuity for the safe blank slate of rupture. Insistence, endurance, keeping on, chronicity as timeishness without obvious historical or futural directionality, without even recognizable agency, are forms of engagement with the times, which is to say, they are ways of extracting, protracting, dilating, or otherwise intensifying everyday existence without promising to be any particular kind of subject in return. As the federal government and industry, following the cues of Fisher and other conservationists, moved in the early twentieth century to regulate the production, conservation, and expenditure of human energy, Stein's (and Melanctha's) mode of chronicity, we might say, chucked all that.

Queerer Chronicities, American Religions

I'd like to call Bartleby's and Stein's modes of defective, imperfect, queer chronicity *chronocatachresis*. *Catachresis* is a literary term, describing the misuse of a word—not just in the sense of making a mistake but also in the sense of purposefully stretching the meaning or function of a word beyond its denotative or even commonsensically metaphoric ones. In "The Woodchuck Song" of my epigraph, the woodchuck "chucking" wood is one example of catachresis: the noun "woodchuck" is possibly derived from the Cree "wuchak," but breaking the syllables apart produces the back-formation "to chuck," a sonic metaphor for chopping wood. "Chuck" originally meant to cluck, to throw, or to tickle gently under the chin, but not actually to chop; hence the stretching of the term toward wood chopping is catachrestic. In the song, the "chucking" then does what it says, refracting backward on the wood to produce the cutting or splitting of the modal verb "would" into other modal verbs, "could" and "should."

There is a vaguely sexual politics to catachresis; the root word *kata* means "down," with the sense of a perversion. And in fact, Foucault (1990b, 53) defines *chresis,* or use, in terms of sexual pleasure: the way a human being regulated his or her pleasures in terms of conduct, regimen, proportion, and timing.[16] Chronocatachresis, then, would name an individual's "perverse" deregulation of temporality—his or her untimeliness in terms of the dominant regimes of time I have elsewhere called chrononormativity and here fleshed out in historical terms by way of the history of human resource management and the movement for racial uplift. Chronocatachresis names a way of misusing, or even misunderstanding, the principles of control over a condition, the management of wayward affects, and the discipline of self-production. Bartleby achieves this misuse by preferring not to quit, not to leave, not to work or eat or do anything at all but be "*always there*" (Melville [1853] 1979, 118; emphasis in source), a chronic condition blighting the lawyer's otherwise safe and snug existence and interrupting the rhythms of his days. Melanctha achieves it by wandering away from both the interminable wait for black liberation and the drumbeat of racial uplift, and by feeling her feelings right when they happen to her.

Interestingly, though, "Melanctha's" Jeff Campbell too has his moment of chronocatachresis, his queerest moment of chronicity. In a rare moment of giving Melanctha credit for her own way of being in the world, Jeff declares, "I got a new feeling now, you been teaching to me, just like I told you once, *just like a new religion to me,* and I see perhaps what really loving is like, like really having everything together, new things, little pieces all different, like I always before been thinking was bad to be having, all go together like, to make one good big feeling" (Stein [1909] 2000, 136; emphasis mine).

"Having everything together" is Jeff's version of "feeling right when it happens to you," a scheme that disrupts the orderly arrangement of time into the sequence of past, present, and future. And Jeff connects it to religion. It's hard to know what denomination Jeff is indexing here—probably none in particular, though the narrator tells us that he has been "raised religious by his people" (Stein [1909] 2000, 105). Certainly, what Jeff describes is not the internalization of a catechism, or the completion of a ritual that installs him into a religious order. It is some kind of sudden indwelling, some moment of what the Baptist tradition, especially in its African American iterations, has called "catching the spirit."[17] And Melanctha too has felt this. Early on in "Melanctha," Stein writes that "Melanctha Herbert always loved too hard and much too often. She was always full with mystery and subtle movements and denials and vague distrusts and complicated disillusions. Then Melanctha would be sudden and impulsive and unbounded in some faith" (91). This last phrase, "unbounded in some faith," seems key to understanding Jeff's religious feeling as well: like marijuana, faith unbinds the body's tempo, and that unbinding produces a feeling of connection with another.

Here, then, is a sensory regime that does not accede fully to either discourse, as it is primarily affective, or biopolitics, as its object is unbound from compulsory forms of sociability rather than bound to them. Importantly, there is no organized church involved in Jeff's religious feeling or Melanctha's unbounded faith, not even a black one. The narrator tells us that "[r]eligion ha[s] never interested Jeff very much" (Stein [1909] 2000, 105), so he does not get his feeling from even the reverse discourse of black Christianity. Nor is "religion" a category of personhood that Jeff or Melanctha can occupy, like that of "the colored people" that indexes their racial belonging—neither one claims to be a Christian, for example. Thus, in this "good big feeling" that Jeff can get when he tunes himself to Melanctha, and in Melanctha's being "unbound in some faith," there is something that eludes total capture by biopolitics, by the discourse of racial uplift, by theological doctrine, and by even the temporal regularity of ritual. This "feeling" is neither past- nor future-oriented: only when Jeff is with Melanctha in this particular, "religious" way can he let go of his sense of being bound by both tradition ("remembering right," as Melanctha puts it) and the idea of the collective future of African Americans, and only when Melanctha finds her particular form of faith can she loosen herself from the strictures of respectability.[18]

This religious feeling reflects the influence of William James on Stein. James, in *Varieties of Religious Feeling,* was interested not in the institutionalized church, or the clergy and its hierarchies, or theology, but in religion as affect: "Religion . . . shall mean for us *the feelings, acts, and experiences of individual men in their solitude so far as they apprehend themselves to stand in relation to whatever they may consider the divine"* (James [1901–2] 1987, 36; emphasis in source). In these lectures, James aimed to capture what he called, invoking Kant, the "sense-content" of religion (56), which he fleetingly correlated with substance use in the way that the contemporary term the "chronic" also does: "Sobriety diminishes, discriminates, and says no; drunkenness expands, unites, and says yes. It is in fact the great exciter of the *Yes* function in man" (348). In other words, the affective state indexed by and inculcated in religion involves a radical loss of self and expansion of relationality. Stein, though, was less concerned with the relation between the human and the divine. Instead, she understood religious feeling as a sense-method through which humans could stand in different relation to one another. Thus when Jeff has "religion," he has something besides his own regimen and Melanctha's excitements alike, and the feeling makes possible, at least momentarily, a collaboration or being-together of two: "They sat in the bright fields and they were happy, they wandered in the woods and they were happy. Jeff always loved in this way to wander. Jeff always loved to watch everything as it was growing, and he loved all the colors in the trees and on the ground, and the little, new, bright colored bugs he found in the moist ground and in the grass he loved to lie on and in which he was always so busy searching. Jeff loved everything that moved and that was still, and that had color, and beauty, and real being" (Stein [1909] 2000, 130). This passage evokes James's description of saintliness as "the outlines of the confining selfhood melt[ing] down" (James [1901–2] 1987, 250). Melanctha and Jeff's religion, here channeling some of transcendentalism in its focus on nature, fosters and depends on the pleasures of feeling together in rhythmic time as well as unbounded space: the repetitions of "they" and "Jeff," as well as the paratactic "ands," strung like beads on a rosary, unify both the passage and the characters. Oddly, here the hyperregulation of time is chronocatacrestic, for the repetends take Melanctha and Jeff out of the times that seem to predestine them for failure (Melanctha) or conventional success (Jeff), and turn them toward the pleasure of one another.

"Melanctha," then, brings us full circle back to the Shakers and to the role of Protestant ecstatic religion in American culture: it may not be accidental after all that its protagonist's name echoes that of the reformer Philip Melanchthon, colleague of Martin Luther. But the reforms this story points to are different from those nailed to the church doors of Wittenberg. What threatens existing orders and allows for new solidarities in both "Melanctha" and Shaker worship is not doctrine, faith, or belief so much as the way that tuning bodies to one another's frequencies, especially temporal ones, allows for the expansion of their boundaries and their merging into one another. As my following, final chapter shows, this is a feature of religion writ large, the feature that allows it to function against the very canons that purportedly authorize it.

SACRA/MENTALITY IN
DJUNA BARNES'S *NIGHTWOOD*

Entirely woven through with elements that are imaginary, erotic,
effective, corporal, sensual, and so on, [the church] is superb!

MICHEL FOUCAULT, "On Religion"

Ecstatic religion, or the ritualized movement that intends to open bodies up to other bodies and to the
spirit(s), might be counterposed to another religious activity, Catholicism's verbal confession by the individual
to a single priest. In the latter, sinful thoughts and acts
are transformed into spoken words of contrition, and
then dissolved into priestly statements of absolution.
Ecstatic religion emanates from active bodies coming together in public or semipublic spaces; the Catholic confession emanates from the still body in the silent booth
in the recesses of the church. Ecstatic religion infuses the
body with affect and fuses it to multiple other bodies;
confession intends to empty the body of desire and its
effects. Yet Foucault (1990a, 58–63) reminds us that the
Catholic confession actually saturated the body with desire; its interrogative tendency to draw out the subtlest
indications of prohibited arousal led to an expansion of
language about sex, and eventually, through sexology

and psychology, to the bundling of lust, fantasy, acts, and object-choice into a kind of person, the homosexual. It is difficult, then, to imagine the regime of modern Western sexuality without the confession.

The work of Americanist scholars such as Peter Coviello (2013), John Mac Kilgore (2016), and Molly McGarry (2012) has clarified the ways that ecstatically embodied belief practices in the United States—nondominant religions from Native American spirituality to Mormonism to the "science" of spiritualism—refuse to accede to the techniques whereby physical acts become sexual identities through the medium of speech.[1] But what if instead of only turning to ecstatic Protestant religions to think beyond *scientia sexualis*, we center other Catholic rites, and ask toward what forms of eroticism and relationality they extend? Having suggested in my first chapter that Shaker dance led to new modes of engroupment, including racialization as what some scholars (see Fine et al. 1997) have called "off white," and having elaborated, across the period between the late eighteenth century and the fin de siècle, some sense-methods attendant to whiteness, to enslavement and its escape, to variously racialized and sexualized historical methods, and to a form of chronicity at once black and queer, in the previous chapter I ended up back at ecstatic religion with "Melanctha." This suggests to me that the long nineteenth century's extralinguistic, sensory modes of belonging and becoming, of which ecstatic religion might be the most extreme example, forge relationalities that do not begin or end with race, gender, or, in particular, sexuality. Yet sitting between the dissident Protestant sects I have discussed or alluded to and a mainline Protestantism that effectively became the secular worldview in post-Puritan America is Catholicism, always a stigmatized religion in the United States. Catholicism accrued stigmatized gendered, racialized, and sexualized meanings here because of its association first with the French, Spanish, and Anglican North American colonizers and their indigenous converts against whom Puritan English settlers defined themselves, then with immigrants and Mexicans from the 1840s onward, and then with antidemocratic, even subversive, "foreign" entanglements abroad during the Progressive era that preceded *Nightwood,* the subject of this chapter.[2] Central to anti-Catholic discourse in the United States has been a vision of Catholicism as suspiciously carnal, with implications that include, in Jenny Franchot's (1994, xxi) description of antebellum objections to it, "novel structures of interiority and public conduct" and "an alternative psychological landscape that offered to an industrializing, individualist society a populated sacramental tradition, a vastly enlarged sense of temporality, and a reconfigured spatiality of confessional, monastery, and cathedral." In Franchot's view, Catholicism's deeply embodied rituals and iconography indexed modes of subjectivity, behavior, collectivity, time, and space that were antithetical to Protestant visions of modernity.

Pace Foucault, then, Catholicism cannot be reduced to the confession, which is only one of the sacraments. Resituating confession into its original sacramental context, we can see that Catholic liturgical practice (not always equivalent to Roman Catholic theology) is in many ways much more "catholic" about bodies, desires, fantasies, and affinities than the dominant Protestant worldview of the New England colonies and eventually the United States as a whole—in ways that contest the regime of modern sexuality and make sacramentality a sense-method of the sort I have been tracking throughout this book. Foucault himself seems to recognize this in the epigraph above, in which he lauds the "imaginary, erotic, effective, corporal, sensual" aspects of the church. William James, in *The Varieties of Religious Experience,* seems to have done so as well, writing that Catholicism "has so many cells with so many different kinds of honey, is so indulgent in its multiform appeals to human nature, that Protestantism will always show to Catholic eyes the almshouse physiognomy" (James [1901–2] 1987, 413). Invoking the science of physiognomy, James anticipates Foucault's understanding of Christianity as the precursor to *scientia sexualis*—correctly keying that early science of the body to a Protestant worldview. But James's gentle pun on monastic cells, which he depicts as bursting with liquid honey, suggests an *ars erotica* inherent in Catholicism, particularly as it centers on immersion in fluids and on drinking and eating, or the two sacraments of baptism and the Eucharist.

This chapter, then, offers up these two, most sensate sacraments—with a detour through the sacramental imposition of hands—as a way out of what I consider a counter-Reformational regime of sexuality, using Djuna Barnes's modernist classic *Nightwood* ([1936] 2006) as a touchstone text, one at the very outer edge of a very long nineteenth century that I have limned in terms of the movement from an eighteenth-century specification of the sensual body as a domain of knowledge and control toward a final consolidation of the homosexual/heterosexual binary in the Anglo-American world by the mid-twentieth century. For no novel knows the history of confession, or understands and repudiates its stakes for the production of modern homosexuality, better than *Nightwood,* which has not generally been read as a meditation on Christianity.[3] *Nightwood,* though, turns over and over again to the motif of genuflection. Its original title was *Bow Down,* which became the title of the first chapter; several of its characters spend their time "going down before the impending and inaccessible" (5); the main female character, Nora Flood, goes down on her knees in horror when she first sees her lover, Robin Vote, with another woman; and Robin eventually "go[es] down" (179) herself, falling to the floor and crawling around in a grotesque chase scene with a dog. These episodes echo *Nightwood*'s central scene, which is explicitly figured as a confession: in a chapter titled "Watchman, What of the Night?," the pathetic and jilted Nora comes to the apartment of her friend Matthew Dante O'Connor, a cross-dressing, defrocked priest and abortionist, to tell the story of her doomed love with Robin. As watchman, Matthew emblematizes what Foucault (1990a) calls the Christian pastoral, the beneficent, all-seeing shepherd who will sacrifice himself, if necessary, for his sheep. His tiny one-room apartment, strewn with women's garments and rusty gynecological tools, also visually condenses Foucault's notion of the confessional as, at once, closet and precursor for the "science" of sexuality (see Veltman 2003). But despite these gestures to the confessional, *Nightwood* ultimately uses religion to reject the regime of sexuality: it does so unsurprisingly by renouncing the confession and its hypervigilance over the body, but also counterintuitively by turning to other sacraments. Barnes illuminates a sacramental point of view—a sacra/mentality—that is the final sense-method I will discuss in this book.

Briefly, sacramentality is an affective experience of the sort that James claimed as religious, though he did not treat the sacraments in his compendium of religious experiences. Considered a visible sign of inward grace, a Christian sacrament is nevertheless not altogether visual. Rather, as a rite, it enacts an embodied relation to the divine and a relation to the body of the divine, one that also inaugurates or affirms relations among those who take part in or witness it. In rethinking the term "sacramentality," I put a slash before "mentality" to indicate that it is not solely the

property of Catholics, Christians, or even people of faith but an incorporative stance toward objects and others, a way of encountering the world
and its people as well as or even instead of the divine. In *Nightwood*, I
will demonstrate below, sacra/mentality puts pressure not only on the
virulent anti-Catholicism seen in the United States from the late eighteenth century up to Barnes's own moment but also on the solidification,
by the 1930s, of the homosexual as a species in medical discourse, if not
as completely so in the vernacular.[4] Finally, on a more contemporary horizon, sacra/mentality contests present-day theoretical configurations of
queerness as radical negativity—theorizations that are profoundly linked
to the secular.

Protestants, Penance, and Prattle

As I've indicated above, Foucault's straight track from the confessional
to the closet may be a result of his focusing so much on the confession
as a ritual of speech rather than of physical and sensory engagement:
his version of the confession is actually somewhat Protestant, or at least
Counter-Reformation Catholic. He treats the Protestant confession as a
continuation of the Catholic one, arguing for "a certain parallelism in the
Catholic and Protestant methods of examination of conscience and pastoral direction," and claiming that "procedures for analyzing concupiscence
and transforming it into discourse were established in both instances"
(Foucault 1990a, 116). But he may have been too fast to conflate the two.
In fact, the medieval reorganization of confession, and eventually the
Protestantization of this religious ritual during the Counter-Reformation,
made modern sexuality possible and foreclosed other possibilities. These
included what Foucault elsewhere calls the uses of pleasure—or at least,
in this case, the use of the body as a sanctioned instrument with which
to achieve transformations both individual and social, to do what queer
theory has called world making.

Early Christian penance was deeply corporeal; the rite emphasized
the public display of repentance in embodied suffering. Foucault himself
has described changes in the rite of penance that precede the Protestant
revolution, arguing that the monastic tradition of *exagoreusis*, or the verbal expression of sin, eventually overtook *exomologesis*, the somatic expression of penitence in early Christianity. And Stephen Haliczer (1996, 8)

identifies the Fourth Lateran Council of 1215 as a turning point in the relation between acts and words. When the council put priestly absolution at the center of the rite of penance, its leaders also began to extend the interrogatory phase: as Haliczer's history of the confession in Spain reveals, after this council there appeared numerous manuals instructing priests and penitents in the elaborately structured process of examining the sinner's conscience and replying appropriately to this examination.[5]

In some ways, early modern Protestants simply made this already-revised Catholic rite of penance into an explicitly secular matter; Martin Luther's *Babylonian Captivity of the Church* (1520) demoted the confession from the sacraments. But more generally, Protestantism refocused Christian attention onto the Word as manifest in Scripture (clearest in the doctrine of *sola scriptura*), and Puritanism especially focused on Scripture oral and aural, interpreted aloud by believers and/or received by witnesses, in ways that had deep ramifications for the rite of penance.[6] The Counter-Reformation Catholic Church, in turn, responded to Protestantism in a particularly Protestant way: the bishops at the Council of Trent (1545–63) made the confession the centerpiece of a renewed emphasis on the sacraments, demanding more frequent and much more detailed *verbal* interrogations and responses, and the rite became more extravagantly linguistic (Foucault 1993, 212–15).[7] When the Protestants stripped the confession of its sacramental status, and then forced the Catholic Church to reconfirm that very status as a specifically oral and aural exchange between priest and penitent, they paved the way for the transformation of acts into the utterances—a process begun in the thirteenth century and culminating in the Counter-Reformation—that would eventually, in the transfer of this process to a medical environment, signal particular identities.

But more importantly for my purposes here, by desacramentalizing confession, Protestants also reined in the sacraments' power to contest both the regime of alliance (marriage and descent) and the regime of sexuality (bodies as objects of knowledge and desire as the key to selfhood). As Franchot's (1994, xxi) invocation of Catholicism's "populated sacramental tradition" suggests, the sacraments conjoin people into and as the body of Christ on a social model that explicitly competes with earthly marriage and family. By contrast, the eventual transformation of sex into discourse isolated and specified individuals as if their erotic life had nothing to do with their extended social relations, though the newly specified were, of course, able to forge new social relations on the very basis of their named identities. The sacraments also foreground nongenealogical models for descent, such as discipleship and apostolic succession. The regime of sexuality, on the other hand, propped up the ideology of reproductive kinship as, by the early twentieth century, it focused more and more on the Oedipal scenario. Finally, while the sacraments have a complex relation to the past, or what Franchot (1994, xxii) calls "a vastly enlarged sense of temporality" insofar as they reanimate historically specific events such as the Last Supper, "sexuality" separated erotic life from the historical process by implanting desire into (and as) a timeless psyche. A close examination of the sacraments themselves, particularly those among which the confessional was originally embedded before its secularization, reveals loops of flight not only beyond marriage and reproduction but also beyond the regime of sexuality, which are as powerful and promising as those of the Protestant evangelical and spiritualist traditions discussed by other Americanists.

A sacrament is a palpable manifestation of God's grace, experienced as an interaction between priest and recipient and sometimes extending itself between or among these recipients. In Catholic doctrine, there are seven of them: baptism, confirmation, Eucharist, penance, holy orders, marriage, and extreme unction. Since Thomas Aquinas, who followed Aristotle's theories of the material, each sacrament has been understood as bipartite, consisting of what the Catholic catechism calls "essential matter" and "form."[8] The essential matter is a substance—water for the baptism; oil for confirmation and extreme unction; bread and wine for the Eucharist; the priest's spoken absolution for penance; the laying on of hands for receiving the holy orders; and the couple's spoken consent for marriage. The form is verbal and in general connected to church authority; indeed, for most sacraments that form is a linguistic performative: "I baptize thee . . ." enacts a baptism; "I confirm thee . . . ," a confirmation; "I do," a marriage. "I absolve thee" transforms penance into absolution; "Accipe spiritum sanctum" ("Receive the Holy Ghost") enacts an ordination; and "I anoint thee" enacts extreme unction.[9] Put differently, the words, when accompanied by the properly sanctified material, *are* the action; the exception is the Eucharist's command, "Eat/drink this and remember me," in which the communion consists of that eating and drinking.

But strikingly, only two sacraments have words as both their essential matter and their form: marriage and penance. Historians of marriage have described the way the Catholic Church seized marriage from the purview of families by demoting tangible, customary signs of agreement between couples' families and the couple itself, such as the dowry, the ring, the handclasp, the father's "handing over" of the bride, and the kiss, and by making the words of consent the validating act.[10] Despite the Council of Trent establishing the necessity of marrying before priest and witnesses, the essential matter of the marriage sacrament is still that of the twelfth century as formulated by Pope Alexander III and theologian Peter Lombard: consent, evidenced by the verbal "I do" of the bride and groom rather than by the priest's "I now pronounce you man and wife" or by consummation (Martos 2001, 374). Penance is equally verbal but, conversely, rests on the priest's words. Since the Fourth Lateran Council of 1215, and as reaffirmed by the Council of Trent, the essential matter of penance has been the priest's statement of absolution rather than the penitent's dramatization or statement of his or her sins.[11] Finally, Catholic marriage and penance are the least tactile of the sacraments: while these two are centered on speaking and hearing, the other five center on touch (of water in baptism, oil in confirmation and extreme unction, and hands in ordination) or taste (of the bread and wine in the Eucharist).

The removal of the somatic and theatrical aspects of marriage and penance in favor of verbalization, their eventual desacralization by the Protestants, and the Counter-Reformation's reclaiming marriage and penance as sacraments in the Protestant terms of aurality and verbosity, are precisely what made these two rituals so transferrable to the civil realm, so useful for a *scientia sexualis* centered on the confession, and eventually for a regime of normalization centered on marriage. Thus a Western *scientia sexualis* stemming from confession and grounded in law and psychiatry has been effulgently linguistic. More recently, a biopolitics of normalization, which exceeds both law and the health professions to encompass statistics and population management, has depended on diminishing the language required from those against whom aberrant species of people are demarcated. Thus heteronormativity has been laconic. In other words, the more that sexual minorities have been spoken about, pressed to speak and through speaking to establish the truth of themselves, the less the "marriageable" have been spoken about and had to speak: culturally, both sexual "deviance" and marriage are organized around a dichotomy between the hyperarticulated and the presumed. This is made particularly stark by the comparative loquaciousness of the confession and terseness of the marital declaration "I do." While the becoming-verbal of confession (and the becoming-tacit of marriage) certainly precede the Protestant Reformation by many centuries, their shift away from embodied acts can be seen as a precursor to Protestantism's diminution of the incarnational, visceral, and visual aspects of Catholicism in favor of a focus on the Word of God as manifest in Scripture. This shift is central to the Counter-Reformation's reorienting of Catholicism itself toward a garrulous penitential scene and, to a lesser extent, a reticent marital one. And as it turns out, *Nightwood* is saturated with this history.

Nightwood's Sacramentalities

Nightwood's only straight marriage is abridged and disastrous: Robin Vote marries the Baron Felix von Volkbein, bears a son, and abandons them both. She does not so much as speak an "I do"; in fact she accepts Baron Felix's proposal of marriage "as if [her] life held no volition for refusal" (Barnes [1936] 2006, 46). But the novel both stylistically mirrors the prolix aspect of the confession (the first thirty pages are a nearly unreadable series of long paragraphs) and comments on it. As the controlling voice of the novel, Matthew O'Connor aligns Protestantism with the word and Catholicism with the sensory, figuring Protestantism in terms of talking. He asks, "What do you listen to in the Protestant church? To the words of a man who has been chosen for his eloquence" (23), and finishes by stating that the Protestant outlook "is as hard, as hard as the gift of gab" (24). By contrast, he figures Catholicism as somatic: it's "already in your blood" (24). He gives Catholicism the fleshy qualities missing from Protestantism, describing the Catholic sinning boldly ("*pecca fortiter*") with his goats, and finishing with a statement that in contrast with Protestantism's "hard gab," Catholicism is "as soft as a goat's hip" (24). But then, just as these distinctions seem firm, they merge in the figure of the Catholic confessional—which I read as a post-Reformation one—where "in sonorous prose, lacking contrition (if you must) you can speak of the condition of the knotty,

tangled soul and be answered in Gothic echoes, mutual and instantaneous " (24).

In other words, *Nightwood* understands that if Catholicism originally seemed promisingly carnal, the Counter-Reformation confession
reduced it to a hollow verbal exchange. We see this recapitulated in the
chapter titled "Watchman, What of the Night?," in which Matthew's
long-winded apologia overtakes Nora's abject declarations of her love
for Robin: she has come to confess to him, but he ends up the penitent.
There is even a second confessional moment in the text: Matthew goes to
an empty church to confess in the form of a masturbation session, pulling
out his penis and making it "face the mystery so it [the mystery] could see
him [the penis] as clear as it saw me" (Barnes [1936] 2006, 140). Here,
Matthew lays bare not so much his sins as his state of morphological ab-
jection, in an act reminiscent of *exomologesis*. Both penitent and priest, he
offers his penis as simultaneously sign and solution: it identifies his sinful
state, and serves as gender-normalizing punishment for his transgender
subjectivity and cross-dressing, the "me" that God "sees" but apparently
cannot see through to Matthew's female soul. Yet for the modern regime
of sexuality within which the novel takes place, this form of confession
fails too; neither oral confession nor penitent acts in a post-Reformation
world can save Matthew. He thus finishes his own chapter-long mono-
logue, "Go Down, Matthew," by renouncing the linguistic, declaring,
"I've not only lived my life for nothing, but I've told it for nothing" (175).

Despite its own torrents of prose, then, *Nightwood* resists the triumph
of verbalization, of sacramental "form." We might think of *Nightwood*
in terms of Barnes's stubborn (and perhaps apocryphal?) statement, "I am
not a lesbian. I just loved Thelma."[12] If being a legible lesbian at that historical moment meant a certain mannishness à la Radclyffe Hall, or an
investment in women's community along the lines of Renée Vivien's and
Natalie Barney's salons, or a couple-centered domestic arrangement like
that of Gertrude Stein and Alice B. Toklas, Djuna Barnes could only ever
fail. Her sexual worldview—the capaciousness of "loving Thelma"—may
have drawn less from the sexological model of the lesbian, the Sapphic
Left Bank's protofeminist revaluation of women's culture, or the ideal
of the Boston marriage, than from her spiritualist grandmother's influence, her own father's bigamy, and her nonconsensual, quasiincestuous
first marriage to her uncle (her father's second wife's brother). Certainly

it encompassed her agonized relationship to Thelma's committed non-monogamy, her own bisexuality, and her exclusion from the upper-class leisure that many of the Left Bank lesbians enjoyed. To what of this complexity could the identity statement "I am a lesbian" compare? And what intricacies of attachment are contained in her seemingly defensive, self-diminishing, pre-lesbian-feminist "just"?

One of those intricacies, I contend, is spiritual. Instead of the verbal form, the novel revalues sacramental matter and proffers the latter as a counterhistory of sexuality: *Nightwood* is the story of Barnes's love for Thelma, written in a sacramental language. Then, too, Barnes's commitment to the sacraments other than confession also has something to do with what T. J. Jackson Lears (1994), Heather Love (2009), and Kevin Floyd (2009) have in different ways made it possible to think of as an affinity for the premodern in protest of modernity's reifications.[13] Following these scholars, we might also call Barnes's counterhistory of sexuality an erotics of counterhistory, insofar as the novel is also deeply invested in questions of the relation between past and present and yet fundamentally lacks the nostalgia of some modernist texts. The novel makes its move toward the historical less through the motif of return to, say, early Christianity, than by renewing the promise of the two sacraments central to Catholicism, and the only two recognized as sacraments by Protestantism: baptism and the Eucharist. In doing so, *Nightwood* makes Protestantism more carnal, more Catholic, less secular. On a more contemporary note, it also intervenes on a (perhaps by now rather predictable) debate in queer theory as to whether eschewing sociability, understood as so totally overwritten by marriage and reproduction as to be unredeemable, actually contests the regime of sexuality. As I'll demonstrate below, the novel makes possible a reading of queer theory's antisocial thesis as itself part and parcel of a secular regime of sexuality—as, indeed, completely wrapped up in the dynamic of confession that girds "sexuality"— and not as the latter's antidote.

Nightwood proffers instead what might be called a *hypersocial thesis* grounded in baptism and the Eucharist as figures for a radically corporealized relationality, an inhabitation *by and of* the other rather than a self-shattering. The basis of this hypersocial thesis is twofold: the plethora of figuration (a different form of "form" than Catholicism's words) opened up by these sacraments, and the vision of bodies and spirits as capable of inhabiting one another in traversals of corporeal boundaries. Moreover, this hypersocial thesis involves something the antisocial thesis cannot account for, the question of history: to inhabit or be inhabited by others includes a visceral reckoning with their pasts. Again, this is an aspect of the most lushly sensate sacraments: whereas marriage orients the betrothed toward a future until death do them part, and penance orients confessors toward the sins of their past, baptism and the Eucharist have a promisingly complex relationship to time and to history.

Baptism, or, the Water of Enjoinment

In *Nightwood,* baptism is initially a reminder of our oceanic origins, our commonality with other species in deep time. Foucault (1980, 30) writes, somewhat opaquely, "It is not through sexuality that we communicate with the orderly and pleasingly profane world of animals." I take this to mean that the animal world has its own extralinguistic system of ordering—one thinks, for instance, of the different roles of bees in a hive—independent of the naming function supposedly granted to Adam by God (and thus "profane"). One way to read sexuality, then, is as the demarcation between the inhuman and the human, the "human" denoting the kinds of entities that aestheticize, nominalize, and categorize not just bodies but the pleasures of the body. A turn toward the animal would thus seem to figure a way out of the prison house of both language and sexuality, which is to say, of the social. And *Nightwood* is often read as a novel of degeneration.[14] Nora's lover, Robin Vote, is the avatar for a devolutionary animality that begins with the phytological and moves through the zoological. Robin first appears in a faint in her apartment, figured as a plant: her body smells like fungi, her flesh has the "texture of plant life," and there is "an effulgence as of phosphorous glowing" around her head (Barnes [1936] 2006, 38). The narrator eventually analogizes Robin to a "beast turning human" (41), yet this process is incomplete, as "she yet carried the quality of the 'way back' as animals do" (44).

But Robin is not just a figure of degeneration, for her temporal qualities do not refer exclusively to the past. Her prehistoric qualities, that is, are matched by her antifutural ones, such that she embodies Lee Edelman's (2004) most trenchant formulations of queerness: she rejects children, going so far as to threaten to smash the doll that her lover Nora Flood gives her as a symbol of the children they cannot have, and she even lets her pets die. In her refusal to be intelligibly human, which is to say, intelligible at all, Robin is fundamentally antisocial, even asocial; the novel refers to her "unpeopled thoughts" (Barnes [1936] 2006, 50), and Nora realizes that Robin "can't 'put herself in another's place,' she herself is the only 'position'; . . . [Robin] knows she is innocent because she can't do anything in relation to anyone but herself" (155). Indeed, Robin is the living emblem of Lacan's (1999, 126) injunction that "there is no such thing as a sexual relation." Finally, Robin escapes figuration altogether. Matthew describes Nora's fatal error regarding Robin as "dress[ing] the unknowable in the garments of the known" (Barnes [1936] 2006, 145). If a figure is something like matter pressed into the service of an idea (and thus very different from the catechism's use of the term "form"), Robin simply refuses to let that process come to fruition. Baron Felix remarks, "I never did have a really clear idea of her at any time. I had an image of her, but that is not the same thing" (119). In sum, Robin links the antihuman, the asocial, and the antifigural, and in doing so she clarifies the way that the antisocial thesis in queer theory has disdained the figure itself.

Robin's becoming animal, that is, is less about degeneration or a departure from history or even humanity, than it is about the fantasy of being unrepresentable, about an iconoclasm that is, I think, the basis of the queer antisocial thesis. We can see that iconoclasm in Leo Bersani's (1987) formulation of *jouissance* as a mode of *askesis*, in which anal sex serves as a rite of penance for the sin of selfhood, shattering the *imago*. We can see it in Edelman's (2004) *sinthomosexual,* which denotes a fundamental resistance to meaning and intelligibility. But as alluring and intellectually rigorous as these formulations are, I find them somewhat unsatisfying in that they are merely the flip side of the same coin: they are part of the complex of renunciation, asceticism, sadomasochism, and transgression of the limits of selfhood that Foucault sometimes suggests as modes of resistance to the regime of sexuality. Ultimately, this complex too depends on the rite of confession—which is to say on the linchpin of the regime of sexuality—for its meaning. It is not that one must confess before having, say, anal sex. Rather, confession has worked, historically, to produce the very ideal of personhood *necessary for* the queerly impersonal, self-unmaking, death-seeking drive to do its work. It is not possible to have the second without the first.

This is especially clear in Foucault's essay "Friendship as a Way of Life": "[Ascesis is] the work that one performs on oneself in order to transform oneself or make the self appear which, happily, one never attains. Can that be our problem today? We've rid ourselves of asceticism. Yet it's up to us to advance into a homosexual ascesis that would make us work on ourselves and invent—I do not say discover—a manner of being that is still improbable" (Foucault [1981] 1984, 137). The language of "oneself," "the self," and "being" still suggests a monadic horizon for queer activities: the product of all this effort is a new and different self, however unattainable, seen as the precursor to and product of new social relations. Bersani, it is fair to say, does return penance to the exomological in his suggestion that anal sex does precisely this work, and he thereby recorporealizes penance in ways that reanimate its sacramental qualities. But the model of self-shattering that the antisocial thesis privileges, as I'm not the first feminist critic to note, is actually very much bound up in the self it seeks to jettison. Finally, Bersani's and Edelman's emphasis on destroying the figure (the ego, the self, the child, the political horizon) makes the antisocial thesis a somewhat reactionary queer theoretical drive toward a high modernist politics of the nonrepresentational. I say "reactionary" because the ideal of nonrepresentation is not, in the end, very far from the politics of self-abstraction that animates liberal, representative democracy; those with the heaviest burden of embodiment are least able to reach even a queer apotheosis of self-negation.[15] On this model, Robin Vote is, if not male, at the very least consummately white.

If the regime of sexuality originates in the confessional and finds its pseudooppositional corollary in asceticism, s/m, defiguration, and other elements of the antisocial thesis, we can of course follow Derrida's (2000) work on hospitality and wonder if another version of friendship, that *hyper*social mode that Foucault posited as homosexuality's real, material work on the world and against the regime of sexuality, resonates in the other sacraments. For Foucault ([1981] 1984, 135) writes, in the same essay on friendship, "Perhaps it would be better to ask oneself, 'What relations, through homosexuality, can be established, invented, multiplied, and modulated?' The problem is not to discover in oneself the truth of one's sex, but, rather, to use one's sexuality henceforth to arrive at a multiplicity of relationships."[16]

Here, Foucault must mean something like "homoerotic life" rather than "homosexuality," as the idea of using one's specification as a kind of person in order to arrive at relationships that dismantle selfhood seems oxymoronic; indeed, the identity-concept that is "homosexuality" has sometimes led us to multiply one kind of relationship only to shut down many others. In comparison to Foucault's words on asceticism, though, here the horizon is promisingly plural: for he focuses on social relations rather than on individual models of selfhood. What Foucault does not consider here is that relations can be established, invented, multiplied, and modulated through uses of the body that do not necessarily conform to what dominant culture recognizes as sex, yet are not personal and intimate in the way that friendship feels either.[17] These uses, or sense-methods, have been the subject of this book thus far, and the sacraments are one of them.

Even friendship, we might note, is never merely personal: while Foucault would insist that radical forms of friendship must operate "outside of institutional relations," by which he means marriage and identity politics as well as school, the military, and the church, no friendship completely escapes the framings of social relations such as race, class, gender, et cetera: as cliques make clear, friendship is always mediated by public forms of intelligibility. There were also times when Foucault suggested that such promising social modes could occur *within* institutional relations. In 1978, for instance, he got into an argument with a hitchhiker about the Catholic Church. The hitchhiker was against it. Foucault ([1978] 1999, 107) responded with the words I have used as my epigraph above: "Entirely woven through with elements that are imaginary, erotic, effective, corporal, sensual, and so on, [the church] is superb!" Here he seems to recognize that the church, like many institutions, contains the contradictions Marx attributed to the capitalist workplace and Foucault himself understood in terms of reverse discourse: the church generates both recognized forms of being and new forms of relationality that are irreducible to what it sanctions (marriage) or condemns (homosexuality). Canon law and the church's interrelations with the state may produce legible and legal subjects, but what Catholics call "the mysteries" go beyond these earthly boundaries, beyond the boundaries between mind and body, and beyond the boundaries between individuals. Yet they are not, for that, intimate in the secular sense of the word. Nor do they constitute friendships per se.

To wrest *Nightwood* out of its frame of degenerate literature and high modernism and resituate it in terms of a sacramental queer hypersociability akin to but not reducible to friendship, let us turn away from the universally admired, unrepresentable androgyne Robin Vote, and toward the much more difficult, weepy, overwrought femme, Nora Flood. A minor character remarks, in the novel's opening chapter, "Wir setzen an dieser Stelle über den Fluss"—something like "We set out in this place, here, over the river" (Barnes [1936] 2006, 17; translation mine). While the allusion is to the river Styx, the wave of passion on which the novel rides is Nora's. Her full name, "Nora Flood," echoes the Old Testament's story of Noah. In Christian theology, the flood that besets Noah prefigures the baptism; one might also say of course that the baptism rewrites aspects of the Hebrew text. Nora is the novel's figure for a sacrament more radical than penitence.

Early in the novel, Nora seems aligned with the verbal and textual: the narrator tells us that as "an early Christian ... [Nora] believed in the word" (Barnes [1936] 2006, 56). But this association of Nora with words morphs into an association with water; Matthew declares that Nora is "of a clean race, of a too eagerly washing people" (91). It's notable that Matthew describes Protestants as "a race," as if washing confers enough bodily likeness on the washers that they may be thought of as a people, with water replacing blood. But Matthew later declares, "We wash away our sense of sin, and what does that bath secure us? Sin, shining bright and hard. In what does a Latin bathe? True dust. We have made the literal error. We have used water, we are thus too sharply reminded. . . . The Anglo-Saxon has made the literal error; using water, he has washed away his page" (96). Though this passage nicely skewers the Anglo rage for spiritual and physical hygiene, oddly, here, baptism washes away the "page," the word earlier associated with Protestantism: in short, the "literal error" of using water and not the word is a promising one. To wash away the page and immerse oneself in the element is, in a sense, to return to the material, the dust in which "the Latin" bathes. Here, "Latin" also invokes both anti-Catholic discourse associating Catholicism with Italy and Spain, and, in its association with dust, a slight distance from Nora's whiteness.

Matthew eventually redeems this dusty (dirty?) version of baptism for something the novel insistently tropes as queer—the night: "I'm an angel on all fours, with a child's feet behind me, seeking my people that have never been made, going down face foremost, drinking the waters of night at the water hole of the damned, and I go into the waters, up to my heart, the terrible waters!" (Barnes [1936] 2006, 102). "Going down" differently than in the confession now, Matthew sees the sacrament of baptism as an act of "seeking my people that have never been made," or those outside of both polity and discourse. Gathering at the font with other outcasts, he enters these unclean waters not to be forgiven but to be conjoined with something, someone, somewhere, beyond the secular and racial imaginations not only of "peoplehood" but also of humanism's humanity. This is, remarkably, what a sacrament *does*: it uses a material substance to invite recipients into both an experience of otherness and a community. Just as the sacrament's proffered otherness is not limited to the earthly but includes the divine, its community is not limited to existing people but encompasses beings who were "never made" as solely human, let alone as a nation—the Apostles, the saints, the angels. Or, in Matthew's case, the damned.

We can see this dual, communitarian and other-extensive aspect of the sacrament, especially baptism, enacted in *Nightwood*'s consistent linkage of humans and nonhumans through water. Robin appears to us first figuratively immersed and transfigured into an animal, "as if sleep were a decay fishing her beneath the visible surface" (Barnes [1936] 2006, 38), the verb "fishing" curiously oscillating between "hunting her like a fish" and "turning her into a fish." In another example of water connecting the human and the inhuman, when Nora first meets Robin in the circus, a lioness comes to the edge of its cage, turns her head toward Robin, goes down on all fours, and, "as if a river were falling behind impassable heat, [the lioness's] eyes flowed in tears that never reached the surface" (60). This scene, in turn, prefigures the novel's famous ending in the ruined chapel on Nora's property, in which Robin goes down on all fours before Nora's dog, and then begins to fight with it as if she herself were a dog. The dog begins to cry, and Robin for the first time cries too, cries with him, "crying in shorter and shorter spaces, moving head to head, until [Robin] gave up, lying out, her hands beside her, her face turned and weeping; and the dog too gave up then, and lay down, his eyes bloodshot, his head flat along her knees" (180).

Why does this final liquidation of the boundary between human and animal, a typical trope in the literature of degeneration, take place in a chapel—and not only in a chapel but in front of "a contrived altar, before a Madonna" (Barnes [1936] 2006, 178), with flowers and toys heaped at her feet and two candles burning? It is because this scene, like the one in Matthew's apartment, figures a sacrament, one as powerful as the confessional but extremely different in its performance and meaning. Baptism is practiced by various Christian sects in at least four different ways—aspersion or sprinkling, affusion or pouring, immersion of part of the body, or total submersion—but its fundamental sign is water flowing to the head. *Nightwood*'s final scene is not one of washing body and soul clean, though, as Matthew has earlier described baptism. Instead, the novel's final scene separates ablution from absolution, and merges with Matthew's figure of the "waters of night."

Crucially, this last baptism through tears finally joins Robin's body with something. Whereas the confession is a technique that, Foucault (1990a) tells us, specified individuals—isolated, intensified, and consolidated acts into monadic identities—baptism is fundamentally a rite of engroupment, of admission to a social field irreducible to the human. Its fundamental work is not on the self, whether to shore it up or to dismantle it; baptism not only *asp*erses but *disp*erses the self. Then, too, the identity it confers, that of "Christian," has little to do with the specification of individuals; there is no postbaptismal apparatus that characterizes the baptized person as a *kind* of Christian (except, redundantly, a baptized one). Robin, then, is baptized at the end of *Nightwood* in boys' clothes, by and with a dog, not into the divine, and not merely into Matthew's community of human inverts, but into an unnameable interspecies form of belonging—very different from the unrepresentability and implicit whiteness with which she earlier seemed so aligned.

Furthermore, the sacraments do not only figure the "matter" of binding humans laterally, "populating" them, in Franchot's words across spatial imaginaries, but also offer a "vastly enlarged sense of temporality" (Franchot 1994, xxi). As the theologian Mark Jordan (2006, 331) reminds us, "A spiritual child through baptism exchanges biological family for the genealogy traced in ritual supersession." "Genealogy" is perhaps the wrong word here, as baptism enfolds the participant into a collective movement through time, whose simultaneous forward propulsion and backward extension have to do with predestination and fulfillment, prophesy and recapitulation, rather than with biological reproduction or even simple descent. Jordan writes, "Baptism inaugurates a series of inhabitations or vicarious performances that reach backwards, sideways, and forwards through an ingathered history" (328). This question of how history can be "ingathered," which is to say crystallized into formations that can illuminate the past, can catalyze the future otherwise, and can create diagonal lies across the temporal field, is crucial to queer theory. It counters not only the (admittedly promising) nonrelationality of the antisocial thesis but also the (much less promising) ahistoricality of that way of construing queer. A queer hypersocial thesis, then, necessarily entails the question of the social as it binds us with what and who have come before us, and will survive after us: *Nightwood* clarifies, again, the role of the sacraments in making this possibility felt—especially in 1936, when "I am a lesbian" might seem to mean, at least on the face of things, restriction to horizontal community.[18]

Imposition, or, the Hands of Historicity

Franchot (1994) reminds us that in anti-Catholic discourse, the Catholic Church was figured as static and resistant to historical change. This was part of how Protestants constructed history itself, a seemingly secular and secularizing concept: as a "text-oriented" (Franchot 1994, 6) progression from the Reformation to the present, dependent on and taking place within the pages of "biblically allusive historical and fictional narratives" (7) that both mimicked and supplanted Scriptural historiography. This seemingly secular but deeply Protestant mode of history is contested by Jordan's notion of "ingathering" the past, a term I take to mean apprehending the past as more than a sequence of events in which one supersedes the next—rather, it means something akin to Walter Benjamin's concept of the convolute, literally a sheaf (Eiland and McLaughlin 1999, xiv). The term "convolute" invokes the leaf in the bud, the event in longitudinal history rolled back over and over on itself in lateral relations such that events of different times can be thought or felt in conjunction.

Following Jordan and Benjamin, then, we might ask what a sacra/mental historicist method would look like.

We might expect that it would look like New Historicism, which also privileges a kind of sideways ingathering of fragments from a single moment in time, reading them as symptoms of a larger cultural logic, in a method with which academics are still reckoning. But as David Aers (2003) has discussed in great depth, New Historicism was elaborated by Catherine Gallagher and Stephen Greenblatt (2001) in direct *opposition* to the sacraments and to sacramental ways of thinking. Gallagher and Greenblatt equate the sacraments with sterile and ahistorical doctrinal formalism, as opposed to living and vital history. Analogizing the art object to the Eucharist, they write, "When the literary text ceases to be [like the Sacrament] a sacred, self-enclosed, and self-justifying miracle, when in the skeptical mood we foster it begins to lose at least some of the special power ascribed to it, its boundaries begin to seem less secure and it loses exclusive rights to the experience of wonder.... [The new historicist project] is concerned with finding the creative power that shapes literary works *outside* the narrow boundaries in which it had hitherto been located, as well as *within* those boundaries" (12). I am sympathetic to the New Historicist project, and remain deeply invested in questions of how texts contain the historicizing seeds of their own undoing.[19] But given Gallagher and Greenblatt's rhetorical divide between a dead formalism and a creative, shaping historicism—a divide that, we might note, always risks inflection by the homo/hetero binary—I think it may not be a coincidence that an antisacramental New Historicism and the New Americanist writing that followed it in the 1990s were not particularly hospitable to queer theory, that it has taken a generation of queer theorists trained under this method some time to formulate other ways of doing and thinking history.[20] At the same time, what queer culture and by extension queer theory may have in common with New Historicism is, paradoxically, something sacramental: a relation to the fragmentary object as the invocation of and invitation to a world (see Muñoz 2009), of which relation queer camp is paradigmatic.

Just as the anecdote is the New Historicist key to what Greenblatt calls speaking with the dead, a camp performance is the reanimation of a historically specific, culturally "dead," ideologically oversaturated object (a Cole Porter song, a Dolly Parton wig, a Wildean gesture, Joan

Crawford as Mommie Dearest).[21] The *Oxford English Dictionary* dates the first usage of "camp" to 1909 as "[o]stentatious, exaggerated, affected, theatrical; effeminate or homosexual," and both this meaning and the practice seem to have emerged in tandem with the gender inversion model of homosexuality.[22] It is impossible to pinpoint just when outmoded or archaic objects became part of that exaggerated performance and affect, but Djuna Barnes's roman à clef *The Ladies Almanack* (1928), which spoofs the Left Bank Parisian lesbian subculture of Natalie Barney and her salons in seventeenth-century Baroque style, suggests that by the first third of the twentieth century, the historicist aspect of camp sensibility—which I have elsewhere called "temporal drag" (Freeman 2010) and David Román (2005, 137) calls "archival drag"—had been consolidated.[23] I suggested in chapter 3 that pseudohistoricist time travel novels and highly stylized historical novels such as *Salammbô* created settings within which alternate possibilities for gender and sexuality could be made into imagined worlds: accordingly, Barnes and the performers she creates in her novels scavenge around more fragmented pasts, picking up individual elements or stylistic gestures to express sexual dissidence.

Camp parts ways with New Historicism, though, by treating its historical fragment as a doorway not just into a "true" past of violence and oppression but also into a series of complex temporal relations: acknowledgments of contemporary paradoxes and struggles, invocations of a future to come, surrogate relations to the dead, nonlinear models of descent (and dissent). In other words, camp has an irreverent sacramental sensibility. In *The Premodern Condition*, Bruce Holsinger (2005, 5–6) has described the sacramental sensibility as one "which finds in discrete past events and surviving relics the wondrous promise of an invisible totality it can only occasionally glimpse in the lived present." In other words, the sacrament takes up something acknowledged to have happened in the past, such as the Last Supper, and uses that fragment as a prismatic lens for two things: for the fleeting presence of utopia in the now (the body of Christ reassembled in the communion), and for a peek at the kingdom of heaven that awaits believers in the future. In fact, recent queer theologians have connected this sacramental sensibility with José Esteban Muñoz's (2009) work on how glimpses of utopian futures appear in ephemeral present-tense performances (see Brintnall, Marchal, and Moore 2017). By resurrecting the term "sacramental," Holsinger points toward ways of knowing that include desires, bodies, and fantasies, and which the stridently secularized historicisms of New Historicism, and even the astringently atheistic philosophies of some continental theory, tend to disavow or displace. Aers points out, correctly, that religious ritual and its treatment of objects are not by any means an avoidance of conflict, contemporaneity, or narrative, three elements crucial to what Gallagher and Greenblatt call "history" and counterpose to religion. Nor do the sacraments avoid diachrony, local contingency, process, or accidental likeness, other aspects of practicing historicisms new and otherwise.

In fact, *Nightwood* is as suffused with the desire to speak with the dead as New Historicism ever was, but understands sacramentality as a way of doing so rather than as a mode of avoidant self-enclosure. Importantly, the novel figures the "doing" of history as an imposition or laying-on of hands. This gesture, the essential matter of the rite of holy orders that admits properly trained men into the formal priesthood, also appears in confirmation, baptism, and extreme unction, and forms a part of the blessing administered by priests to penitents, the married couple, communion takers, and so on. The laying on of hands is another visible sign of the Holy Spirit, understood as a means of conveying that spirit to the newly ordained. It is also sometimes interpreted as a way of imparting ministerial gifts, or charism; some theologians describe it as an ongoing conduit between recipient and divine source.[24] Its role as a means of power transferred from one priest to the next also gives it a kind of supercessionary character going back to the original Apostles: in this sense the laying on of hands conveys something both eternal (divinity) and historical (succession).

In *Nightwood,* hands are the relay for a less purely monumental or sequential movement between past and present. About Robin, Felix observes, "When she touched a thing, her hands seemed to take the place of the eye. He thought: 'she has the touch of the blind who, because they see more with their fingers, forget more in their minds.' Her fingers would go forward, hesitate, tremble, as if they had found a face in the dark. When her hand finally came to rest, the palm closed; it was as if she had stopped a crying mouth" (Barnes [1936] 2006, 45–46). Robin's hand, her touch, overtakes the visible, supplanting both eye and "crying mouth" or speaking instrument. In a Nietzschean ([1873–76] 1997) mode of amnesia as a catalyst for experiencing the present, Robin's touch also stays the movement of memory. Importantly, *Nightwood*'s regime of palpability contains within it a kind of forgetting of the cognitive, or remembering of the visceral, that founds the novel's alternatives to genealogy, lineal descent, and history proper. Here is one example, one of the most beautiful passages in the novel, and a complex reimagining of the imposition of hands: "As an amputated hand cannot be disowned because it is experiencing a futurity, of which the victim is its forebear, so Robin was an amputation that Nora could not renounce. As the wrist longs, so her heart longed" (Barnes [1936] 2006, 64).

In this elaborate synecdoche, hand and wrist are cleaved in both senses of the word. They cannot be severed, yet their separation is necessary to assert the difference between their futures: the hand is experiencing a futurity of which the wrist can only be an ancestor. But rather than touching in a forward movement, here the hand longs physically backward through the wrist, wishing itself extensive enough to meet the wrist not in the past but in a future that precludes it (else the hand would not be "amputated," and Nora cannot renounce Robin precisely *because* Robin is an amputation and Nora feels her as a phantom limb). The hand, that touch that enables forgetting "with the mind," though not apparently with the body, opens up a past of suffering, and a future of rejoining. Both memory and futurity here are metacarpal.

In *Nightwood*, then, the laying on of hands gets transmuted from a means of signifying a relation to the divine or bestowing the gifts of ministry to a way of palpably (and erotically, given the significance of hands for lesbian sex) reorganizing relations between past and present. The gesture, appearing only fleetingly, nevertheless links the affiliative aspect of the baptism to the complexly filiative work of the Eucharist.

Blood, or Food

Matthew O'Connor's distinction between Protestantism and Catholicism turns on the figure of blood ("in the blood"), explicitly counterposed to words ("the gift of gab"). But what does it mean to say that Catholicism—perhaps even Christianity—is "in the blood?" How can Christianity be sanguinary, when it has been so consistently theorized and theologized as a form of sodality beyond biological kinship? In fact, the new covenant is supposed to be a counterimaginary to family. In its substitution of the bonds of faith for those of genealogy, Christianity also counters what we now know as the eugenic concept of "race," or the idea that something corporeal connects earthly families across the boundaries of both domicile and historical moment. In some ways, then, the bread and wine of Christian theology are simply another version of the baptismal waters, insofar as they posit belonging as a relationship of shared fluids superseding both the fictions of sperm and blood that organize the meanings of kinship, and the imposition of hands, insofar as this represents descent as a matter of surrogation.

Here are the words the priest speaks at the Eucharist, quoting Christ at the last supper:

> On the day before he was to suffer,
> he took bread in his holy and venerable hands,
> and with eyes raised to heaven
> to you, O God, his almighty Father,
> giving you thanks, he said the blessing,
> broke the bread
> and gave it to his disciples, saying:
> TAKE THIS, ALL OF YOU, AND EAT OF IT,
> FOR THIS IS MY BODY,
> WHICH WILL BE GIVEN UP FOR YOU.
>
> In a similar way, when supper was ended,
> he took this precious chalice
> in his holy and venerable hands,
> and once more giving you thanks, he said the blessing
> and gave the chalice to his disciples, saying:
> TAKE THIS, ALL OF YOU, AND DRINK FROM IT,
> FOR THIS IS THE CHALICE OF MY BLOOD,
> THE BLOOD OF THE NEW AND ETERNAL COVENANT,
> WHICH WILL BE POURED OUT FOR YOU AND FOR MANY
> FOR THE FORGIVENESS OF SINS.
> DO THIS IN MEMORY OF ME. (Catholic Church 2011, 639)

It's easy, and tempting, to see this eaten body and poured-out blood as a radical reorganization of corporeal connectivity beyond both family and race, and indeed this is what I've been suggesting. But *Nightwood* complicates this sacrament by reminding us of the role of the Jew in blood theology. The novel's figure for blood as lineage, kinship, and descent is Robin's husband Felix von Volkbein, the fake Baron born on a bed stitched with the emblems of a made-up aristocracy. Far from being a nobleman, Felix's father Guido is "a Jew of Italian descent" (Barnes [1936] 2006, 4), whose lineage is entirely fictional: his borrowed name, Volkbein, contains the figure of a biologized people, a "volk"; he has stolen a coat of arms and invented a "list of progenitors . . . who had never existed" (5–6); and the portraits of his father and mother that eventually hang in his dining room are "reproductions of two intrepid and ancient actors" (9–10) that he found in a dusty attic. Guido also carries a handkerchief whose color scheme indexes the running of the Jews at Corso in 1466, making him what the narrator calls, in racialized terms, "the sum total of what is the Jew . . . black with the pain of a participation that, four centuries later, made him a victim, as he felt . . . the degradation by which his people had survived" (4–5). Here we see the stereotype of the Jew as Sander Gilman (1991) has described it: figuratively black, mired in history, incurably bound to racial ties (or as the novel puts it, "heavy with impermissible blood" [5]), greedy, duplicitous, supplicating, and eternally victimized.

So what, then, do Christians consume when they figuratively drink the blood of a Jew? In one of the novel's most complex statements about the Eucharist, *Nightwood*'s narrator remarks, "The Christian traffic in retribution has made the Jew's history a commodity; it is the medium through which he receives, at the necessary moment, the serum of his own past that he may offer it again as his blood" (Barnes [1936] 2006, 13). Here, retribution, or penance, turns out to be a means of recirculating the past when it is rethought as a means of injecting the penitent (here, the Jew) with the "serum," the blood, of *history*. The past, marked as Jewish, becomes the sacramental blood of Christ. In other words, Barnes rethinks penance in precisely Eucharistic terms, as a sacrificial offering of blood that reanimates a community, as sacraments do. But Barnes also rethinks the Eucharist as an offering of history, of pastness itself, in ways that the New Historicist description of the sacrament as merely formal belies. Barnes's problematic formulation that Jewish sacrifice is the bedrock of a "commodified" Christian redemption seems to damn Jews and

Christians in the same breath, but it does suggest that the sacraments are deeply, complexly historicist.

Nightwood also recognizes this process as in keeping with capitalism. According to Matthew O'Connor, the function of Christians is to "bring up from that depth charming and fantastic superstitions through which the slowly and tirelessly milling Jew once more becomes the 'collector' of his own past" (Barnes [1936] 2006, 13). Disturbingly, here Christians recycle histories of suffering and exclusion into objects of consumption resold to their original owners—retelling the Old Testament as the New, we can presume. And they do so in ways that exactly follow the movement of the commodity-fetish: A Jew's "undoing," Matthew declares, "is never profitable until some *goy* has put it back into such shape that it can again be offered as a 'sign'" (13). He continues, "A Jew's undoing is never his own, it is God's; his rehabilitation is never his own, it is a Christian's" (13). And, of course, the commodity-fetish is precisely the thing that obscures histories of suffering—the relation between owner and laborer—in a fantasy that the subject can be renewed, eternally, by the product: it is the form of formalism itself. This is certainly one way to read the sacramental, perhaps one in keeping with Gallagher and Greenblatt's (2001) way, and the novel understands that the sacrament *can* be, simply, an uncomplicated reincorporation and sanctification of the Jew. Indeed, as Gil Anidjar (2009, 48) persuasively argues, the drinking of sacramental blood is not actually separable from later, racializing figurations of blood purity: Eucharist and eugenics—etymologically *eu-* (good) *charism* (grace) and *eu-* (good) *gens* (people) respectively—are not that far apart. Early Christians imagined themselves as those who, by drinking the pure blood of Christ, became themselves a pure people. In this sense, Barnes's choice of the term "serum" is not incidental: a serum is actually plasma purged of clotting agents, used as an antitoxin, and Barnes seems to imagine the Eucharist as, precisely and paradoxically, a Jewish offering made to purge a people of Jewishness. Here we can see again the off-whiteness of Catholicism in its entanglement, despite its invocations of blood purity, with a racialized Judaism.

Yet *Nightwood*'s other images of the Eucharist emphasize the quality of the host as *food* rather than as purified serum, and thus turn it other ways. It is notable that nobody in the novel seems to consume any meals, though Matthew mentions eating a salad and everyone drinks like a fish. Instead, people are troped as edible: for instance, the circus performer Frau Mann has "a skin that was the pattern of her costume, a bodice of lozenges, red and yellow . . . one somehow felt they ran through her as the design runs through hard holiday candies" (Barnes [1936] 2006, 16). A more directly sacramental image of receiving the past through the incorporative gestures of the Eucharist by eating people is reiterated in the first account of Robin Vote: "Such a woman is the infected carrier of the past . . . we feel that we could eat her, she who is eaten death returning, for only then do we put our face close to the blood on the lips of our forefathers" (41). Here, the image of "eaten death returning" is a way to come into contact with the savagery of our ancestors, with the violence and impurity indexed by the blood on their lips that could indicate either their cannibalism or their own version of a brutal Eucharist, or both. This passage proposes eating the other not only as a movement beyond language—as Foucault ([1981] 1984, 136) describes friendship, two people meeting "without terms or convenient words, with nothing to assure them about the meaning of the movement that carries them toward each other"—but also as time travel, a means of quite literally tasting the blood of the past. In other words, in *Nightwood*'s economy of sacra/mental friendship, the encounter with the other must include an encounter with his or her past, and without the Christian recycling of this into a commodity. Foucault's (136) description of friendship as "the formation of new alliances and the tying together of unforeseen lines of force," then, is perhaps not temporally thick enough, not as rich as the blood on the lips of Robin's predecessors.

What we have here is the image of a sacrament as something more than a palpable means of infusing a people with otherness such that they feel a visceral sense of belonging to one another and to God, important as that might be for countermanding marital and genealogical notions of togetherness. Instead, what I am describing as the sense-method of a Barnesian sacra/mentality includes the rupturing bodily encounters both excised from the rite of penance by the organized church, and indicative of what it means to really *host* the other, which includes opening oneself to the pain of their past. *Nightwood*'s counterpoint to the regime of sexuality, with the latter's verbalization of everything, is something like cannibalism, a completely different use of the mouth—though I'd argue that it is a mutual and reciprocal eating in which neither party is completely dead. Thus for *Nightwood*, cannibalism is less a shattering of the self than a remixing of it. This is what I would like to stress as crucial to a queer hypersociability that countermands both the sexological, taxonomic imperative of the fin de siècle and modernism, and the current queer antisocial thesis: *Nightwood*'s method of affinity risks wounding encounters between bodies, and encounters between previously wounded bodies. Yet its queer hypersociability is not afraid of risking images of wholeness in the figure, or of taking the figure too literally (or, indeed, of taking the figure into the body). It understands that history hurts, but the gustatory trope allows for other experiences of history, including that of satisfaction. And it does not disavow connections between humans, and between humans and others, that some might call merely religious.

We can see a glimpse of this queer sociability that I am linking to a sacramental outlook in Matthew's statement that "Nora will leave [Robin] some day, but though those two are buried at opposite ends of the earth, one dog will find them both" (Barnes [1936] 2006, 113). What links Robin and Nora is not a rosy vision of a shared subjectivity achieved by eating the same substance, nor an exalted spiritual state of living together after death, but a shared susceptibility to *being eaten* by the same creature. Here again, animals lead us to the extralinguistic aspect of the sacramental, and its ability, as a sense-method, to provide connective tissue between the dead and the living, the past and the present. And it is Nora, again, who figures the passion of giving her body and blood to be eaten for this purpose: "Nora robbed herself for everyone; incapable of giving herself warning, she was continually turning about to find herself diminished.... She was by fate one of those people who are born unprovided for, except in the provision of herself" (57–58). This figure of eating impurity, of offering the body as necessarily impure because human food, throws a wrench into any fantasy of confession as communication, as language purified of power relations—if indeed one could have such a fantasy after Foucault. The narrator insists that Nora's "good is incommunicable" (57), that her passions "ma[k]e the seventh day immediate" (58) in a way that obviates questions of belief and makes faith a material matter. The narrator continues, "To 'confess' to her was an act even more secret than the communication provided by a priest ... she recorded without reproach or accusation, being shorn of self-reproach or self-accusation" (58). In the figure of a confession that is "more secret" than the "communication provided by a priest," the pun on "communication" (which means both to converse and to administer the sacraments) suggests that Nora offers up and receives a Eucharist of a visceral, nonverbal kind.

In all, then, *Nightwood* moves from the confessional whereby acts, fantasies, and desires turn into discourse; through the baptism whereby immersion in, drinking of, and exchanging water enables a reconfiguration of the social; through the laying on of hands whereby the past is a visceral encounter; to the Eucharist, where consumption remixes both selfhood and the present. Tracking this, I have asked: if sexuality and its other in the project of ascesis both emerge from the rite of confession, what would the other that Foucault calls friendship, and I am calling queer hypersociability, look like if imagined in terms of the rite of the Eucharist, a sense-method that seems opposed to ecstatic religion but shares the latter's fantasies about how bodies can be conjoined through material means? It would, I have suggested, look more engaged with pastness, violence, and memory, and involve collisions of bodies with one another and with spirit and animal, rather than just like sex as we know it. If New Historicism also emerged from a rejection of that Eucharist, what would a Eucharistic imagining of the historical look like, and what is its purchase for queer theory? It would not counterpose the figural and the historical but exploit the trace of the visceral in the sign for new forms of connectivity, insisting that the queer and the social are inseparable. I think *Nightwood* helps immensely in thinking about these questions. The sacra/mentality of Djuna Barnes lies in her commitment to the tangible, the perceptible: in her version of history, we leave our body and our blood to be eaten by the dogs.

RHYTHM TRAVEL

In Amiri Baraka's short-short story "Rhythm Travel"
([1995] 2009), an African American man uses timing
to time travel—specifically, he seizes musical meter as
a way to simultaneously move from historical scene to
historical scene and to join with groups of people who
preceded him and will succeed him. After manifesting
himself before the story's narrator as Theolonius Monk's
"Misterioso" (1958), the unnamed traveler declares,
"Dis visibility, be unseen. But now I can be around anyway, perceived, felt, heard. I can be the music" (Baraka
[1995] 2009, 148). Through this technology—which
he names, in its various developmental stages in rapid
succession, "Molecular Anyscape. The Resoulocator . . .
T-Disappear" (148)—the man has solved the problem
of visibility that plagues the spectacularized African
American male, creating an "unseen" visibility, a sense-
method for evincing himself into historically specific
scenes of sociability. His latest improvements, he tells

the narrator, have "pushed the Anyscape into Rhythm Spectroscopic Transformation" (149). While the science here is shaky, the idea encoded in this name is that sound can be parsed into discrete units on a spectrum, rhythmic items which become exchangeable for one another across time. This allows the traveler to enter other historical moments by becoming a piece of period music and then reappearing "anywhere and anytime" (149) that particular music plays—much as *Of One Blood*'s Dianthe Lusk seems to have traveled across time from ancient Ethiopia by way of sing-ing, except that here the emphasis is not on lyrics or melody but on the beat. As Baraka (1994 [2009], 123) puts it elsewhere, "Rhythm is the most basic, the shortest of all stories, the Be & At." In other words, rhythm, "beat," is both manifestation (be) and location (at), which makes some sense of why it allows Baraka's rhythm traveler to go places.

While "Rhythm Travel" is a late twentieth-century work of Afrofu-turist science fiction, it is worth pausing to note the way it gathers to-gether the themes I have been pursuing in this book. First, it develops the idea that being together with others is a matter of keeping in time with them. Baraka recognizes that timing is crucial not only to how respon-sive flesh becomes constituted into bodiliness and subjectivity but also to engroupment—to how bodies come together, and how subjectivities are constituted and modified in that coming together. As he writes in an essay, rhythm is sociability in a nutshell, for it is "the splitting of the one into two" (Baraka [1994] 2009, 122). In other words, there is no rhythm without more than one sonic or kinesthetic event, and rhythm is what conjoins them; similarly, the body becomes ex-tensive, stretching out-ward in rhythmic response, becoming more than itself. Timing, then, is a constitutive aspect of how bodies become oriented toward one another both synchronically and diachronically, how they come to feel tempo-rally coincident or connected across historical eras.

"Rhythm Travel" links this process to the two outer historical edges of this book, an admittedly somewhat underspecified period of enslave-ment and an early twentieth century specified by the date 1920. As to the first, Baraka's unnamed traveler describes becoming the slave song "Take This Hammer" and being "sung" into the scene, as he echoes slaves dig-ging a well to the musical accompaniment of their own voices: "They were singing this and I begin to echo. A big hollow echo, a sorta blue shattering echo" (Baraka [1995] 2009, 150). "Shattered" out of their misery by this transhistorical call-and-response, the slaves "got to smilin because it made them feel good," while the owners and overseers take on a rhythm of their own, "turn[ing] their heads sharply back and forth, looking behind them and at the slaves" (150). Here, timing has momentarily united the slaves to one another and to their freeborn descendants, while deindividualizing their white captors into a head-bobbing, paranoid mass. In a second historical allusion, Baraka's traveler finances the improvements on his technology by robbing banks, a nod to W. E. B. Du Bois's science fiction short story "The Comet" ([1920] 1999), whose protagonist is a messenger serving a bank. Yet another moment of homage to Du Bois appears when the traveler remarks, "You probably heard of the Scatting Comet" (Baraka [1995] 2009, 150), turning the comet away from the doom it portends in Du Bois's story and toward another rhythmic act in which the body, including the human voice, is an instrument for sociability rather than a signifier of it. Whereas Du Bois's comet emits toxic gases that kill off almost the entirety of New York City, Baraka's Scatting Comet invites the traveler and the narrator into a scene of possibility. As the traveler assures the narrator in the story's last lines, "Ain't no danger. Just don't pick a corny tune" (150).

"Rhythm Travel" also nicely condenses the themes of this book because it implicitly endorses the idea of biopolitics as a merger of two developments in the organization of time: discipline, which oriented living bodies toward one another through inculcating synchrony between their movements, and historical time, which oriented living bodies toward the dead and the unborn through inculcating a sense of temporal sequence, consequence, and succession. Thought in terms of time, biopolitics consists of managing populations first via individual disciplinary techniques, then through large-scale coordination of their activities, and finally by their ideological situation on a timeline of those consigned either to ahistoricity/obsolescence or modernity/futurity—the timeline of race. In his trip to the plantation, Baraka's time traveler uses the foundation of discipline, the rhythmic activity of keeping together in time, to enter the era of slavery in which he, his compatriots, and his predecessors count as ahistorical waste, and to bring them some momentary pleasure. In his trip to the Scatting Comet, he also enters the scientific future, claiming, "I turned into some Sun Ra and hung out inside gravity" (Baraka [1995] 2009, 150). Becoming the music of Sun Ra, the traveler can unmake a law that is both physiological and political: the downward pull of gravity has special purchase for a population terrorized by the mob hangings that emerged after the Civil War, and hanging "out" rather than "down," being "inside" of a force rather than the object of it, suggests an ability to bend it other ways.

These kinds of acts are exactly what I have been tracking in this book: I have been interested in small-scale temporal coincidences between bodies, achieved through corporeal praxes opening out from face-to-face community toward the larger population and toward other moments on the historical timeline. Through representations of the Shakers, I have demonstrated how dance was used for face-to-face recruitment away from the norms of Protestant-secular, heterogendered whiteness. Through nineteenth-century African American literature, I have shown how miming death was used as a wedge against social death. Through Twain's and Hopkins's early science fiction novels, I have tracked how amateur historiography, for which time travel is a figure, worked against dominant historicisms and their racial implications. Through Melville's and Stein's tales of debility, I have suggested a queer and crip chronicity that countered the rhythms of racial uplift and human resource management. And through Djuna Barnes's modernist novel shot through with Catholic sensibilities, I have laid out how the sacramental contested the Protestant secularity of the regime of sexuality itself.

Taken together, these chapters remind us that the nineteenth century was not just a drama of national space and scale, inflected by imperialism, capitalism, and Manifest Destiny (even as these too are temporal constructs). It was also a drama of temporality, in which bodies were timed into official and minor forms of belonging, and arranged in historical relation to one another—a drama whose opening and closing curtains do not neatly correspond with the turn of centuries but tangle with one another as regimes of secularity, race, and health, among other forms of power, rise and consolidate. My hope is that this book also matters for the present, insofar as it allows us to conceptualize social formation beyond and beside the linguistic, as an embodied and affective process. Sense-methods are not just for the past. They are for now, for being around otherwise: perceived, felt, heard.

NOTES

....

Introduction

1 See, e.g., the *Rule of St. Benedict* (6th century AD), which prescribes the eight canonical hours for prayers and hours for meals. Foucault's second and third volumes of *The History of Sexuality* also describe the regimes of self-care and bodily
exercise that, while not precisely equivalent to the timetable, greatly precede the
prison timetable he uses as a figure for modern discipline. See Foucault 1990b and
1990c.

2 Thompson 1967 dates the uneven emergence of time-discipline somewhat earlier, at
the turn of the eighteenth century.

3 I thank my second anonymous reader for Duke University Press for this formulation.

4 Foucault (1979, 155) is rather breezy about what preceded this new body, the
"mechanical body."

5 "The time of each must be adjusted to the time of the others in such a way that the
maximum quality of forces may be extracted from each and combined with the
optimum result" (Foucault 1979, 164).

6 The majority of essays in Gregg and Seigworth's *The Affect Studies Reader* (2010)
engage with the concept of habitus.

7 In the first volume of *The History of Sexuality* (1990a), Foucault describes cultures
with an *ars erotica* as non-Western. In the second two volumes (Foucault 1990b and
1990c), he considers the *ars erotica* of ancient Greece and their reformulations under
Roman rule, respectively, but with an emphasis on practices of selfhood and self-
knowledge rather than on collective action, making them less useful for this project
than they might otherwise be.

8 Here, I am reversing Hardt and Negri's (2004, 94–95) distinction between bio*power*
as sovereign order, separate from society, and bio*politics* as immanent, relational, and
potentially oppositional, precisely because in much recent queer-theoretical work,
"biopolitics" has been centered on the state.

9 I owe this formulation to my first anonymous reader at Duke University Press.

10 A working bibliography on American sentimental culture would include E. Barnes
1997; Berlant 2008; Burgett 1998; Carby 1987; Coviello 2005; Douglas 1977; Ellison
1999; Hendler 2001; Howard 1999; Luciano 2007; Noble 2000; Romero 1997; S.
Samuels 1992; Schuller 2017; S. M. Smith 1999; and Tate 1992. Schuller 2017 has

made a compelling case that sentimentalism was first and foremost a racializing discourse, with gender dimorphism following as an effect of whiteness.

11 I have learned the most about the racialization of sentiment from Schuller 2017 and S. M. Smith 1999.

12 Anderson 1982; Luciano 2007; and Kete 2000 are astute about the role of mourning ritual in organizing collectively-felt time. On collecting and tourism as part of the inculcation of historical feeling, see Lockwood 2015. Brief histories of the practice of historical reenactment can be found in McCalman and Pickering 2010. For a beautiful theorization of historical reenactment, see Schneider 2011. The history of *tableaux vivants* is detailed in Holmström 1967, 209–63.

13 On femme receptivity, see Cvetkovich 2003, 49–82.

14 Thanks to Dana Luciano for bringing this connection to my attention.

15 For an assertion that the gay white male archive and the antisocial thesis are linked, see Halberstam in Caserio, Edelman, Halberstam, and Muñoz 2006.

Chapter 1. Shake It Off

1 For example, "An Indian Tune" (undated) ran "Quo we lorezum qwini /qui qwini qwe qwini qwe / Hock a nick a hick nick / qwini qwi qwo cum" (Andrews [1963] 2011, 74), while "Arkumshaw's Farewell" (also undated) featured the lyrics "Me tanke de white man for who me did fess / Me tank de good Elder who he did address / Me feel poor and needy me want me soul save / An now lest me weary de white man me leave" (Andrews [1963] 2011, 75).

2 On the Mormons, see Coviello 2013; Bentley 2002; and Hickman 2014. On the heteroreproductive timing of the period, see Luciano 2007.

3 Jagose 2012 offers another example outside the historical scope of this chapter, focusing on the promotion of simultaneous orgasms in marriage and sex manuals of the early twentieth century.

4 On celibacy as a form of sociability in reform cultures, see Kahan 2013.

Chapter 2. The Gift of Constant Escape

1 See, for example, Holland 2000; Luciano 2003; Parham 2008.

2 On surrogation, see Roach 1996.

3 See Harris 1881a. This American tale dates from at least the nineteenth century but has its roots in West African storytelling as well as other traditions; the folklorist D. L Ashliman characterizes it as Aarne-Thompson-Uther type 1 and traces it to nineteenth-century Europe, Scotland, Scandinavia, and Palestine, as well as India's *Panchatantra,* compiled between the third and fifth centuries AD (see Ashliman 2000–2018). For the African version, see Courlander and Prempeh 1957. The Bahamas version starring Boukee is from Parsons 1918. Variants are also catalogued in Green 2006.

4 I thank my second anonymous reader for Duke University Press for this formulation.

5　I thank my second anonymous reader for Duke University Press for helping me think through a more precise version of this paragraph.

6　Genovese ([1974] 1976) cites Nietzsche 1927, 432; Troeltsch 1950; and Kautsky 1953. See Genovese (1974) 1976, 707–8, notes 5, 7, and 8.

7　Several theorists of black domesticity have explored how black women, including Jacobs, both exploited and subverted domestic ideology. See, for example, Carby 1987; DuCille 1993; and Reid-Pharr 1999.

8　For an analysis of how Douglass's and Jacobs's narratives understand marriage as a complicated and not always salutary relation to the state, see Coviello 2013.

9　This is somewhat different than Hartman's beautiful "The Time of Slavery" (2002). Hartman means to situate the temporality of slavery in the present, for black Europeans and Americans. Jacobs, writing contemporaneously with slavery, means to repudiate the deathly form of domesticity.

10　Here, of course, I am thinking about Michael Brown, who on August 9, 2014, in Ferguson, Missouri, was shot twelve times by police officer Darren Dean Wilson despite being unarmed. Brown's body was left in the road for four hours. See Hunn and Bell 2014.

11　In Fanon's ([1952] 1994) *Black Skin, White Masks,* the narrator describes being hailed as a "Negro" by a taunting white child, an experience that, far from confirming and consolidating his bodily imago, ruptures it. The scene famously reverses Lacan's mirror stage, in which the child experiences its separateness and bodily boundaries through an alienated mirror image. Thus the affirmation of blackness is, in Fanon's terms, a negation of psychic and bodily wholeness.

12　The most comprehensive explanation of Afropessimism, which attributes the term to Saidiya Hartman and explains the original meaning, is Wilderson 2010; see especially 346–47n9.

13　See also Hartman (2002, 759), which argues in a slightly different vein vis-à-vis African ancestors that "we are coeval with the dead."

14　The most forceful articulations of the relationship between blackness and non- or antihumanity, besides Fanon, are Wynter 1984 and (1992) 1994; and Wilderson 2010. Various other ways of formulating this include Chandler 2008; Gordon 2010; Hartman 2003; Sexton 2008; and Spillers 1987. I mean here not to reduce these works of scholarship to one another but to mark them as being in a larger conversation.

15　See, for example, Richard Wright's *Native Son* ([1940] 2005).

16　I owe this formulation to my second reader for Duke University Press.

17　See Mbembe (2003, 23): "The slave nevertheless is able to draw almost any object, instrument, language, or gesture into a performance and then stylize it." See also much of Fred Moten's work; for example, Moten 2003, 2008a, 2008b.

18　I name Moten an Afro-optimist in the playful spirit of queer studies, where "queer optimism" (see Snediker 2009 for the phrase) has been described as a response to the antisocial thesis, and following Sexton 2011.

19 Cohen (1997) makes much the same point in "Punks, Bulldaggers, and Welfare Queens," where she argues that a queer politics based on radical outsiderness to heterosexuality cannot recognize the ways that even the marital-reproductive black family is never accorded full heteronormativity.

20 In the bibliography, I list this first edition under Charles Stearns's names, following critical assessment that this edition contains a great deal of Stearns's writing, and to distinguish it from the 1851 version, in which Brown apparently had a greater hand. Quotations are from the 2008 edition of the 1851 version.

21 See, for example, Brooks 2006, 71.

22 The credit for locating the figures of Brown and his box—figures 2.1–2.5—belongs to Ruggles 2003. I thank him for this work, and hope to build on it by closely interpreting the images.

23 I am reading Brown's performances with his box, which preceded his stage work as a mesmerist and practitioner of electro-biology, as a deliberately incomplete enactment of the "fugitive," much in the way Britt Rusert (2017) reads Brown's later stage work as "fugitive science."

24 On polyrhythm, see Arom 1991. On the slave songs, see, famously, Du Bois (1903) 1997.

25 The racial element of the zombie myth is that *voudon*, or "voodoo," makes zombification possible.

Chapter 3. Feeling Historicisms

1 Collins (1986) distinguishes between narratives where time travel is explicitly rendered as a hallucination, thought experiment, or dream, and fictions of explicitly physical time travel.

2 The works Twain read before writing *Connecticut Yankee* include William Edward Hartpole Lecky's *History of European Morals,* Hippolyte Taine's *The Ancient Regime,* Carlyle's *The French Revolution,* George Standring's *People's History of English Aristocracy,* and Charles Ball's *Slavery in the United States.* For a comprehensive bibliography of Twain's historical readings that is probably in need of updating, see J. D. Williams 1965.

3 For a good account of this process, see Kahan 2017.

4 The name Amyas is derived from the Latin *amare,* "to love."

5 "Yankee" (n.), etymology, *Oxford English Dictionary*, last accessed November 13, 2018, http://www.oed.com/viewdictionaryentry/Entry/231174.

6 "Hank" (n.), definitions 7 and 4a respectively (rare or dialect), *Oxford English Dictionary,* last accessed November 13, 2018, http://www.oed.com/viewdictionaryentry/Entry/83999.

7 On precedent, casuistry, and romantic historiography, see Goode 2009; on amateur historiography, see B. G. Smith 1998; on the dangers of pleasure, see, for example Horkheimer and Adorno 1969. On queer theory's dangerous ahistoricism, see especially Morton 1993.

8 I owe the phrase "the sexuality of history" to Goode 2009.

9 On antitheatricality in the *Eighteenth Brumaire,* see Parker 1991.

10 On the Reconstruction-era domestic romance, see Carby 1987 and Tate 1992. On science fiction as emerging in the nineteenth century after Mary Shelley's *Franken-stein* (1818), see, e.g., Spree 1973 and Scholes and Rabkin 1977. Works by African American authors that imagine alternative futures rather than pasts include Martin Delany's *Blake, or the Huts of America* (1859), Frances Ellen Watkins Harper's *Iola Leroy* (1892), and Sutton E. Griggs's *Imperium in Imperio* (1899).

11 Alternate history is history that would have followed if a particular event had tran-spired, a kind of temporal twist on future-set speculative fiction.

12 On mesmerism as a trope for rape and other sexual violations, see S. M. Smith 1999; as Smith demonstrates, this is especially evident in Hawthorne's *The House of the Seven Gables* (1851).

13 I'm alluding here to Walter Benn Michaels's (1987) classic reading of late nineteenth-century literature in terms of crises over the gold standard, *The Gold Standard and the Logic of Naturalism,* and Philip K. Fisher's (1985) historicist reading of popular American literature in terms of the realities it made palatable, *Hard Facts: Setting and Form in the American Novel.*

14 On turns to the archaic, obsolete, and negative in the literature of same-sex love, see Love 2009. For an elegant theory of queer anachronism, see Rohy 2009.

Chapter 4. The Sense of Unending

1 "Chronic" (adj), definition 1, *Oxford English Dictionary,* last accessed December 17, 2018, http://www.oed.com/view/Entry/32570.

2 For a beautiful meditation on the way chronic illness transforms time, see Samuels 2017.

3 As it turns out, I am not the first critic to consider "Bartleby, the Scrivener" and Stein together in terms of chronicity, which I discovered midway through drafting this chapter. Michael Snediker, in a brilliantly quirky essay on Melville (including "Bartleby"), Stein (though not "Melanctha"), and chronic pain, focuses on "pre-fer" as in "like," and "like" in terms of "the inexorable everydayness of chronic pain" (Snediker 2015, 2). For Snediker, the opacity and resistance of the word "like"— the modern-day "prefer"—a seemingly transparent and inconsequential word that actually "pulses in and out of legibility" (3), makes it good for thinking about the body whose utility and functions cannot be taken for granted. He reads Melville as an author who "treats the word *like,* even when it behaves grammatically as it should, as a word resistant to disappearing into its function" (13), which is precisely Stein's linguistic project as well. Where I would differ from Snediker is in pivoting a bit from bodily pain and toward other chronic conditions often named as psycho-logical that we might attribute to Bartleby and Melanctha—laziness? recalcitrance? anhedonia?—and through these, toward the chronic as a malady of tense and time. In other words, if for Snediker, Melville and Stein both pursue a resistance to ableist

notions of bodily function through their use of repetition, for me, this project is fundamentally a sensory and temporal one, which can produce bodies whose tenselessness is precisely their way of apprehending and transforming their contexts.

4 My interest in linguistic defectiveness is inspired, in part, by Chen 2012. For a detailed and rigorous consideration of tense in American literature, see Weinstein 2015.

5 For an extended meditation on this question, see Arsić 2007.

6 Contemporary disability activists refer to this as the "spoon theory" of energy: people with disabilities wake up with a limited amount of energy, metaphorized as a handful of spoons. Every task costs a spoon, and when the spoons run out, the person has no choice but to rest and replenish. See Miserandino 2003.

7 Irving Fisher does not use this phrase, but does refer to "vital resources" and consistently analogizes the population to the country's "lands, waters, minerals, and forests" (I. Fisher 1908, 1). The *Oxford English Dictionary* cites the first use of "human resources" as 1915. ("Human resources" (n.), definition 1, *Oxford English Dictionary*, last accessed December 17, 2018, http://www.oed.com/view/Entry/274632).

8 The Greek compound is my speculation; name dictionaries give no documented etymology for "Melanctha." Philipp Schwarzerdt (whose last name, meaning "black earth" in German, was changed to Melanchthon, or "black earth" in Greek, in honor of his proficiency in the latter language) was a contemporary and friend of Martin Luther.

9 On Stein and cubism, see Steiner 1978 and Dubnick 1984.

10 Ironically, Wiedman (2010, 52) advocates the promotion of "cardiovascular fitness, nutritional balance, and reasonable stress levels" at the individual and various collective levels.

11 For an excellent reading of "Melanctha" along these lines, see Fleissner 2004.

12 In fact, Bartleby's lumpen endurance resonates quite a bit with Lauren Berlant's (2011) "cruel optimism," the condition of attachment to that which prevents one's thriving.

13 "Chronic" (adj.), definition no. 3 (*transf.*), *Oxford English Dictionary*, last accessed December 17, 2018, http://www.oed.com/view/Entry/32570.

14 "Chronic" (adj.), draft addition, June 2007, *Oxford English Dictionary*, last accessed December 17, 2018, http://www.oed.com/view/Entry/32570.

15 Urbandictionary.com gives the following definitions: "sinthetek," entry 4 (March 16, 2005); "Diego," entry 8 #3 (July 18, 2003), "Oki3," entry 57 (July 22, 2006), at http://www.urbandictionary.com/define.php?term=chronic.

16 The phrase "chresis aphrodesion" translates as "the use of pleasure," the title of the second volume of *The History of Sexuality* (Foucault 1990b).

17 For an expansive sense of how breath, spirit, and religious ritual create new forms of sociability, see Crawley 2016.

18 This version of faith interestingly connects to Harney and Moten's (2013, 97–98) concept of "the feel," a sensation of visceral interconnection among black bodies whose ancestral history includes being crushed together in the ship's hold during the Middle Passage.

Chapter 5. Sacra/mentality in Djuna Barnes's *Nightwood*

1   On Native Americans' speech as "enthusiastic," I have learned from Kilgore 2017;
    on the Mormons, see Coviello (2013, 104–28) and Freeman (2002); on spiritualism,
    see McGarry 2012. I've also written about the Oneida Perfectionists in some of the
    same terms; see Freeman 2004.

2   See Franchot 1994; Nordstrom 2006.

3   The exception is Veltman 2003. The extant bibliography on *Nightwood*'s exploration
    of Judaism, by contrast, is large. It includes Trubowitz 2012; Hanrahan 2001; and
    Altman 1993. In terms of Catholicism, *Nightwood* has also been read as a neode-
    cadent text (see Blyn 2008), and decadence is complexly entwined with Catholi-
    cism (see Hanson 1997). But nobody has taken *Nightwood* seriously as, in some
    ways, a Catholic theology, or perhaps a countertheology of Catholicism.

4   Chauncey (1995) contends that until World War II, sexuality was not fully consoli-
    dated under the homo/hetero divide but was understood in gay male communities
    and by the dominant culture on a model of gender inversion, with "queer" signi-
    fying sexual interest in other men but normative gender presentation, and "fairy"
    signifying a more stigmatized gender inversion accompanied by an interest in other
    men.

5   Foucault (1990a, 58) also cites the Fourth Lateran Council as a turning point.

6   Kibbey (1986, 7) writes that for Puritans in the English colonies, salvation was "es-
    sentially a linguistic event," in which listeners' relation to their own language was
    transformed in a "conversion from one system of meaning to another." But of course
    any scholar of early modern literature and culture will recognize that my schematic
    division of Catholics into "the material" and Protestants into "the textual" is an
    oversimplification. As Kearney (2009, 22) has argued, Protestants struggled with
    the problem that the text itself is material, and also believed that responses to the
    Word would and should be somatic (34). I think it is fair, though, to say that non-
    verbal transactions are less important to Protestants than to even post-Reformation
    Catholics.

7   For detailed renditions of the same story, see both Haliczer 1996 and Martos 2001.

8   For a concise history of each sacrament, see Martos 2001; on Aquinas in particular,
    see Martos 2001, 60–64.

9   For an enumeration of the matter and form of each sacrament, see Catholic Church
    2011.

10 In addition to Martos 2001, 351–80, see Coontz 2006, 106–7; Goody 1983 makes a
    compelling argument that the Catholic Church became involved in marriage regu-
    lation and rites because they wanted to wrestle large tracts of land away from aristo-
    cratic landholders, with uninheritable lands defaulting automatically to the Church.

11 On penance and the two Councils, see Martos 2001, 295 and 308–12.

12 Thelma Wood, her lover. See Field 1983, 137.

13 On antimodern premodernism, see Lears 1994; on identifications with the sexual
    formations made obsolete by the hetero/homo divide, see Love 2009; on the

reification of "sexuality" as part of a larger aspect of the system of production, see Floyd 2009.

14 Persuasive readings along these lines include Seitler (2008, 94–128) and Stockton (2009).

15 I take my understanding of disembodiment as a relay to citizenship from Warner 1990b and Berlant 2008.

16 Note that by "sexuality" here Foucault means not the regime of knowledge/power but something more like "erotic acts."

17 Interestingly, Bersani and Phillips (2008) offer up the analytic scene as just this promising kind of impersonal relational mode. But again, it's all talk—and thereby conforms to a Protestant split between an apprehending and cognizing mind and a body that cannot take on this function. In this sense it repudiates Freud's compelling claims about the symptom as a means of bodily knowledge and communication. More promising is their discussion of the original scene for the impersonal, the disinterested love of God theorized by Catholic mystics in the late seventeenth century as *le pur amor*, in which love of God does not depend on whether God is merciful or vengeful to humans: love is, here, indifferent to reward or punishment for that love. But though they analogize that kind of love to "bareback" (condom-free) sex between men, Bersani and Phillips do not elaborate upon the role of bodily acts. It does seem crucial that they cite Saint Catherine of Genoa's inability, as a follower of pure love, to confess her sins (51–53).

18 This would, of course, be wrong. For a moving account of how pre-Stonewall lesbians and gay men understood themselves as connected to historical periods, populations, and figures not their own, see Nealon 2001.

19 For example, a masterful, though not precisely New Historicist, account of how historical elements deconstruct the morality of Hawthorne's tales and sketches is Colacurcio 1984.

20 While the New Americanists by no means excluded sexuality or queer theory from consideration, I think it is fair to say that their suspicion of the aesthetic made it difficult to claim certain queer strategies as directly political or, indeed, historicizing. I consider Dinshaw 1999 and Nealon 2001 to be the inaugural books in the shift toward considering queer modes of historiography. McGarry 2012 is a splendid example of queer theory, religious studies, and historiographical questions reinflecting one another.

21 I have argued elsewhere, following the lead of R. Dyer 1986 and Ross 1989, that camp is best understood as a queer archival practice, albeit without the reverence for preservation that accompanies archival work. See Freeman 2010.

22 "Camp" (adj.), *Oxford English Dictionary,* last accessed December 19, 2018, http://www.oed.com/view/Entry/26746.

23 When I was writing *Time Binds,* I somehow failed to come across David Román's formulation of archival drag, for which I apologize to him.

24 On the history and theological disputes over the laying on of hands, see Tipei 2009.

REFERENCES

Abelove, Henry. 1992. *The Evangelist of Desire: John Wesley and the Methodists*. Stanford, CA: Stanford University Press.

Abelove, Henry. 2003. "Some Speculations on the History of Sexual Intercourse during the Long Eighteenth Century in England." In *Deep Gossip*, 21–28. Minneapolis: University of Minnesota Press.

Abelove, Henry. 2008. "Yankee Doodle Dandy." *Massachusetts Review* 49:13–21.

Abraham, Nicolas. 1995. "Rhythmizing Consciousness: An Essay on the Temporality of Rhythm." In *Rhythms: On the Work, Translation, and Psychoanalysis*, translated by Benjamin Thigpen and Nicholas T. Rand, 65–103. Stanford, CA: Stanford University Press.

Aers, David. 2003. "New Historicism and the Eucharist." *Journal of Medieval and Early Modern Studies* 33 (2): 241–59.

Agamben, Giorgio. 1998. *Homo Sacer: Sovereign Power and Bare Life*. Stanford, CA: Stanford University Press.

Ahmed, Sara. 2006. *Queer Phenomenology: Orientations, Objects, Others*. Durham, NC: Duke University Press.

Alaimo, Stacy. 2010. *Bodily Natures: Science, Environment, and the Material Self*. Bloomington, IN: Indiana University Press.

Altman, Meryl. 1993. "A Book of Repulsive Jews? Rereading *Nightwood*." *Review of Contemporary Fiction* 13 (3): 160–71.

Anderson, Benedict. 1982. *Imagined Communities: Reflections on the Origin and Spread of Nationalism*. New York: Verso Books.

Andrews, Edward Deming. (1963) 2011. *The People Called Shakers: A Search for the Perfect Society*. New York: Dover.

Andrews, Edward Deming. 1972. "The Shaker Mission to the Shawnee Indians." *Winterthur Portfolio* 7:113–28.

"Andy's Review." 2010. Online review of Gertrude Stein's *Three Lives and Tender Buttons*. Goodreads, September. Accessed December 20, 2018. http://www.goodreads.com/review/show/120595050.

Anidjar, Gil. 2009. "We Have Never Been Jewish: An Essay in Asymmetric Hematology." In *Jewish Blood: Reality and Metaphor in History, Religion, and, Culture*, edited by Mitchell B. Hart, 31–56. New York: Routledge.

Anonymous. 1795. "A Short Account of the People Known by the Name of Shakers, or Shaking Quakers." *Theological Magazine, or, Synopsis of Modern Religious Sentiment.* September/October, 81–87.

Anonymous. (1847) 2013. "The Shaker Concert." *Norfolk Democrat* (Dedham, MA), 5 February, 3. Reprinted in Goodwillie 2013, 3:165–66.

Arom, Simha. 1991. *African Polyphony and Polyrhythm: Musical Structure and Methodology.* Translated by Martin Thom, Barbara Tuckett, and Raymond Boyd. Cambridge: Cambridge University Press.

Arsić, Branka. 2007. *Passive Constitutions, or 7 1/2 Times Bartleby.* Stanford, CA: Stanford University Press.

Ashliman, D. L. 2000–2018. "Playing Dead: Folktales of Aarne-Thompson-Uther Type 1 and Related Stories." Accessed December 20, 2018. http://www.pitt.edu/~dash/type0001.html.

Baerman, Matthew, and Greville G. Corbett. 2010. "Introduction: Defectiveness: Typology and Diachrony." In *Defective Paradigms: Missing Forms and What They Tell Us,* 1–18. Oxford: Oxford University Press.

Baraka, Amiri. (1994) 2009. "Northern Iowa: Short Story and Poetry." In *Tales of the Out and Gone,* 119–23. Brooklyn, NY: Akashic Books.

Baraka, Amiri. (1995) 2009. "Rhythm Travel." In *Tales of the Out and Gone,* 148–50. Brooklyn, NY: Akashic Books.

Barnes, Djuna. (1936) 2006. *Nightwood.* New York: New Directions.

Barnes, Elizabeth. 1997. *States of Sympathy: Seduction and Democracy in the American Novel.* New York: Columbia University Press.

Barthes, Roland. 2013. *How to Live Together: Novelistic Simulations of Some Everyday Spaces.* Translated by Kate Briggs. New York: Columbia University Press.

Bataille, Georges. 1986. *Erotism: Death and Sensuality.* San Francisco, CA: City Lights Publishing.

Beaver, Harold. 1981. "Homosexual Signs (*In Memory of Roland Barthes*)." *Critical Inquiry* 8 (1): 99–119.

Bederman, Gail. 1995. *Manliness and Civilization: A Cultural History of Gender and Race in the United States, 1880–1917.* Chicago, IL: University of Chicago Press.

Beecher, Catharine. 1841. *A Treatise on Domestic Economy.* Boston, MA: Marsh, Capen, Lyon, and Webb.

Benjamin, Walter. (1936) 1968. "The Work of Art in the Age of Mechanical Reproduction." In *Illuminations; Essays and Reflections,* edited and with introduction by Hannah Arendt, translated by Harry Zohn, 217–42. New York: Harcourt, Brace, and World.

Benjamin, Walter. (1950) 1968. "Theses on the Philosophy of History." In *Illuminations; Essays and Reflections,* edited and with an introduction by Hannah Arendt, translated by Harry Zohn, 253–64. New York: Harcourt, Brace, and World.

Benjamin, Walter. (1963) 2009. *The Origin of German Tragic Drama.* Translated by John Osborne. New York: Verso.

Bentley, Nancy. 2002. "Marriage as Treason: Polygamy, Nation, and the Novel." In *The Futures of American Studies,* edited by Donald E. Pease and Robyn Wiegman, 341–70. Durham, NC: Duke University Press.

Berlant, Lauren. 2008. "National Brands, National Body: *Imitation of Life.*" In *The Female Complaint: The Unfinished Business of Sentimentality in American Culture,* 107–44. Durham, NC: Duke University Press.

Berlant, Lauren. 2011. *Cruel Optimism.* Durham, NC: Duke University Press.

Bersani, Leo. (1986) 1990. *The Freudian Body: Psychoanalysis and Art.* Reprint, New York: Columbia University Press.

Bersani, Leo. 1987. "Is the Rectum a Grave?" *October* 43:197–222.

Bersani, Leo, and Adam Phillips. 2008. *Intimacies.* Chicago, IL: University of Chicago Press.

Bibb, Henry. (1850) 2001. *Narrative of the Life and Adventures of Henry Bibb.* New York: Published by the Author. Reprinted in 2001 as *The Life and Adventures of Henry Bibb, an American Slave.* Madison: University of Wisconsin Press.

Blackburn, Absolem H. (1812) 2013. *A Brief Account of the Rise, Progress, Doctrines, and Practices of the People Usually Denominated Shakers.* Flemingsburg, KY: A. Crookshanks. Reprinted in Goodwillie 2013, 2:233–58.

Black Lives Matter. n.d. "Herstory." BlackLivesMatter.com. Accessed December 20, 2018. https://blacklivesmatter.com/about/herstory/.

Blakemore, Erin. "There Are only Two Shakers Left in the World." *Smithsonian Magazine* online, January 6, 2017. Accessed December 20, 2018. http://www.smithsonianmag.com/smart-news/there-are-only-two-shakers-left-world-180961701/.

Blassingame, John W. 1972. *The Slave Community: Plantation Life in the Antebellum South.* New York: Oxford University Press.

Blyn, Robin. 2008. "*Nightwood*'s Freak Dandies: Decadence in the 1930s." *Modernism/Modernity* 15 (3): 503–26.

Boone, Joseph Allen. 2014. *The Homoerotics of Orientalism.* New York: Columbia University Press.

Bostwick, Homer. 1860. *A Treatise on the Nature and Treatment of Seminal Diseases.* New York: Rogers.

Bourdieu, Pierre. 1977. *Outline of a Theory of Practice.* Translated by Richard Nice. Cambridge: Cambridge University Press.

Brennan, Teresa. 2004. *The Transmission of Affect.* Ithaca, NY: Cornell University Press.

Brintnall, Kent, Joseph Marchal, and Stephen D. Moore, eds. 2017. *Sexual Disorientations: Queer Temporalities, Affects, Theologies.* New York: Fordham University Press.

Britton, Wesley. 1992. "Carlyle, Clemens, and Dickens: Mark Twain's Francophobia, the French Revolution, and Determinism." *Studies in American Fiction* 20:197–204.

Brooks, Daphne A. 2006. *Bodies in Dissent: Spectacular Performances of Race and Freedom, 1850–1910.* Durham, NC: Duke University Press.

Brown, Gillian. 1992. *Domestic Individualism: Imagining Self in Nineteenth-Century America*. Berkeley: University of California Press.

Brown, Henry Box. (1851) 2008. *Narrative of Henry Box Brown, Written by Himself*. Edited and with an introduction by John Ernest. Chapel Hill: University of North Carolina Press.

Brown, Thomas. 1812. *An Account of the People Called Shakers*. Troy, NY: Parker and Bliss.

Browning, Barbara. 1998. *Infectious Rhythm: Metaphors of Contagion and the Spread of African Culture*. New York: Routledge.

Bruce, Dickson D., Jr. 1984a. "Ancient Africa and the Early Black American Historians, 1883–1915." *American Quarterly* 36 (5): 684–99.

Bruce, Dickson D., Jr. 1984b. "The Ironic Conception of American History: The Early Black Historians, 1883–1915." *Journal of Negro History* 69 (2): 53–62.

Budd, Michael Anton. 1997. *The Sculpture Machine: Physical Culture and Body Politics in the Age of Empire*. New York: New York University Press.

Burgett, Bruce. 1998. *Sentimental Bodies: Sex, Gender, and Citizenship in the Early Republic*. Princeton, NJ: Princeton University Press.

Butler, Judith. (1990) 2006. *Gender Trouble: Feminism and the Subversion of Identity*. New York: Routledge.

Butler, Judith. 2011. *Bodies That Matter: On the Discursive Limits of Sex*. New York: Routledge.

Butler, Judith. 2015. *Notes toward a Performative Theory of Assembly*. Cambridge, MA: Harvard University Press.

Butler, Octavia. 2000. *Lilith's Brood*. 1st trade ed. New York: Grand Central.

Carby, Hazel. 1987. *Reconstructing Womanhood: The Emergence of the Afro-American Woman Novelist*. New York: Oxford University Press.

Caserio, Robert, Lee Edelman, Judith Halberstam, and José Esteban Muñoz. 2006. "The Anti-Social Thesis in Queer Theory." *PMLA* 121 (3): 819–28.

Castronovo, Russ. 2000. "Sexual Purity, White Men, and Slavery: Emerson and the Self-Reliant Body." *Prospects: An Annual of American Cultural Studies* 25:193–227.

Catholic Church. 2011. *The Roman Missal*. 3rd typical ed., chapel ed. Chicago, IL: Liturgy Training Publications.

Chandler, Nahum. 2008. "Of Exorbitance: The Problem of the Negro as a Problem for Thought." *Criticism* 50 (3): 345–410.

Chauncey, George. 1995. *Gay New York: Gender, Urban Culture, and the Making of the Gay Male World, 1880–1940*. New York: Basic Books.

Chen, Mel. 2012. *Animacies: Biopolitics, Racial Mattering, and Queer Affect*. Durham, NC: Duke University Press.

Cheng, Anne Anlin. 2009. "Skins, Tattoos, and Susceptibility." *Representations* 108 (1): 98–119.

Chesnutt, Charles. 2011. *The Conjure Stories*. New York: W. W. Norton.

Clark, Christopher. (1812) 2013. *A Shock to Shakerism: Or, a Serious Reflection on the Idolatry of Ann Lee of Manchester*. Reprinted in Goodwillie 2013, 2: 5–80.

Cohen, Cathy. 1997. "Punks, Bulldaggers, and Welfare Queens: The Radical Potential of Queer Politics?" *GLQ* 3 (4): 287–302.

Colacurcio, Michael J. 1984. *The Province of Piety.* Cambridge, MA: Harvard University Press.

Collins, William J. 1986. "Hank Morgan in the Garden of Forking Paths: *A Connecticut Yankee in King Arthur's Court* as Alternative History." *Modern Fiction Studies* 32 (1): 109–14.

Comrie, Bernard. 1976. *Aspect: An Introduction to the Study of Verbal Aspect and Related Problems.* Cambridge: Cambridge University Press.

Coole, Diana, and Samantha Frost, eds. 2010. *The New Materialisms: Ontology, Agency, and Politics.* Durham, NC: Duke University Press.

Coontz, Stephanie. 2006. *Marriage, A History: How Love Conquered Marriage.* New York: Penguin Books.

Courlander, Harold, and Albert Kofi Prempeh, eds. 1957. *The Hat-Shaking Dance and Other Tales from the Gold Coast.* New York: Harcourt, Brace.

Coviello, Peter. 2005. *Intimacy in America: Dreams of Affiliation in Antebellum Literature.* Minneapolis: University of Minnesota Press.

Coviello, Peter. 2013. *Tomorrow's Parties: Sex and the Untimely in Nineteenth-Century America.* New York: New York University Press.

Crawley, Ashon. 2016. *Blackpentecostal Breath: The Aesthetics of Possibility.* New York: Fordham University Press.

Cvetkovich, Ann. 2003. *An Archive of Feelings: Trauma, Sexuality, and Lesbian Public Cultures.* Durham, NC: Duke University Press.

Davies, John Gordon, P. Van Zyl, and F. M. Young. 1984. *A Shaker Service Reconstructed.* Birmingham, UK: Institute for the Study of Worship and Religious Architecture.

Dean, Tim. 2000. *Beyond Sexuality.* Chicago, IL: University of Chicago Press.

Dean, Tim. 2009. *Unlimited Intimacy: Reflections on the Subculture of Barebacking.* Chicago, IL: University of Chicago Press.

Dean, Tim, Hal Foster, Kaja Silverman, and Leo Bersani. 1997. "A Conversation with Leo Bersani." *October* 82: 3–16.

Deleuze, Gilles. 1997. "Bartleby; or, The Formula." In *Essays Critical and Clinical,* translated by Daniel W. Smith and Michael A. Greco, 68–90. Minneapolis: University of Minnesota Press.

Deleuze, Gilles, and Félix Guattari. 1988. *A Thousand Plateaus.* Translated by Brian Massumi. London: Athlone Press.

Derrida, Jacques. 1998. "That Dangerous Supplement." In *Of Grammatology,* translated by Gayatri Chakravorty Spivak, 141–64. Baltimore, MD: Johns Hopkins University Press.

Derrida, Jacques. 2000. *Of Hospitality: Anne Dufourmantelle Invites Jacques Derrida to Respond.* Translated by Rachel Bowlby. Stanford, CA: Stanford University Press.

Dickens, Charles. (1842) 2001. *American Notes for General Circulation.* New York: Penguin Classics.

Dinshaw, Carolyn. 1999. *Getting Medieval: Sexualities and Communities, Pre- and Postmodern*. Durham, NC: Duke University Press.

Dinshaw, Carolyn. 2012. *How Soon Is Now? Medieval Texts, Amateur Readers, and the Queerness of Time*. Durham, NC: Duke University Press.

Doane, Mary Ann. 2002. *The Emergence of Cinematic Time: Modernity, Contingency, the Archive*. Cambridge, MA: Harvard University Press.

Douglas, Ann. 1977. *The Feminization of American Culture*. New York: Anchor Press/ Doubleday.

Douglass, Frederick. (1845) 1982. *Narrative of the Life of Frederick Douglass, an American Slave*. Edited by Henry Louis Gates. New York: Penguin.

Dubnick, Randa K. 1984. *The Structure of Obscurity: Gertrude Stein, Language, and Cubism*. Urbana: University of Illinois Press.

Du Bois, W. E. B. (1903) 1997. *The Souls of Black Folk*. Edited and with an introduction by David W. Blight and Robert Gooding-Williams. New York: Bedford / St. Martin's.

Du Bois, W. E. B. (1920) 1999. "The Comet." In *Darkwater: Voices from within the Veil*, 149–60. New York: Dover.

duCille, Ann. 1993. *The Coupling Convention: Sex, Text, and Tradition in Black Women's Fiction*. New York: Oxford University Press.

During, Simon. 2010. "Mimic Toil: Eighteenth-Century Preconditions for the Modern Historical Reenactment." In *Historical Reenactment: From Realism to the Affective Turn*, edited by Iaian McCalman and Paul A. Pickering, 180–99. Basingstoke, UK: Palgrave Macmillan.

Dydo, Ulla E. 2008. *Gertrude Stein: The Language That Rises*. Evanston, IL: Northwestern University Press.

Dyer, Mary M. 1847. *The Rise and Progress of the Serpent from the Garden of Eden, to the Present Day*. Concord, NH: printed for the author.

Dyer, Richard. 1986. *Heavenly Bodies: Film Stars and Society*. New York: St. Martin's.

Dyer, Richard. 1997. "The White Man's Muscles." In *Race and the Subject of Masculinity*, edited by Harry Stecopoulos, 286–314. Durham, NC: Duke University Press.

Edelman, Lee. 2004. *No Future: Queer Theory and the Death Drive*. Durham, NC: Duke University Press.

Eiland, Howard, and Kevin McLaughlin. 1999. Translators' foreword to *The Arcades Project*, by Walter Benjamin, ix–xiv. Cambridge, MA: Belknap Press.

Elkins, Hervey. (1853) 2010. *Fifteen Years in the Senior Order of Shakers*. Hanover, NH: Dartmouth University Press.

Ellison, Julie. 1999. *Cato's Tears and the Making of Anglo-American Emotion*. Chicago, IL: University of Chicago Press.

Ernest, John. 2007. "Outside the Box: Henry Box Brown and the Politics of Anti-Slavery Agency." *Arizona Quarterly* 63 (4): 1–24.

Fanon, Frantz. (1952) 1994. *Black Skin, White Masks*. Translated by Constance Farrington. New York: Grove Press.

Field, Andrew. 1983. *Djuna: The Life and Times of Djuna Barnes*. New York: Putnam.

Fine, Michelle, Lois Weiss, Linda C. Powell, and L. Mun Wong, eds. 1997. *Off-White: Readings on Race, Power, and Society*. New York: Routledge.

Fisher, Irving. 1908. *Report on National Vitality, Its Wastes and Conservation*. Washington, DC: National Conservation Commission.

Fisher, Philip K. 1985. *Hard Facts: Setting and Form in the American Novel*. New York: Oxford University Press.

Fleissner, Jennifer. 2004. *Women, Compulsion, Modernity: The Moment of American Naturalism*. Chicago, IL: University of Chicago Press.

Floyd, Kevin. 2009. *The Reification of Desire: Toward a Queer Marxism*. Minneapolis: University of Minnesota Press.

Forster, E. M. (1924) 2005. *A Passage to India*. Edited by Oliver Stallybrass. New York: Penguin Classics.

Foucault, Michel. (1976) 1997. *Society Must Be Defended: Lectures at the Collège de France, 1975–1976*. Edited by Mauro Bertani and Alessandro Fontana. Translated by David Macey. New York: Picador.

Foucault, Michel. (1978) 1999. "On Religion." In *Religion and Culture*, edited by Jeremy R. Carrette, 106–9. New York: Routledge.

Foucault, Michel. (1978–79) 2008. *The Birth of Biopolitics: Lectures at the Collège de France, 1975–1976*. Edited by Michel Senellart. Translated by Graham Burchell. New York: Picador.

Foucault, Michel. 1979. *Discipline and Punish: The Birth of the Prison*. Translated by Alan Sheridan. New York: Vintage.

Foucault, Michel. 1980. "A Preface to Transgression." In *Language, Counter-memory, Practice: Selected Essays and Interviews*, edited by Robert Bouchard, 29–52. Ithaca, NY: Cornell University Press.

Foucault, Michel. (1981) 1984. "Friendship as a Way of Life." Translated by John Johnston. In *The Foucault Reader*, edited by Paul Rabinow, 135–40. New York: Pantheon.

Foucault, Michel. 1990a. *The History of Sexuality*. Vol. 1, *The Will to Knowledge*. Translated by Robert Hurley. New York: Vintage.

Foucault, Michel. 1990b. *The History of Sexuality*. Vol. 2, *The Uses of Pleasure*. Translated by Robert Hurley. New York: Vintage.

Foucault, Michel. 1990c. *The History of Sexuality*. Vol. 3, *The Care of the Self*. Translated by Robert Hurley. New York: Vintage.

Foucault, Michel. 1993. "About the Beginning of the Hermeneutics of the Self: Two Lectures at Dartmouth." *Political Theory* 21 (2): 198–227.

Franchot, Jenny. 1994. *Roads to Rome: The Antebellum Protestant Encounter with Catholicism*. Berkeley: University of California Press.

Franken, Claudia. 2000. *Gertrude Stein, Writer and Thinker*. Berlin: LIT Verlag.

Freeman, Elizabeth. 2002. *The Wedding Complex: Forms of Belonging in Modern American Culture*. Durham, NC: Duke University Press.

Freeman, Elizabeth. 2004. "The Whole(y) Family: Economies of Kinship in the Progressive Era." *American Literary History* 16 (4): 619–47.

Freeman, Elizabeth. 2010. *Time Binds: Queer Temporalities, Queer Histories.* Durham, NC: Duke University Press.

Freud, Sigmund. (1905) 1975. *Three Essays on the Theory of Sexuality.* New York: Basic Books.

Freud, Sigmund. (1914) 1950. "Remembering, Repeating, and Working-Through." In *The Standard Edition of the Complete Psychological Works of Sigmund Freud,* vol. 12, edited by James Strachey, 147–56. London: Hogarth Press.

Freud, Sigmund. (1920) 1964. "Beyond the Pleasure Principle." In *The Standard Edition of the Complete Psychological Works of Sigmund Freud,* vol. 18, edited by James Strachey, 1–64. London: Hogarth Press.

Fulton, Joe B. 2000. *Mark Twain in the Margins: "The Quarry Farm Marginalia" and "A Connecticut Yankee in King Arthur's Court."* Tuscaloosa: University of Alabama Press.

Gaines, Kevin Kelly. 1996. *Uplifting the Race: Black Leadership, Politics, and Culture in the Twentieth Century.* 2nd ed. Chapel Hill: University of North Carolina Press.

Gallagher, Catherine, and Stephen Greenblatt. 2001. *Practicing New Historicism.* Chicago, IL: University of Chicago Press.

Garcia, Angela. 2010. *The Pastoral Clinic: Addiction and Dispossession along the Rio Grande.* Berkeley: University of California Press.

Gates, Henry Louis. 1988. *The Signifying Monkey: A Theory of African-American Literary Criticism.* New York: Oxford University Press.

Gelder, Ann. 1989. "Justifying the Page." *Qui Parle: Critical Humanities and Social Sciences* 3: 168–84.

Genovese, Eugene. (1974) 1976. *Roll, Jordan, Roll: The World the Slaves Made.* New York: Vintage.

Gibbs, Anna. 2010. "After Affect: Sympathy, Synchrony, and Mimetic Communication." In *The Affect Studies Reader,* edited by Melissa Gregg and Gregory Seigworth, 186–205. Durham, NC: Duke University Press.

Gilman, Sander L. 1991. *The Jew's Body.* New York: Routledge.

Gomez, Jewelle. 1991. *The Gilda Stories.* Ithaca, NY: Firebrand Books.

Goode, Mike. 2009. *Sentimental Masculinity and the Rise of History, 1790–1890.* Cambridge: Cambridge University Press.

Goodwillie, Christian, ed. 2013. *Writings of Shaker Apostates and Anti-Shakers, 1782–1850.* 3 vols. London: Pickering and Chatto.

Goody, Jack. 1983. *The Development of the Family and Marriage in Europe.* Cambridge: Cambridge University Press.

Gordon, Lewis. 2010. "Theory in Black: Teleological Suspensions in Philosophy of Culture." *Qui Parle: Critical Humanities and Social Sciences* 18 (2): 193–214.

"Great Moral Curiosity! Shaker Concert!" 1847. *Maine Cultivator and Hallowell Gazette,* 3.

Green, Harvey. 1986. *Fit for America: Fitness, Sport, and American Society.* New York: Pantheon.

Green, Thomas A. 2006. *The Greenwood Library of American Folktales.* 4 vols. San Francisco: Greenwood Press.

Gregg, Melissa, and Gregory Seigworth. 2010. "An Inventory of Shimmers." In *The Affect Studies Reader,* edited by Melissa Gregg and Gregory Seigworth, 1–25. Durham, NC: Duke University Press.

Griggs, Sutton E. (1899) 2003. *Imperium in Imperio.* New York: Modern Library.

Grosz, Elizabeth. 1994. *Volatile Bodies: Toward a Corporeal Feminism.* Bloomington, IN: Indiana University Press.

Grosz, Elizabeth. 2004. *The Nick of Time: Politics, Evolution, and the Untimely.* Durham, NC: Duke University Press.

Haliczer, Stephen. 1996. *Sexuality in the Confessional: A Sacrament Profaned.* New York: Oxford University Press.

Hanrahan, Mairéad. 2001. "Djuna Barnes's *Nightwood: The Cruci-Fiction of the Jew.*" *Paragraph: A Journal of Modern Critical Theory* 21 (1): 32–49.

Hanson, Ellis. 1997. *Decadence and Catholicism.* Cambridge, MA: Harvard University Press.

Hardt, Michael and Antonio Negri. 2004. *Multitude: War and Democracy in the Age of Empire.* New York: Penguin Press.

Harney, Stefano, and Fred Moten. 2013. *The Undercommons: Fugitive Planning and Black Study.* Wivenhoe, UK: Minor Compositions.

Harris, Joel Chandler. 1881a. "Mr. Fox Goes Hunting, but Mr. Rabbit Bags the Game." In *Uncle Remus: His Songs and His Sayings: The Folk-Lore of the Old Plantation,* 70–72. New York: D. Appleton.

Harris, Joel Chandler. 1881b. "The Wonderful Tar-Baby Story." In *Uncle Remus: His Songs and His Sayings: The Folk-Lore of the Old Plantation,* 23–25. New York: D. Appleton.

Hartman, Saidiya V. 1997. *Scenes of Subjection: Terror, Slavery, and Self-Making in Nineteenth-Century America.* New York: Oxford University Press.

Hartman, Saidiya V. 2002. "The Time of Slavery." *South Atlantic Quarterly* 101 (4): 757–77.

Hartman, Saidiya V. 2003. "'The Position of the Unthought: An Interview with Saidiya V. Hartman. By Frank B. Wilderson III." *Qui Parle: Critical Humanities and Social Sciences* 13 (2): 183–201.

Hartman, Saidiya V. 2008. *Lose Your Mother: A Journey along the Atlantic Slave Route.* New York: Farrar, Strauss, and Giroux.

Hedin, Raymond. 1982. "Strategies of Form in the American Slave Narrative." In *The Art of the Slave Narrative: Original Essays in Criticism and Theory,* edited by John Sekora and Darwin T. Turner, 25–35. Macomb, IL: Western Illinois University Press.

Hegel, G. W. F. (1837) 1981. *Lectures on the Philosophy of World History.* Translated by H. B. Nisbet. Cambridge: Cambridge University Press.

Hendler, Glenn. 2001. *Public Sentiments: Structures of Feeling in Nineteenth-Century American Literature.* Chapel Hill: University of North Carolina Press.

Hickman, Jared. 2014. "The Book of Mormon as Amerindian Apocalypse." *American Literature* 86: 429–61.

Hocquenghem, Guy. (1972) 1993. *Homosexual Desire*. Durham, NC. Duke University Press.

Holland, Sharon. 2000. *Raising the Dead: Readings of Death and (Black) Subjectivity*. Durham, NC: Duke University Press.

Holmström, Kirstin Gram. 1967. *Monodrama, Attitudes, Tableaux Vivants*. Stockholm: Almqvist and Wiksell.

Holsinger, Bruce W. 2005. *The Premodern Condition: Medievalism and the Making of Theory*. Chicago, IL: University of Chicago Press.

Hopkins, Pauline. (1903) 1988. *Of One Blood*. In *The Magazine Novels of Pauline Hopkins*, 439–621. New York: Oxford University Press.

Horkheimer, Max, and Theodor Adorno. 1969. *The Dialectic of Enlightenment*. London: Continuum.

Horsman, Reginald. 1981. *Race and Manifest Destiny: The Origins of American Racial Anglo-Saxonism*. Cambridge, MA: Harvard University Press.

Howard, June. 1999. "What Is Sentimentality?" *American Literary History* 11(1): 63–81.

Hsu, Hsuan. 2015. *Sitting in Darkness: Mark Twain's Asia and Comparative Racialization*. New York: New York University Press.

Huffer, Lynne. 2009. *Mad for Foucault: Rethinking the Foundations of Queer Theory*. New York: Columbia University Press.

Hunn, David, and Kim Bell. 2014. "Why Was Michael Brown's Body Left There for Hours?" *St. Louis Dispatch,* September 14. Accessed December 20, 2018. http://www.stltoday.com/news/local/crime-and-courts/why-was-michael-brown-s-body-left-there-for-hours/article_0b73ec58-c6a1-516e-882f-74d18a4246e0.html.

Jackson, Jean E. 2005. "Stigma, Liminality, and Chronic Pain: Mind-Body Borderlands." *American Ethnologist* 32 (3): 332–53.

Jacobs, Harriet A. (1861) 1987. *Incidents in the Life of a Slave Girl, Written by Herself.* Edited by Jean Fagin Yellin. Cambridge, MA: Harvard University Press.

Jagose, Annamarie. 2012. *Orgasmology*. Durham, NC: Duke University Press.

Jain, S. Lochlann. 2013. *Malignant: How Cancer Becomes Us*. Berkeley: University of California Press.

Jameson, Fredric. 1982. *The Political Unconscious: Narrative as Socially Symbolic Act*. Ithaca, NY: Cornell University Press.

James, William. (1901–2) 1987. *The Variety of Religious Experience: A Study in Human Nature*. In *William James: Writings 1902–1910,* edited by Bruce Kuklick, 1–477. New York: Literary Classics of the United States, Inc.

Jefferson, Thomas. (1785) 1998. *Notes on the State of Virginia*. New York: Penguin.

Jordan, Mark D. 2006. "Sacramental Characters." *Studies in Christian Ethics* 19 (3): 323–38.

Judy, Ronald. 1991. "Kant and the Negro." *Surfaces* 1 (online). Accessed December 20, 2018. http://www.pum.umontreal.ca/revues/surfaces/vol1/judy.html.

Kahan, Benjamin. 2013. *Celibacies: American Modernism and Sexual Life*. Durham, NC: Duke University Press.

Kahan, Benjamin. 2017. "Conjectures on the Sexual World System." *GLQ* 23 (3): 327–57.

Kant, Immanuel, Marcus Weigelt, and F. Max Müller. (1871) 2007. *Critique of Pure Reason*. London: Penguin.

Kautsky, Karl. (1908) 1953. *Foundations of Christianity*. Translated by H. F. Mins. New York: Russell and Russell.

Kearney, James. 2009. *The Incarnate Text: Imagining the Book in Reformation England*. Philadelphia: University of Pennsylvania Press.

Kete, Mary Louise. 2000. *Sentimental Collaborations: Mourning and Middle-Class Identity in Nineteenth-Century America*. Durham, NC: Duke University Press.

Kibbey, Ann. 1986. *The Interpretation of Material Shapes in Puritanism: A Study of Rhetoric, Prejudice, and Violence*. Cambridge: Cambridge University Press.

Kilgore, John Mac. 2016. *Mania for Freedom: American Literatures of Enthusiasm from the Revolution to the Civil War*. Chapel Hill: University of North Carolina Press.

Kracauer, Siegfried. 1975. "The Mass Ornament." Translated by Barbara Correll and Jack Zipes. *New German Critique* 5: 67–76.

Kreiger, Georgia. 2008. "Playing Dead: Harriet Jacobs's Survival Strategy in *Incidents in the Life of a Slave Girl*." *African American Review* 42 (3/4): 607–21.

Lacan, Jacques. 1999. *On Feminine Sexuality: The Limits of Love and Knowledge*. Edited by Jacques-Alain Miller. Translated by Bruce Fink. New York: W. W. Norton.

Laplanche, Jean. (1970) 1976. *Life and Death in Psychoanalysis*. Translated by Jeffrey Mehlman. Baltimore: Johns Hopkins University Press.

Laqueur, Thomas. 2004. *Solitary Sex: A Cultural History of Masturbation*. Brooklyn, NY: Zone Books.

Lears, T. J. Jackson. 1994. *No Place of Grace: Antimodernism and the Transformation of American Culture, 1880–1920*. Chicago, IL: University of Chicago Press.

Lefebvre, Henri. 2004. *Rhythmanalysis: Space, Time, and Everyday Life*. London: Continuum Books.

Lemke, Thomas. 2011. *Biopolitics: An Advanced Introduction*. New York: New York University Press.

Lockwood, J. Samaine. 2015. *Archives of Desire: The Queer Historical Work of New England Regionalism*. Chapel Hill: University of North Carolina Press.

Lorch, Fred W. 1958. "Hawaiian Feudalism and Mark Twain's *A Connecticut Yankee in King Arthur's Court*." *American Literature* 30: 50–66.

Lorde, Audre. (1978) 2007. "The Uses of the Erotic: The Erotic as Power." In *Sister Outsider: Essays and Speeches by Audre Lorde*, 53–59. Reprint, Freedom, CA: The Crossing Press.

Lorenz, Chris. 2009. "Scientific Historiography." In *A Companion to the Philosophy of History and Historiography*, edited by Aviezer Tucker, 393–403. New York: Blackwell.

Love, Heather. 2009. *Feeling Backward: Loss and the Politics of Queer History*. Cambridge, MA: Harvard University Press.

Luciano, Dana. 2003. "Passing Shadows: Melancholy Nationality and Black Publicity in Pauline E. Hopkins's *Of One Blood*." In *Loss: The Psychic and Social Contexts of Melancholia,* edited by David Eng and David Kazanjian, 148–87. Berkeley: University of California Press.

Luciano, Dana. 2007. *Arranging Grief: Sacred Time and the Body in Nineteenth-Century America.* New York: New York University Press.

Madden, Etta. 1998. *Bodies of Life: Shaker Literature and Literacies.* Westport, CT: Greenwood Press.

Manderson, Lenore, and Carolyn Smith-Morris. 2010. "Introduction: Chronicity and the Experience of Illness." In *Chronic Conditions, Fluid States: Chronicity and the Anthropology of Illness,* edited by Lenore Manderson and Carolyn Smith-Morris, 1–18. New Brunswick, NJ: Rutgers University Press.

Marriott, David. 2011. "Inventions of Existence: Sylvia Wynter, Frantz Fanon, Sociogeny, and 'the Damned.'" *CR: The New Centennial Review* 11 (3): 45–89.

Martos, Joseph. 2001. *Doors to the Sacred: A Historical Introduction to Sacraments in the Catholic Church.* Rev. ed. Liguori, MO: Liguori/Triumph Press.

Marx, Karl. (1869) 1963. *The Eighteenth Brumaire of Louis Bonaparte.* New York: International.

Marx, Karl, and Friedrich Engels. (1845–46) 1970. *The German Ideology.* Edited by Christopher John Arthur. New York: International.

Massumi, Brian. 2002. *Parables for the Virtual: Movement, Affect, Sensation.* Durham, NC: Duke University Press.

Mauss, Marcel. 1973. "Techniques of the Body." *Economy and Society* 2 (1): 70–88.

Mbembe, Achille. 2003. "Necropolitics." Translated by Libby Meintjes. *Public Culture* 15 (1): 11–40.

McCalman, Iain, and Paul Pickering, eds. 2010. *Historical Reenactment: From Realism to the Affective Turn.* New York: Palgrave Macmillan.

McGarry, Molly. 2012. *Ghosts of Futures Past: Spiritualism and the Cultural Politics of Nineteenth-Century America.* Berkeley: University of California Press.

McNeill, William H. 1997. *Keeping Together in Time: Dance and Drill in Human History.* Cambridge, MA: Harvard University Press.

Meillassoux, Claude. 1975. *L'Esclavage en Afrique précoloniale.* Paris: François Maspero.

Melville, Herman. (1853) 1979. "Bartleby, the Scrivener: A Story of Wall Street." In *Billy Budd and Other Tales,* 103–40. New York: Penguin.

Michaels, Walter Benn. 1987. *The Gold Standard and the Logic of Naturalism: American Literature at the Turn of the Century.* Berkeley: University of California Press.

Military Field Manuals, 1782–1899. 2007. CD-ROM. Beverly Hills, CA: BACM Research.

Mirzoeff, Nicholas D. 2015. "#BlackLivesMatter Is Breathing New Life into the Die-In." *New Republic,* August 10. Accessed December 20, 2018. https://newrepublic.com/article/122513/blacklivesmatter-breathing-new-life-die.

Miserandino, Christine. 2003. "The Spoon Theory." Butyoudontlooksick.com. Accessed December 20, 2018. https://butyoudontlooksick.com/articles/written-by-christine/the-spoon-theory/.

Morrison, Toni. 1987. *Beloved.* New York: Knopf.

Morse, Theodore F., and Robert Hobart Davis. 1903. "The Woodchuck Song." New York: Howley, Haviland, and Dresser.

Morton, Donald. 1993. "The Politics of Queer Theory in the Postmodern Moment." *Genders* 17:121–50.

Moses, Omri. 2014. *Out of Character: Modernism, Vitalism, Psychic Life.* Stanford, CA: Stanford University Press.

Moskowitz, Sally. 2005. "Playing Dead: An Unconscious Fantasy, Bodily Focused Defenses, and Their Roots in Infancy." *Journal of the American Psychoanalytic Association* 53 (3): 891–916.

Moten, Fred. 2003. *In the Break: The Aesthetics of the Black Radical Tradition.* Minneapolis: University of Minnesota Press.

Moten, Fred. 2008a. "Black Op." *PMLA* 123 (5): 1743–47.

Moten, Fred. 2008b. "The Case of Blackness." *Criticism* 50 (2): 177–218.

Muñoz, José Esteban. 2000. "Feeling Brown: Ethnicity and Affect in Ricardo Bracho's *The Sweetest Hangover (and Other STDs)." Theatre Journal* 52 (1): 67–79.

Muñoz, José Esteban. 2009. *Cruising Utopia: The Then and the There of Queer Futurity.* New York: New York University Press.

Nealon, Christopher. 2001. *Foundlings: Lesbian and Gay Historical Emotion before Stonewall.* Durham, NC: Duke University Press.

Newton, Esther. 1984. "The Mythic Mannish Lesbian: Radclyffe Hall and the New Woman." *Signs* 9: 557–75.

Ngai, Sianne. 2005. *Ugly Feelings.* Cambridge, MA: Harvard University Press.

Nietzsche, Friedrich. (1873–76) 1997. "The Uses and Disadvantages of History for Life." In *Untimely Meditations,* edited by Daniel Breazeale, 59–123. Translated by R. J. Hollingdale. Cambridge: Cambridge University Press.

Nietzsche, Friedrich. (1908) 1992. *Ecce Homo: How One Becomes What One Is.* Rev. ed. Translated and with an introduction and notes by R. J. Hollingdale. New York: Penguin.

Nietzsche, Friedrich. 1927. "Beyond Good and Evil." Translated by Helen Zimmern. In *The Philosophy of Nietzsche,* edited by Willard Huntington Wright, 369–616. New York: Modern Library.

Noble, Marianne. 2000. *The Masochistic Pleasures of Sentimental Literature.* Princeton, NJ: Princeton University Press.

Nordstrom, Justin. 2006. *Danger on the Doorstep: Anti-Catholicism and American Print Culture in the Progressive Era.* Notre Dame, IN: University of Notre Dame Press.

Novick, Kerry Kelley, and Jack Novick. 1987. "The Essence of Masochism." *Psychoanalytic Study of the Child* 42:353–84.

Obermeier, Anita. 1998. "Medieval Narrative Conventions and the Putative Antimedievalism of Twain's *Connecticut Yankee.*" In *Reinventing the Middle Ages and the Renaissance: Constructions of the Medieval and Early Modern Periods,* edited by William F. Gentrup, 223–39. Turnhout, Belgium: Brepols.

O'Malley, Michael. 1990. *Keeping Watch: A History of American Time.* Washington, DC: Smithsonian Institution Press.

Orpheus. (c. 3rd century BC–2nd century AD) 1792. Hymn 86, "To Death." In *The Hymns of Orpheus, Translated from the Original Greek,* translated by Thomas Taylor, 224–27. London: printed for the author.

Palmer, F. R. 2001. *Mood and Modality.* Cambridge: Cambridge University Press.

Panagia, Davide. 2009. *The Political Life of Sensation.* Durham, NC: Duke University Press.

Parham, Marisa. 2008. *Haunting and Displacement in African American Literature and Culture.* New York: Routledge.

Parker, Andrew. 1991. "Unthinking Sex: Marx, Engels, and the Scene of Writing." *Social Text* 29: 28–45.

Parsons, Elsie Clews, ed. 1918. *Folk Tales of Andros Island, Bahamas.* New York: American Folklore Society.

Patterson, Daniel W. 1979. *The Shaker Spiritual.* Princeton, NJ: Princeton University Press.

Patterson, Orlando. 1982. *Slavery and Social Death: A Comparative Study.* Cambridge, MA: Harvard University Press.

Pfitzer, Gregory M. 2008. *Popular History and the Literary Marketplace, 1840–1920.* Amherst: University of Massachusetts Press.

"Playing Dead Twice in the Road." 2006. In *The Greenwood Library of American Folktales,* vol. 1, *The Northeast, the Midwest, and the Mid-Atlantic,* edited by Thomas A. Green, 285–87. Westport, CT: Greenwood Publishing Group.

Pratt, Lloyd. 2009. *Archives of American Time: Literature and Modernity in the Nineteenth Century.* Philadelphia, PA: University of Pennsylvania Press.

Preston, Ann. 1849. *Cousin Ann's Stories for Children.* Philadelphia, PA: J. M. McKim.

Protevi, John. 2009. *Political Affect: Connecting the Social and Somatic.* Minneapolis: University of Minnesota Press.

Puar, Jasbir. 2007. *Terrorist Assemblages: Homonationalism in Queer Times.* Durham, NC: Duke University Press.

Rathbun, Caleb. (1796) 2013. "Caleb Rathbun Aged Nearly Seventeen Years, the Son of Valentine Rathbun. Jun. Maketh Oath." *Western Star* (Stockbridge, MA), April 5, 4. Reprinted in Goodwillie 2013, 1: 139–41.

Rathbun, Valentine. 1781. *An Account of the Matter, Form, and Manner of a Strange New Religion.* Providence, RI: Bennett Wheeler.

Reid-Pharr, Robert. 1999. *Conjugal Union: The Body, the House, and the Black American.* New York: Oxford University Press.

Rifkin, Mark. 2011. *When Did Indians Become Straight? Kinship, the History of Sexuality, and Native Sovereignty.* New York: Oxford University Press.

Roach, Joseph. 1996. *Cities of the Dead: Circum-Atlantic Performance.* New York: Columbia University Press.

Robinson, Charles E. 1893. *A Concise History of the United Society of Believers Called Shakers.* East Canterbury, NH: [self-published].

Rohy, Valerie. 2009. *Anachronism and Its Others: Sexuality, Race, and Temporality.* Albany, NY: SUNY Press.

Román, David. 2005. *Performance in America: Contemporary U.S. Culture and the Performing Arts.* Durham, NC: Duke University Press.

Romero, Lora. 1997. *Home Fronts: Domesticity and Its Critics in the Antebellum United States.* Durham, NC: Duke University Press.

Rosen, George. 1972. "The Committee of One Hundred on National Health and the Campaign for a National Health Department, 1906–1912." *American Journal of Public Health* 62 (2): 261–63.

Rosenberg, Jordy (Jordana). 2011. *Critical Enthusiasm: Capital Accumulation and the Transformation of Religious Passion.* New York: Oxford University Press.

Ross, Andrew. 1989. "The Uses of Camp." In *No Respect: Intellectuals and Popular Culture,* 135–70. New York: Routledge.

Rowe, John Carlos. 1995. "How the Boss Played the Game: Twain's Critique of Imperialism in *A Connecticut Yankee in King Arthur's Court.*" In *The Cambridge Companion to Twain*, edited by Forrest Robinson, 175–92. Cambridge: Cambridge University Press.

Ruggles, Jeffrey. 2003. *The Unboxing of Henry Brown.* Richmond: Library of Virginia.

Rusert, Britt. 2017. *Fugitive Science: Empiricism and Freedom in Early African American Culture.* New York: New York University Press.

Rush, Benjamin. 1812. *Medical Inquiries and Observations, upon Diseases of the Mind.* Philadelphia, PA: Kimber and Richardson.

Samuels, Ellen. 2017. "Six Ways of Looking at Crip Time." *Disability Studies Quarterly* 37, no. 3 (online).

Samuels, Shirley, ed. 1992. *The Culture of Sentiment: Race, Gender, and Sexuality in 19th Century America.* New York: Oxford University Press.

Scales, William. (1789) 2013. "Mystery of the People Called Shakers." *Boston Gazette and the Country Journal,* June 15, 1. Reprinted in Goodwillie 2013, 1: 119–22.

Schivelbusch, Wolfgang. (1977) 1986. *The Railway Journey: Time, Space, and Industrialization in the Nineteenth Century.* Berkeley: University of California Press.

Schneider, Rebecca. 2011. *Performing Remains: Art and War in Times of Historical Reenactment.* New York: Routledge.

Scholes, Robert, and Eric S. Rabkin. 1977. *Science Fiction: History-Science-Vision.* New York: Oxford University Press.

Schuller, Kyla. 2017. *The Biopolitics of Feeling: Race, Sex, and Science in the Nineteenth Century.* Durham, NC: Duke University Press.

Scott, Bonnie G. 1998. *The Gender of History: Men, Women, and Historical Practice.* Cambridge, MA: Harvard University Press.

Sedgwick, Catharine Maria. (1824) 1969. *Redwood: A Tale.* 2 vols. Reprint, New York: Garrett Press.

Sedgwick, Eve Kosofsky. 1991. "Jane Austen and the Masturbating Girl." *Critical Inquiry* 17: 818–37.

Sedgwick, Eve Kosofsky. 1997. "Paranoid Reading and Reparative Reading; or, You're So Paranoid, You Probably Think This Introduction Is about You." In *Novel Gazing: Queer Readings in Fiction*, edited by Eve Kosofsky Sedgwick, 1–40. Durham, NC: Duke University Press.

Sedgwick, Eve Kosofsky. 2003. *Touching Feeling.* Durham, NC: Duke University Press.

Seitler, Dana. 2008. *Atavistic Tendencies: The Culture of Science in American Modernity.* Minneapolis: University of Minnesota Press.

Seltzer, Mark. 1992. *Bodies and Machines.* New York: Routledge.

Sexton, Jared. 2008. *Amalgamation Schemes: Antiblackness and the Critique of Multiracialism.* Minneapolis: University of Minnesota Press.

Sexton, Jared. 2011. "The Social Life of Social Death: On Afropessimism and Black Optimism." *Tensions* 5: 1–47.

Shell, Marc. 1995. *The End of Kinship: "Measure for Measure," Incest, and the Ideal of Universal Siblinghood.* Baltimore, MD: Johns Hopkins University Press.

Sherman, Stuart. 1997. *Telling Time: Clocks, Diaries, and English Diurnal Form, 1660–1785.* Chicago, IL: University of Chicago Press.

"A Short Account of the People Known as Shakers, or Shaking Quakers." 1795. *Theological Magazine* 1 (2): 81–87.

Smith, Bonnie G. 1998. *The Gender of History: Men, Women, and Historical Practice.* Cambridge, MA: Harvard University Press.

Smith, James. (1810) 2013. *Remarkable Occurrences Lately Discovered among the People Called Shakers.* Reprinted in Goodwillie 2013, 1: 189–99.

Smith, Mark M. 1997. *Mastered by the Clock: Time, Slavery, and Freedom in the American South.* Chapel Hill: University of North Carolina Press.

Smith, Shawn Michelle. 1999. *American Archives: Gender, Race, and Class in Visual Culture.* Princeton, NJ: Princeton University Press.

Snead, James. 2003. "On Repetition and Black Culture." In *Racist Traces and Other Writing: European Pedigrees and African Contagions,* edited by James Snead, Kara Keeling, Colin McCabe, and Cornell West, 11–33. New York: Palgrave Macmillan.

Snediker, Michael. 2009. *Queer Optimism: Lyric Personhood and Other Felicitous Persuasions.* Minneapolis: University of Minnesota Press.

Snediker, Michael. 2015. "Queer Philology and Chronic Pain: Bersani, Melville, Blanchot." *Qui Parle: Critical Humanities and Social Sciences* 23 (2): 1–27.

Solomons, Leon, and Gertrude Stein. 1896. "Normal Motor Automatism." *Psychological Review* 3: 492–512.

Somerville, Siobhan. 2000. *Queering the Color Line.* Durham, NC: Duke University Press.

Spillers, Hortense. 1984. "Interstices: A Small Drama of Words." In *Pleasure and Danger,* edited by Carole Vance, 73–100. New York: Pandora/HarperCollins.

Spillers, Hortense. 1987. "Mama's Baby, Papa's Maybe: An American Grammar Book." *Diacritics* 17 (2): 64–81.

Stearns, Charles. 1849. *Narrative of Henry Box Brown, Who Escaped from Slavery, Enclosed in a Box 3 Feet Long and 2 Wide, Written from a Statement of Facts Made by Himself, with Remarks upon the Remedy for Slavery, by Charles Stearns.* Boston, MA: Brown and Stearns.

Stein, Gertrude. 1898. "Cultivated Motor Automatism: A Study of Character in Its Relation to Attention." *Psychological Review* 5: 295–306.

Stein, Gertrude. (1903) 1993. *The Making of Americans.* Excerpted in Gertrude Stein and Ulla Dydo, *A Stein Reader,* 17–99. Chicago, IL: Northwestern University Press.

Stein, Gertrude. (1909) 2000. "Melanctha: Each One as She May." In *Three Lives,* edited by Linda Wagner-Martin, 87–187. New York: Bedford/St. Martin's.

Stein, Gertrude. (1913) 1922. "Sacred Emily." In *Geography and Plays,* 178–88. Boston, MA: Four Seas.

Stein, Gertrude. (c. 1922) 1993. "Saints and Singing: A Play." In Gertrude Stein and Ulla Dydo, *A Stein Reader,* 383–99. Chicago, IL: Northwestern University Press.

Stein, Gertrude. (1934) 1985. "Portraits and Repetition." In *Lectures in America,* 165–206. Boston, MA: Beacon Press.

Stein, Gertrude. (1935) 1993. "Composition as Explanation." In Gertrude Stein and Ulla Dydo, *A Stein Reader,* 495–503. Chicago, IL: Northwestern University Press.

Stein, Stephen J. 1992. *The Shaker Experience in America: A History of the United Society of Believers.* New Haven, CT: Yale University Press.

Steiner, Wendy. 1978. *Exact Resemblance to Exact Resemblance: The Literary Portraiture of Gertrude Stein.* New Haven, CT: Yale University Press.

Stockton, Kathryn Bond. 2009. *The Queer Child: Growing Sideways in the Twentieth Century.* Durham, NC: Duke University Press.

Stoler, Ann Laura. 1995. *Race and the Education of Desire: Foucault's History of Sexuality and the Colonial Order of Things.* Durham, NC: Duke University Press.

Stone, Horatio. (1846) 2013. *Lo Here and Lo There! Or, The Grave of the Heart.* Reprinted in Goodwillie 2013, 3: 113–64.

Stowe, Harriet Beecher. 1852. *Uncle Tom's Cabin.* Boston, MA: John P. Jewett. "Uncle Tom's Cabin in American Culture." Accessed December 20, 2018. http://utc.iath .virginia.edu/uncletom/utfihbsa40t.html.

Strogatz, Steven H. 2004. *Sync: How Order Emerges from Chaos in the Universe, Nature, and Daily Life.* Reprint, New York: Hachette.

Tate, Claudia. 1992. *Domestic Allegories of Political Desire: The Black Heroine's Text at the Turn of the Century.* New York: Oxford University Press.

Taves, Ann. 1999. *Fits, Trances, & Visions: Experiencing Religion and Explaining Experience from Wesley to James.* Princeton, NJ: Princeton University Press.

Thompson, E. P. 1967. "Time, Work-Discipline, and Industrial Capitalism." *Past and Present* 38: 56–97.

Tipei, John Fleter. 2009. *The Laying on of Hands in the New Testament: Its Significance, Techniques, and Effects.* Lanham, MD: University Press of America.

Tissot, Samuel. (1758) 1832. *Onanism.* New York: Collins and Hannay.

Tolliver, Cedric R. 2015. "The Racial Ends of History: Melancholic Historical Practice in Pauline Hopkins's *Of One Blood.*" *Arizona Quarterly* 71 (1): 25–52.

Tompkins, Kyla Wazana. 2014. "Eat, Sex, Race." In *Unsettled States: Nineteenth-Century American Literary Studies,* edited by Dana Luciano and Ivy Wilson, 245–74. New York: New York University Press.

Trevarthen, Colwyn. 1999/2000. "Musicality and the Intrinsic Motive Pulse: Evidence from Human Psychobiology and Infant Communication." In "Rhythms, Musical Narrative, and the Origins of Human Communication," Special issue, *Musicae Scientae*, 157–213.

Troeltsch, Ernst. 1950. *The Social Teaching of the Christian Churches.* Translated by Olive Wyon. 2 vols. London: Allen and Unwin.

Trollope, Frances. (1832) 2003. *Domestic Manners of the Americans.* New York: Dover Publications.

Trubowitz, Lara. 2012. *Civil Antisemitism, Modernism, and British Culture, 1902–1939.* New York: Palgrave Macmillan.

Twain, Mark. (1879) 1976. "Some Thoughts on the Science of Onanism." In *The Mammoth Cod, and Address to the Stomach Club,* edited by Gershon Legman, 23–25. Milwaukee, WI: Maledicta Press.

Twain, Mark. 1885. "The Private History of a Campaign That Failed." *Century Magazine* 31: 193–203.

Twain, Mark. (1889) 1982. *A Connecticut Yankee in King Arthur's Court.* Edited by Alison Ensor. New York: W. W. Norton.

Veltman, Laura J. 2003. "'The Bible Lies the One Way, but the Night-Gown the Other': Dr. Matthew O'Connor, Confession, and Gender in Djuna Barnes's *Nightwood.*" *Modern Fiction Studies* 49 (2): 204–27.

von Steuben, Friedrich Wilhelm. 1779. *Regulations for the Order and Discipline of the Troops of the United States.* Philadelphia, PA: Styner and Cist.

"W." 1873. "The Shaker Paradox." *Oneida Circular*, March 17, 1873, 91.

Warner, Michael. 1990a. "Homo-Narcissism, or, Heterosexuality." In *Engendering Men: The Question of Male Feminist Criticism,* edited by Joseph Boone and Michael Cadden, 190–206. New York: Routledge.

Warner, Michael. 1990b. *The Letters of the Republic: Publication and the Public Sphere in Eighteenth-Century America.* Cambridge, MA: Harvard University Press.

Weinstein, Cindy. 1995. "Twain in the Man-Factory." In *The Literature of Labor and the Labor of Literature,* 129–72. Cambridge: Cambridge University Press.

Weinstein, Cindy. 2015. *Time, Tense, and American Literature: When Is Now?* Cambridge: Cambridge University Press.

Welter, Barbara. 1976. *Dimity Convictions: The American Woman in the Nineteenth Century.* Athens: Ohio University Press.

Wergland, Glendyne R. 2011. *Sisters in the Faith: Shaker Women and the Equality of the Sexes.* Amherst: University of Massachusetts Press.

Wiedman, Dennis. 2010. "Globalizing the Chronicities of Modernity: Diabetes and the Metabolic Syndrome." In *Chronic Conditions, Fluid States: Chronicity and the Anthropology of Illness,* edited by Lenore Manderson and Carolyn Smith-Morris, 38–53. New Brunswick, NJ: Rutgers University Press.

Wilderson, Frank B., III. 2010. *Red, White, and Black: Cinema and the Structure of U.S. Antagonisms.* Durham, NC: Duke University Press.

Williams, George Washington. 1883. *History of the Negro Race in America.* 2 vols. New York: G. P. Putnam's Sons.

Williams, James D. 1965. "The Use of History in Mark Twain's *A Connecticut Yankee.*" *PMLA* 80: 102–10.

Williams, Raymond. 1977. "Structures of Feeling." In *Marxism and Literature,* 128–35. New York: Oxford University Press.

Wooster Group. 2015. Rehearsal at St. Ann's Warehouse. The Wooster Group, April 27. http://thewoostergroup.org/blog/2015/04/27/early-shaker-spirituals-at-st-anns -warehouse-dance-rehearsal-with-costume-detail/.

Wright, Richard. (1940) 2005. *Native Son.* New York: Harper Perennial.

Wynter, Sylvia. 1984. "The Ceremony Must Be Found: After Humanism." *Boundary 2* 12 (3) and 13 (1): 19–70.

Wynter, Sylvia. 1994 (1992). "No Humans Involved: An Open Letter to My Colleagues." *Forum N.H.I: Knowledge for the 21st Century,* 1 (1): 42–71.

Youmans, Peter. (1826) 2013. *An Appeal to Scripture and Common Sense, or, A Death Blow to Shakerism.* s.l, s.n. Reprinted in Goodwillie 2013, 2:305–14.

debility, 17, 127, 135, 139–40, 190. *See also* capacity

de Genlis, Madame, 49

Delany, Martin, 195n10

Deleuze, Gilles, 4–5, 13, 15

Derrida, Jacques, 171

de Staël, Germaine, 95

Dickens, Charles, 43–44, 47

die-ins, 85

Dinshaw, Carolyn, 95, 102, 198n20

disability, 16–17, 126–27, 196n6. *See also* blindness; debility

disability studies, 16

disciplinary power, 1–8, 11, 15, 17, 20–26, 50, 63, 88, 95, 99, 117, 122, 133, 140, 149, 155, 189, 191. *See also* docile body

docile body, 3, 22. *See also* disciplinary power

domesticity, 4, 10, 20, 24, 28, 69, 106, 147, 149, 167; racialized, 24, 59–60, 193n7, 193n9

Douglass, Frederick, 58

drag, 104, 108, 119; archival, 178, 198n23; temporal, 103, 178

Dr. Dre: *The Chronic*, 147–48

Du Bois, W. E. B., 83; "The Comet," 189

Duchamp, Marcel: *Nude Descending a Staircase (No. 2)*, 136–37

Dydo, Ulla, 144

Dyer, Richard, 198n21

ecstasy, 21, 29, 30–31, 49, 153, 157–59, 186

Edelman, Lee, 12–14, 58, 61–62, 65–66, 169–71

Egypt, 106, 111

Eighteenth Brumaire of Louis Bonaparte (Marx), 103–4

Emancipation, 47, 58, 63, 79

Emerson, Ralph Waldo, 99

encryption, 53–54, 107–8

Engels, Friedrich, 103

England, 37, 76, 90–92, 97, 99, 117, 159, 197n6; Liverpool, 29. *See also* Great Britain

engroupment, 4–5, 11–12, 15, 17, 19, 77, 159, 175, 188

entrainment, 5, 26, 34

Ernest, John, 69

erotohistoriography, 89–90, 107, 124

Ethiopia, 23, 52, 106, 107, 109–11, 113–15, 117–18, 120, 188

Eucharist, 25, 160, 164–65, 168–69, 177, 180–86

eugenics, 24, 61, 124, 132, 135, 139, 152, 181, 183

Europe, 20, 29, 35, 36, 40, 42, 49–50, 87, 96, 107, 110, 114, 192n3, 193n9. *See also* *individual countries*

exagoreusis, 162

exomologesis, 162, 167

ex-slave narratives, 18–19, 22, 51–84, 88

Fanon, Frantz, 61, 63, 65, 82–84, 111, 193n11, 193n14

Federal Commission on the Conservation of Natural Resources, 131–32

femininity, 16, 59, 95, 134. *See also* femmes

feminism, 3, 16, 167–68, 171

femmes, 16, 173

feudalism, 102, 104–5, 119

Fisher, Irving, 131, 154, 196n7; *Report on National Vitality, Its Wastes and Conservation*, 132–35, 140–41

Fisher, Philip K., 195n13

Flaubert, Gustave: *Salammbô*, 122, 178

Floyd, Kevin, 168

folk tales, 19, 55

Forster, E. M.: *A Passage to India*, 42

Foucault, Michel, 9, 20, 184–86, 191n1, 191n4, 197n5; on ars erotica, 191n7; on biohistory, 15; on biopolitics, 32, 56, 139; on confession, 158, 160–62, 175; on disciplinary power *vs.* biopower, 1–8, 26, 50; on non-conceptual knowl-

historicism, 103–8, 119, 121–22, 178–79, 183, 190, 195n13; New Historicism, 177, 182, 186, 198n19

historiography, 8, 21–22, 74, 108, 115, 117–18, 121–22, 198n20; Africanist, 106–7; amateur, 17, 23, 89, 91, 95, 103, 107, 116, 119, 123, 190; erotohistoriography, 89–90, 107, 124; masturbation and, 102, 111–12; Scriptural, 176

Hocquenghem, Guy, 13

Holford, Castello, 91

Holsinger, Bruce, 178

Holy Spirit, 29, 35, 164, 179

homosexuality, 6, 13, 18, 25, 61, 66, 95, 121, 159, 161–62, 170–72, 178. *See also* gay men; lesbians

Hopkins, Pauline Elizabeth, 18–19; *Of One Blood*, 23, 52, 89–90, 105–22, 124, 188, 190

Huffer, Lynne, 13

humanism, 22, 54, 63–65, 79, 87, 107, 174

human resources, 24, 132, 155, 190, 196n7

hypersociability, 12–17, 25, 168–73, 176, 185–86. *See also* queer hypersociability

ideology, 9, 37, 59–60, 66, 92, 99, 118–19, 164, 177, 189, 193n7

ideorrhythmy, 38

Imbert, Anthony: "Shakers near Lebanon, State of New York," 45–49

imperialism, 24, 91–92, 106–7, 121, 122–24, 190; French, 103; Roman, 104; US, 21, 74, 105, 118. *See also* colonialism; Manifest Destiny

impressibility, 10, 31, 33

ingathering, 16, 176–77

insistence (Dydo), 144–45

intimacy, 9, 30, 81, 172–73

Israelites (historical), 38

Jackson, Jean E., 125

Jackson, Rebecca Cox, 47

Jacobs, Harriet, 22; *Incidents in the Life of a Slave Girl*, 54, 58–60, 67, 69, 193nn7–9

Jain, S. Lochlann, 125

James, Henry, 18

James, William, 145, 156–57, 160–61

Jameson, Fredric, 118

Jefferson, Thomas, 63

Jesus. *See* Christ

Jim Crow, 78, 80, 139

Johns Hopkins School of Medicine, 137, 147

Jordan, Mark, 175–77

jouissance, 170

Judaism, 182–83, 197n3

Kant, Immanuel, 63, 156

Kearney, James, 197n6

Kibbey, Ann, 197n6

Kilgore, John Mac, 35, 159

Kreiger, Georgia, 59, 81

Kush: Telassar, 107, 110–12, 115–17, 122, 124

Lacan, Jacques, 12–13, 170, 193

Lamarckian theory, 31

Laplanche, Jean, 13

Laqueur, Thomas, 100, 102

laying on of hands, 25, 34, 164, 179–80, 186

Lears, T. J. Jackson, 168

Lecky, William Edward Hartpole, 194n2

Lee, Ann, 29, 34, 36, 39–41

Lee, William, 39

Lefebvre, Henri, 147

Le Morte d'Arthur (Malory), 105

lesbians, 16–17, 25, 114, 121, 135, 167–68, 176, 178, 180, 198n18

liberalism, 1, 3, 5, 22, 107, 171

libido, 90, 98, 105, 116–22

Life Extension Institute, 132

living dead, 52, 56. *See also* zombies

Locke, John, 30–31

Lombard, Peter, 165

long nineteenth century, 8, 17–23, 51, 127, 159–60
Lorde, Audre, 17
Lossing, Benson John, 47–**48**
Love, Heather, 168
Luciano, Dana, 7, 9–10, 56–57, 87, 106–7, 192n14
Luther, Martin, 103, 157, 196n8; *Babylonian Captivity of the Church*, 163

Madden, Etta, 34
magic, 69, 88, 96
Maine, 45; Sabbathday Lake, 40
Maine Cultivator and Hallowell Gazette, 45
Manifest Destiny, 190. *See also* colonialism; imperialism
Marriott, David, 63, 75
Martin, Trayvon: murder, 84–85
Marx, Karl, 103
Marxism, 14
masculinity, 24, 92–93, 95, 104, 123
Massachusetts: Boston, 71, 74, 167; Hancock, 51
masturbation, 23, 93, 96–104, 107, 109, 111, 118–19, 121, 167
materialism, 14, 107
Mauss, Marcel, 5
Mbembe, Achille, 7, 53, 56, 193n17
McGarry, Molly, 159, 198n20
McNeill, William H., 50
Meacham, Joseph, 39, 44
Meillassoux, Claude, 53, 55
melancholia, 53–55, 68, 90, 107, 120, 135
Melanchthon, Philip, 135, 157, 196n8
Melville, Herman, 19; "Bartleby the Scrivener," 18, 21, 24, 126–36, 138, 143, 145–46, 148–49, 154–55, 190, 195n3, 196n12
mesmerism, 69, 108–9, 108–10, 112–15, 120, 194n23
Methodists, 28
methodology, of book, 12–17. *See also* sense-methods

metronomics, 7, 49
Michaels, Walter Benn, 99, 195n13
Michal (biblical), 38
Middle Ages, 2, 23, 91, 94–97, 102, 104, 119, 162
Middle Passage, 53, 65, 74, 77, 85, 87, 196n18
minstrelsy, 45, 64, 69
Mirzoeff, Nicholas, 85
"Missing One's Coach: An Anachronism," 88–89
Missouri, 104; Ferguson, 193n10; Marion County, 91
modernism, 18, 25, 136, 160, 168, 171, 173, 185, 190
Monk, Theolonius: "Misterioso," 187
monotony, 41–42, 44–45, 49–53
Morgan, J. Pierpont, 93
Morgan le Fay, 96
Mormonism, 28, 159
Morris, William: *A Dream of John Bell*, 88
Morrison, Toni, 114
Morse, Theodore F.: "The Woodchuck Song," 124
Moses, Omri, 143, 145
Moskowitz, Sally, 81–83
Moten, Fred, 12, 14, 52, 62, 66, 81, 152, 193n18, 196n18
Motley, John, 106
Muñoz, José Esteban, 65, 152, 178

nationalism, 24, 121
necropolitics, 56–57
Negri, Antonio, 191n8
Nell, William Cooper: *The Colored Patriots of the American Revolution*, 88; *Services of Colored Americans in the Wars of 1776 and 1812*, 88
New Americanism, 177, 198n20
New England, 21, 43, 97, 160
New Historicism, 177, 182, 186, 198n19
new materialisms, 4–5

New York City, 189

New Yorker, 27–**28**

New York State, 28, 46; New Lebanon, 42, 45–**46**, 51

Nietzsche, Friedrich, 87, 120–21, 179

Noah (biblical), 173

Norman Conquest, 104

Norton, J. Pease, 131

Novick, Jack, 83

Novick, Kerry Kelly, 83

Oedipus, 164

Onania (pamphlet), 100

Oneida Community, 28, 197n1

Orpheus, 57

Oxford English Dictionary, 147, 178, 196n7

Paige typesetting machine, 105

Panagia, Davide, 5

Paris Commune, 93–94

Parkman, Francis, 106

Parton, Dolly, 177

Patterson, Orlando, 22, 53, 59, 62–63, 77

Paul (biblical), 103

Pennsylvania: Philadelphia, 68, 71–**73**

performativity, 11–12, 22, 64, 66, 74, 164

Phillips, Adam, 198n17

playing dead, 17, 22, 52–87, 107–9, 113, 123

Plessy v. Ferguson, 78

Porter, Cole, 177

Prescott, William, 106

Progressive Era, 123, 141, 159

proprioception, 8, 11, 37

Protestantism, 21, 29–30, 157, 159–60, 162–65, 168, 173, 180, 190, 198n17; Protestant Reformation, 135, 166–67, 176, 197n6. *See also* Anglican Church; Baptists; Methodists; Quakers; Shakers

psychoanalysis, 37, 81, 83, 135

Puar, Jasbir, 5, 13, 56, 127, 139, 141, 148

public health, 131–32, 134, 141

Puritans, 21, 96, 159, 163, 197n6

Quakers, 29

queer hypersociability, 12–17, 25, 168–73, 176, 185–86

queer theory, 5, 12, 14, 22, 54, 61, 64, 66, 90, 103, 168, 170, 176–77, 186, 193n18, 198n20

race, 8, 10, 17, 54, 85–86, 87, 88, 159, 172, 189, 194n25; in Barnes's novel, 173–74, 182–83; in Bibb's autobiography, 21, 60–68; biopolitics of, 31–32; in Brown's autobiography, 21, 68–77; domesticity and, 24, 59–60, 193n7, 193n9; eugenics and, 139, 181; in folk tales, 55–57; gendered, 21, 24, 47–49, 53, 59–61, 64, 95, 104, 109, 190, 191n10, 193n7; in Griggs's novel, 21, 77–84; in Hopkin's novel, 23, 97–98, 106–17, 119–20; invention of, 15; in Jacobs's autobiography, 21, 58–60; in Melville's story, 130, 135, 190; performativity and, 66; sentimental culture and, 9; sexualized, 7, 80; Shakers and, 21–22, 30–31, 35–36, 41–49, 52–53, 98, 159, 190; in Stein's novella, 24, 126, 135–36, 139–41, 151–52, 156, 190; in Twain's novel, 23, 94, 97–98, 120. *See also* Afropessimism; racial uplift; racism; slavery

racial uplift, 8, 24, 126, 152, 155–56, 190

racism, 45, 47, 53, 63, 75, 84, 120, 139–40. *See also* Jim Crow; minstrelsy; slavery; white supremacy

Rathbun, Caleb, 32, 35

Rathbun, Valentine, Jr., 32–33

Rathbun, Valentine, Sr., 36; *An Account of the Matter, Form, and Manner of a Strange New Religion*, 32–33

Reconstruction, 23–24, 53–54, 78, 93, 98, 107, 141

reenactment, 15, 18–19, 22–23, 68, 89, 95, 105, 192n12

reproduction, 8, 10, 22–23, 50, 56, 64, 81, 101, 117, 120–21, 126, 140–41, 149, 152,

Stockton, Kathryn Bond, 144
Stoddard, Charles Warren, 18
Stoler, Ann Laura, 6–7, 15
Stomach Club, 93–94, 96, 101
Stone, Horatio, 35
Stowe, Harriet Beecher, 60; *Uncle Tom's Cabin*, 58
subjectification, 8, 15
Sun Ra, 189
synchrony, 5, 7, 11, 14, 33–36, 41, 47, 49, 188–89

tableaux vivants, 15, 89
Taft, William Howard, 132
Taine, Hippolyte, 194n2
"Take This Hammer," 188
Tar-Baby, 60, 84
Tate, Claudia, 120
Taylorism, 2, 22
Tecumseh, 35
temporal drag, 103, 178
thanatomimesis, 81, 85, 88, 107, 109, 113
Thanatos, 57
Thoreau, Henry David, 18
timetables, 1–2, 26, 191n1
Tissot, Samuel, 102
Toklas, Alice B., 167
Tolliver, Cedric, 105–6
Tompkins, Kyla, 98
Tuskegee University, 79
Twain, Mark (Samuel Langhorne Clemens), 18–19, 190; *The Adventures of Huckleberry Finn*, 90; *The Adventures of Tom Sawyer*, 90; *The Chronicle of Young Satan*, 90; *A Connecticut Yankee in King Arthur's Court*, 23, 89–119, 121–22, 194n2; *The Gilded Age*, 100; *No. 44, the Mysterious Stranger*, 90; *Personal Recollections of Joan of Arc*, 90; *The Prince and the Pauper*, 90, 98; "The Private History of a Campaign That Failed," 91–93; *Pudd'nhead*

Wilson, 90; "Some Thoughts on the Science of Onanism," 93

"Uncle Ned" (song), 69
Union Army, 91
United Society of Believers. *See* Shakers
Urban Dictionary online, 148

Vendôme Column, 93–94, 96
vitality, 24, 80, 126, 128–29, 132–34, 146, 152, 177, 196n7
Volney, Constantin François de, 106

Wall Street, 21, 129–30
War of 1812, 23, 88
Washington, Booker T., 79
Wells, H. G., 91
Welter, Barbara, 59
white supremacy, 53, 55, 57, 63–64, 80, 113–14
Whitman, Walt, 18
Whittaker, James, 39
Wiedman, Dennis, 141, 196n8
Wilde, Oscar, 177
Wilderson, Frank B., III, 53, 63–66, 68, 79–80, 83–84, 86, 193n12
Williams, George Washington: *History of the Negro Race in America from 1619 to 1880*, 88, 106
Williams, Raymond, 111
Wilson, Darren Dean: killing of Michael Brown, 193n10
"The Woodchuck Song," 124
Woolf, Virginia: *Orlando*, 122
Wooster Group, 40
World War II, 20, 197n4
Wright, Richard: *Native Son*, 81

"Yankee Doodle Dandy" (song), 97
Youmans, Peter, 35

zombies, 79, 194n25. *See also* living dead